Social Development in India

Professor Anil S. Navale
(Date of Birth: 15 October 1943)

Social Development in India

Critical Assessment

Essays in Honour of Professor Anil S. Navale

Editor
Chhaya Patel

RAWAT PUBLICATIONS
Jaipur • New Delhi • Bangalore • Guwahati • Kolkata

ISBN 978-81-316-0748-0

Published by
Prem Rawat for **Rawat Publications**
Satyam Apts, Sector 3, Jawahar Nagar, Jaipur 302 004 (India)
Phone: 0141 265 1748 / 7006 Fax: 0141 265 1748
E-mail: info@rawatbooks.com
Website: www.rawatbooks.com

New Delhi Office
4858/24, Ansari Road, Daryaganj, New Delhi 110 002
Phone: 011 2326 3290

Also at *Bangalore, Guwahati* and *Kolkata*

Typeset by Rawat Computers, Jaipur
Printed at Nice Printing Press, New Delhi

Contents

Foreword

For any country, historically the task of winning freedom, becoming independent and achieving *rashtra-nirman* (nation-building) and *rashtriya ekikaran* (national integration) is a complex and daunting one. In most cases, it usually takes a long historical journey of laborious, painful and hard struggle. It often passes through a course of evolutionary ups and downs. In such a course, it takes a mammoth toll of human and material sacrifices. As an immediate instance of such a process, we are well aware of the time taken and challenges faced by Indian freedom struggle and movement before Independence from British rule was achieved in August 1947. In many ways, historically the case of India's Independence, freedom and nation-building is truly exceptional and remarkable.

I should hasten to state that equally challenging and remarkable is India's story of post-Independence period. The path of nation-building and national-integration in a society like that of India which has enormously rich social, economic, cultural, ethnic, religious and regional diversities and a plurality that is unparalleled in modern history. Authoritarian and communist-socialist countries could deal with these sub-nationality-like diversities by use of force, violence and threats. But countries (like India) having become newly democratic nation-states and having a millennia old civilization of peaceful and harmonious co-existence among several ethnic, religious, regional and social communities, have found the task of national integration particularly more complex, sensitive and challenging.

The story of Indian nation-building is so rich that it has the potential to become an ideal lesson for those countries which are struggling hard and are caught in the whirlpool of challenging disintegrative processes. This is not to imply that the challenges of nation-building, integration and consolidation in India are over. It is in the least so. External border disputes inherited from history and internal disputes over water and land among the states have periodically defied Indian leadership and government till date. Many challenges like integration of Junagarh, Hyderabad and Goa are successfully met, but some like Manipur, Nagaland, Jammu & Kashmir have remained to be completely resolved once and for all.

The nation could be structurally constituted and created as a political entity by mechanical process on one opportune historical moment, but its emotional and organic integration is found to be a long complex task. We have examples of Canada, the UK and East European countries where we find the demands for more autonomy, disintegration and/or separation being periodically made. The role of state and society has become crucial in forging and sustaining the emotional bondage between peoples and regions of diverse composition. Innovative, tolerant and ingenious initiatives are needed on the part of one and all concerned. The limitations and shortcomings of state/government efforts towards national integration have to be supplemented by enlightened sections and organizations of the civil society. Partnerships among government and non-government organizations in the domains of their respective strengths have to be the order of the contemporary day.

In short, the objectives of nation-building and national integration cannot be left to the political parties, politicians and politics alone – howsoever committed or concerned they may claim to be. It invariably requires involvement and participation by equally committed, concerned and social service-oriented organizations based in schools, colleges, universities, industry, religio-cultural sectors and youth bodies. Emotional integration and unification of the nation can be achieved by planning creative and genuinely interactive national schemes and programme. Farmers, workers, students, professionals, technocrats, bureaucrats, women, minorities, members and office-bearers of local democracy in villages, *talukas*, districts and cities and will have to (once in a while) step out of their own respective basic field and interact with their counterparts in other regions of the country. We need too much of interaction in order to foster feelings of *Bhartiyata* and Indianness in mutual interest as the citizens of the republic. It must be done in such a manner that the nation and the region/state, both co-exist, co-habit and co-flourish without impinging on the other.

As the country's eminent historian Ramachandra Guha argues and maintains, a country which is desirous of becoming a great democratic nation of unity, peace and harmony cannot afford to forget its history. All those small and big participants involved in its process of shaping the destiny of the nation by small acts too must equally be remembered. As many streams make the big river, many streams of small efforts like those of Professor Navale also contribute towards making a great institution and a great nation – if not today then tomorrow. We must remember such small-place-heroes not only as a mark of our collective gratitude towards them but in our self-interest of letting the future generations know as to what has gone into ensuring their future.

This rather unusually long thematic backdrop in the opening part of the Foreword (to this edited volume) was necessary to construct an appreciative but objective context and perspective. The edited book by Professor Chhaya Patel is brought out to felicitate Professor Anil S. Navale, who has been a multi-talented social work professional of Baroda city and its famous Faculty of Social Work at The Maharaja Sayajirao University of Baroda, Baroda. In order to highlight Professor Navale's multi-dimensional contribution, I believe, this backdrop will not be out of place. Professor Navale's lifelong work, indeed, needed to be documented and thereby appreciated. This volume contains 18 chapters written by his eminent fellow professionals and scholars of social work subject. These chapters together are analysing the relevance and contribution of five inter-related interesting themes of youth – National Service Scheme (NSS), Corporate Social Responsibility (CSR), Non-Government Organisation (NGOs), People Living with HIV/AIDS (PLHA) and Gandhi.

We must also remember that what was good and useful yesterday may not be so today or tomorrow. The NSS is losing its appeal to the youth is a case in point. New winds of global changes are bound to bring about such adverse effects. The onus is on us to have a re-look at the tool and judge its utility. Similarly, Gandhian relevance also needs to be questioned. *Swadeshi* and home grown production has clear inherent limits. Modern industries have a great role to play in mitigating poverty and raising the standard of life of the people who have been deprived from centuries and are yet awaiting the fruits of freedom.

We have entered into the phase in which industry is going to play a pivotal role. The institutions of state and society are on the back seat. Through CSR, the industry and corporate houses are poised to make a big intervention in social development of the country. The chapters in this volume on various aspects of CSR have made timely analyses of its potential and contribution. Industry by its very nature and temperament is an organized institution. This characteristic of industry is surely going to make a huge impact on social and economic development of the country in coming years.

The NGOs, it seems, will always be needed in a vast country like ours. There are people and the areas in the country where outreach is not in good shape. It is the NGOs who go there and serve the people. Some chapters have brought out the conceptual and operational relevance of the NGOs very well. It has enhanced the value of the *festschrift*. As stated earlier, the comprehensive objectives of social development can be best achieved in triangular partnership of market (or say economy, corporate or industries), polity (political parties, government, public sphere, state) and civil society (NGOs, SHOs, CVOs, voluntary organizations). The skill and courage lies in striking a balance among the three, so that no segment develops tendency to dominate and exploit the other. In a globalized era, the national boundaries have become meaningless

Youth activities are the spice of a nation's energy, hope and struggle to rise. The NSS under the purposeful leadership of Professor Navale has made such wonderful and commendable achievements that it makes us all Barodians very proud of him. It is an inspiring story. In our country, somehow making speeches has acquired undue priority and emphasis. It needs to be stressed that action is equally important.

During my tenure as the Vice Chancellor of the MSU, I had an opportunity to interact with Professor Navale and he immensely impressed me with his knowledge, attitude and devotion to his duties. He brought various proposals to start the new courses having a foresight. I supported him to the hilt. The outcome of which is now evident. The students of Faculty of Social Work of the MSU are in great demand. The credit goes, among others, undoubtedly to Professor Navale.

The collection of essays in this volume is the most befitting tribute paid to his academic work and active contribution to social development. I congratulate the editor of this *festschrift*, Professor Chhaya Patel, for undertaking academically and professionally such a noble and timely project.

I feel quite honoured to write the Foreword to such a wonderfully edited *festschrift*.

Dr Anil Kane
Former Vice Chancellor,
The Maharaja Sayajirao University of Baroda, Baroda.
President Emeritus, World Wind Energy Association, Bonn, Germany.

Acknowledgements

First and foremost, I would like to thank Professor Anil S. Navale for agreeing to the idea of bringing out a *festschrift* in his honour and granting consent to edit this volume. This project was conceived a few years ago. I am extremely grateful to all the eminent writers for their contribution in form of chapters for this *festschrift* volume. I wish to particularly mention the fact that the patience they have shown during all these years of awaiting the publishing of this volume is truly appreciated. I wish to offer my sincere apologies to all the esteemed contributors for the inordinate delay in the project.

Dr Anil Kane, former Vice Chancellor, The Maharaja Sayajirao University of Baroda, Baroda; President Emeritus, World Wind Energy Association, Bonn, Germany, and a well-known technocrat has done a great honour and favour by writing a Foreword for this volume. We are extremely grateful to Dr Kane for having agreed to write it and then giving it within a very short time. I also thank my doctoral student and colleague Nida Faruqui, Assistant Professor, Faculty of Social Work, who amidst her busy schedule, cheerfully and readily helped me as and when I requested her during various stages of this publication. I thank my office colleagues at the Faculty of Social Work, Mr Madhukar Mahajan and Mrs Dipti D. Sakharikar, for their periodically sought computer help and administrative inputs. I place on record my sincere thanks to the publisher and his team for doing a good professional job of publishing this *festschrift*.

I feel indebted to my family for having stood behind me in support and encouragement. My mother Anandiben Rambhai Patel, despite being in her advanced age has been the moral force and inspiration behind my modest academic pursuits like this one. My two lovely daughters – Prachi and Bhoomi – often missed on my family time with them but understandingly have lived with it. Prachi also did typing for part of the manuscript. Bhoomi developed self-dependence and thereby spared me from many motherly routines of parental concerns and care. Priyavadan, my husband, has given continuous academic encouragement, guidance and ungrudging help in proof-reading the manuscript despite his own academic and administrative engagements.

I hope this academically ambitious and thematically chequered compilation of essays on such relevant contemporary sub-themes as youth, women, CSR, NGOs, tribal society, PLHA and Gandhi will be of interest to all those who are engaged in the complex, challenging and herculean task of first making sense of and then achieving social development in India.

Baroda **Chhaya Patel**

Contributors

A.S. Kohli, Professor, Department of Social Work and Dean, Faculty of Social Sciences, Jamia Millia Islamia University, New Delhi.

C.Thomas Abraham, Head, Department of Adult Education, Mahatma Gandhi University, Kottayam, Kerala.

Chhaya Patel, Professor, Faculty of Social Work, The M.S. University of Baroda, Baroda, Gujarat.

D.P. Singh, Professor and Head, Department of Social Work, Punjabi University, Patiala, Punjab.

H.S. Suresh, Assistant Programme Advisor, NSS Regional Centre, Ministry of Youth Affairs and Sports, Government of India, Bangalore.

Jagadish B. Deputy Manager, Employee Relations Department, Human Resource Division, Toyota Kirloskar Motor Private Limited, Plot No. 1, Bidadi Industrial Area, Ramanagar District.

Jayshree B. Thakore, Former Professor and Head, Labour Welfare Department, Gujarat University, Ahmedabad.

Koteswara Raju Penmetsa, Principal, DNR Autonomous College and Post-Graduate Courses and Research Centre, Bhimavaram, Andhra Pradesh.

Mahajan P. Mani, Professor (Social Work), School of Gandhian Thought and Development Studies, Mahatma Gandhi University, Kottayam, Kerala.

Mital Petiwale, Visiting Faculty, Faculty of Social Work, The M.S. University of Baroda, Baroda, Gujarat.

Ram Kumar Balyan, Management Educator and Technocrat, CPIMR, Ahmedabad.

R.B.S. Verma, Professor and Head, Department of Social Work, Jain Vishva Bharati University, Ladnun, Rajasthan.

R.D. Sampath Kumar, Director, Centre for Study of Social Exclusion and Inclusive Policy, and Professor, Department of Social Work, Andhra University, Visakhapatnam.

Ritu Mor, Research Scholar, Department of Education and Community Service, Punjabi University, Patiala, Punjab.

Sangeeta Sharma Dhaor, Assistant Professor, Department of Social Work, Bhimrao Ambedkar College, University of Delhi, Delhi.

Sanjai Bhatt, Professor and Head, Department of Social Work, University of Delhi, Delhi.

Sreepriya C.K., School of Gandhian Thought and Development Studies, Mahatma Gandhi University, Kottayam, Kerala.

Sudarshan Iyengar, Former Vice Chancellor, Gujarat Vidyapeeth, Ashram Road, Ahmedabad.

Surendra Singh, Former Vice Chancellor, Mahatma Gandhi Kashi Vidyapith, Varanasi.

Y.S. Siddegowda, Professor, Department of Studies in Social Work, University of Mysore, Manasagangothri, Mysore.

CHAPTER 1

Introduction

CHHAYA PATEL

Festschrift: An Ennobling Academic Tradition

We, in the profession of knowing, learning, teaching, researching, theorizing and practising social sciences, have inherited a very noble tradition of bidding a befitting farewell to an outstanding retiring colleague by writing and/or compiling essays in his or her honour as a tribute to and memory of our long productive institutional association. In social work profession, the Tata Institute of Social Sciences, Mumbai, brought out a Special Issue of *The Indian Journal of Social Work,* edited by Professor Murli Desai, to felicitate Professor Armaity S. Desai and to celebrate the 60th anniversary of the Journal. The following memorable and resounding words of the editor express this sentiment profoundly:

> It is a great privilege and pleasure for me to write this editorial for the Special Issue of *The Indian Journal of Social Work* (IJSW), on 'Social Work Education', in felicitation of Prof Armaity S. Desai. This event is a confluence of two developments. One is, that Prof Desai has achieved the ultimate in her outstanding career, as a social work educator by providing leadership to the University Grants Commission (UGC) for four years, when she retired from it in April 1999. This called for her long overdue felicitation. The second development was the completion of 60 years of uninterrupted publishing by the IJSW, a pioneering medium of social work literature in India. This called for a celebration. What better celebration could the IJSW have than publish a Special Issue in felicitation of Prof Desai? (Desai 2000: 137)

The eminent scholars of social work profession like Katherine A. Kendall, P.D. Kulkarni, David Cox, Shankar Pathak, Ralph Garber, Manohar S. Pawar, Murli Desai, Gracy Fernandes and several other scholars wrote articles and some others presented bouquets of appreciative words in honour of her and the IJSW.

Similarly, the eminent sociologists, political scientists and social scientists like M.N. Srinivas (Shah et al. 1996–1998), Alice Thorner (Patel et al. 2002), I.P. Desai (Shah 1997), Rajni Kothari (Sheth and Nandy 1996), A.M. Shah (Baviskar and Patel 2010), Jan Breman (Shah et al. 2002), A.R. Desai (Shah 1990), A.P. Rana (Bajpai and Shukul 1995), Indira Patel (Patel 1999 and 2009) and a few others are honoured by *festschrifts* (in some cases in multiple volumes) which have enriched the pool of literature in the subject and have become distinct memorable milestones in academic publishing history. Pioneering and prominent scholars of other social sciences like economics and history too have been honoured by the fellow academicians by bringing out excellent edited volumes of seminal essays. This small list of eminent scholars felicitated by equally eminent editors and fellow scholars form one type of *festschrifts* wherein the binding factor in most cases is that of belonging to the same discipline of sociology, political science, history, economics or social work.

There is another type of *festschrifts* too which is altogether a different and unique category in itself. In this category, the editors and contributors to the *festschrift* volume are all very well-known and eminent scholars of international repute, but the so honoured felicitee or the felicitated scholar is not so well known in the formal, institutional and popular circles of academic world. In Western India, we have a *festschrift* volume edited by Upendra Baxi and Bhikhu C. Parekh (1995) in honour of Raojibhai Patel, who was formally only a teacher of mathematics at The M.S. University of Baroda, Gujarat, but was an outstanding teacher (across the usual borders of the disciplines), himself a scholar and scholarship-builder among the young seekers of knowledge and truth, humanist and progressive thinker and an activist who promoted and safeguarded such democratic values as freedom, rights, equality and justice throughout his fully lived productive life. Though there are not many examples of this particular genre of *festschrift* in our knowledge, it is a fairly exemplary one. Parekh has sketched an excellent and comprehensive appreciation of Raojibhai in the following rather long quote:

> Although a mathematician by training ... he is also a philosopher, a social theorist, and a student of Indian history and politics. Having

> read widely and thought deeply, he has clearly worked-out views. Like Socrates, to whom he bears considerable physical resemblance, he is a passionate thinker, constantly probing large philosophical questions, challenging fashionable dogmas, and bringing a fresh and powerful intellect to the analysis of contemporary political and ideological issues.
>
> ... Frustrated by the intellectual mediocrity of the official university, keen and intelligent young students and lecturers belonging to diverse disciplines gravitated towards him ..., discussing Locke, Hume, Marx, Russell, Carnap, M.N. Roy, Karl Popper, Buddhism, Hinduism, Gandhi, Nehru, and of course Indian politics.
>
> ... Raojibhai, 'Mota' as he was affectionately called, played many roles, possible only in an Indian context. He was a teacher though never a guru, for he was too rebellious and rationalist for that .... He was an eternal rebel challenging not only the prevalent intellectual orthodoxies and social practices but also the university authorities; ... He was also as student, constantly reading; thinking, seeking information, borrowing books, asking service, admitting mistakes and circulating drafts of his articles. Thanks to all this, members of the 'Mota School' developed powerful emotional bonds with him. ... Socrates had only one Plato; Raojibhai can claim at least half a dozen. (1995: 432–435)

According to *Bhagavad Gita,* it is immature to think that knowledge and action are different. Wisdom lies in seeing the both as the same. It is observed that, in most cases, the great philosophers, thinkers, theorists, academics, intellectuals or men of ideas rarely are the men of action. The leisurely comforts of rocking in proverbial 'arm chair', placed on ivory towers, and gazing at the far away located macro frontiers and probing deep into the micro recesses of social realities in order to create a new dreamy, utopian vision is one part of the intellectual engagement. But, equally important, if not less, is the other part, i.e. getting off from the high towers and arm chairs and grounding the ideas or visions into some form of concrete action. The following continuing words of Parekh about Raojibhai Mota illuminate and bring out this combination knowledge/action so cogently and vividly:

> At the political (or say activist) level, Raojibhai's great achievement consists in founding the Baroda University Teachers' Association and turning it into powerful tool of academic and social

> transformation. Under his leadership, the Association took on the university authorities ..., challenged the city bosses, fought against the corrupt teachers, and helped create a healthy academic environment. ... Thanks to (these) ... efforts, the Government of Gujarat (changed) the policy of nominating political stooges as Vice-chancellors .... It is his abiding regret that this policy proved short-lived, and that (the) teachers' associations have degenerated into trade unions aggressively fighting only for their salaries and forming damaging alliances with corrupt students' unions.

This rather unusually long citation of a text is intended to highlight the many-splendored scope and varied nature of Indian intellectual and academic life, almost co-existing as a parallel university with the existing one; and which is capable of giving us such pleasant surprises as the outstanding early phase 'graduates' of 'Mota School'/alternative university such as Bhikhu Parekh, Rajni Kothari, D.L. Sheth, Prakash Desai, Dhaval Mehta and others. Later on, under the auspices of Baroda Study Group, led by V.N. Kothari and P.J. Patel the Socratic tradition of seeking knowledge *a la* symposium mode continued in which 'Mota' would invariably be present and actively participate in the proceedings.

The *festschrifts* do not always enjoy all embracing or uncritical reception. It is just in the fitness of the academic profession and advancement of the frontiers of knowledge that nothing passes without being subjected to critical scrutiny of any such idea or an action in public domain. If this were not to happen, the whole effort runs the risk of turning into idol-like hero worship or performing the *aarti* (religious obeisance of a kind) of the favourite deity by the faith-blinded disciples of a sect. We are in a happy state that the domain of academics is blessed with such scholars like Brass (2003) who stand at the other end of the effort and look at it critically without reducing the degree of respect or honour of the scholars felicitated. Brass' strong and caustic words are harsh but quite realistic and useful as they sound a warning bell for all those engaged in the business of producing the *festschrifts*:

> Of the many and varied kinds of text, the festschrift is probably the nearest equivalent to a vanity publication. The gulf between on the one hand the public image of academic practice as a virtuous pursuit of knowledge, and on the other the private reality informing much academic practice – venality and opportunism, intellectual appropriation and suppression – is perhaps nowhere so much in evidence.

> All too often, the festschrift amounts to nothing more than the demonstration of fealty on the part of a group of clients rounded up by a powerful individual approaching retirement, who ... insists on one last public outpouring of deference.
>
> ... The only really transparent approach to this kind of celebratory volume is that adopted some 30 years ago by Frank Manuel (1972: ix), Professor of History at New York University, who confessed unashamedly that: 'This is my sixtieth birthday; but since the temper of the times is not conducive to the gathering of an appropriate Festschrift by my students, I thought I would prepare one for myself'. This declaration of intent to blow his own trumpet, in the absence of others who would agree to blow it for him, is commendably forthright and a somewhat rare admission in academic life. ... One of the more enduring clichés circulating in the academy is that – in so far as a festschrift has any meaning – most of those who get one do not deserve this, while many of those whose work actually merits this kind of recognition never receive such a volume (2003: 220–221).

Though sycophancy is not viewed and considered as a desirable value or a trait, it is often found quite rampant. It takes disguised and sophisticated forms. Hardly any realm of human affairs – be it cultural, political, religious or social – is free from its risks. Some hardcore temporal realms like 'political' and 'social' are particularly vulnerable to its evil presence. If so, then how can academia, which is so deeply steeped into the temporal realms like 'political' and 'social' can be free from its affliction is definitely a moot issue. Hence, Brass, how so much ever sound crude and rude, seems to be right in some of his observations. The world of academia is plagued by the malady of sycophancy. However, it must be stated in clear and unequivocal terms that the *festschrifts* referred to and discussed here in this section are a basket of big exception to Brass' otherwise appreciable assessment. Honouring and felicitating a retired or retiring teacher, mentor, colleague, scholar of great repute and contributor to the creation, sustenance or well-being of the institution and the discipline is certainly not a case of sycophancy or trumped up false importance. It is, indeed, a case of genuine as well as universal appreciation and expression of noble thoughts on the parting occasion. Collapsing of national boundaries and geographies, as seen in some cases, is not a small feat. It is also, indeed, one of the most ennobling and fulfilling academic traditions and practices among the entire participating fraternity of social science professionals, intellectuals, scholars and academics.

There is also a third dimension of academic life in Indian context in which orientation to social initiative, intervention and action as well as institution-building, sustaining and expanding is given primacy (often at the cost of one's own leisurely pursued academic interest and output in terms of theoretical and philosophical reflections, writings and publishing). The same M.S. University of Baroda had several academics who chose to devote themselves to building their particular departments or faculties and spent a life time making them congenial places for many young and the competent scholars to work, contribute and flourish. Their energies were channelled into creating favourable administration and governance structures for facilitating academic and research investigations in otherwise prevalent bureaucratic and conservative environment in the university system. In this sense, the present edited volume is a *festschrift* of a different genre than the two types of it discussed above.

About this *Festschrift*

Social work is such a subject-area which has to be preponderant in favour of process, fact, evidence, and/or empiric rather than being concerned with *only* the normative, theoretical, ideological or philosophical orientations. Practice of social work has come to acquire primacy as compared to the studies of pure theory in such social sciences as sociology, political science, economics, etc. This is not to state and claim that there is no interest in examining theory-fact interplay and relationship between the two in studies done in social work. However, as in case of all other social sciences, the emphasis and balance between the two often gets skewed. Empiric or fact dominates over the concerns of the theory. This volume is conceived as an attempt to pay tribute to a teacher, mentor and colleague who epitomized the empirical practice (of course, guided and informed by latent theoretical, ideological and philosophical orientations) of social work and interwove it so closely and finely that lines of distinctions between the personal and the institutional boundaries blurred and often got merged.

Hence, a few words about the genesis of this volume are in order. The onus of explaining the rationale for the production of such a volume of essays is on the editor's shoulders. Here is the story of its genesis. It was, indeed, a great privilege and pleasure to publish a successful and fairly well received *festschrift* volume of essays in 1999 in honour of an eminent and outstanding teacher, professional and practitioner of social work, (Late) Professor Indira Patel of Baroda

School of Social Work, The M.S. University of Baroda, Baroda (Patel 1999). To our pleasant surprise, it was reprinted in 2009. In that *festschrift*, I had then expressed a few brief and sketchy thoughts on my academic association and appreciation of Professor Navale which was as follows:

> Between 1985 and 1990, I was deeply involved in exploring and choosing an area of research for my doctoral degree .... With the aim of doing Ph.D., I came back to Vadodara and again joined the Faculty of Social Work. It was in this connection that I began meeting my teachers and (now) senior colleagues .... Professor Anil Navale, ... Head and Dean, Faculty of Social Work; Coordinator, UGC-DRS Programme in Social Work; and Honorary Director, National Service Scheme, M.S. University of Baroda, Vadodara, was the first person to bring me closer to Professor Indira Patel by involving me in numerous academically related activities and programmes. He convinced me that there is a lot more to learn from 'Ben' (as he, like many others, called her) .... I owe a very special word of thanks to Prof Navale, as looking back; I feel I would have missed a major lesson in my life, had I not come in contact with Indiraben. This apart, the credit for initiating me in into the field of social work teaching, practice and profession goes to Professor Navale. I worked with him in the NSS and acquired important insights into the issues that are usually encountered in the field (Patel 1999 and 2009: 11–12).

I then had not the slightest inkling of stretching it further in future and transforming it into a full scale edited volume in his honour after the passage of several years of his formal retirement. I have a great pleasure in coming up with second such edited volume in honour of Professor Anil S. Navale from the Baroda School of Social Work. The original objectives and intentions in producing this particular *festschrift* were quite ambitious. But the thematically quite diverse and chequered response from the contributors as well as an inadvertent delay in its compilation, production and publication has altered its character, content and composition. I shoulder complete responsibility for this delay and owe a sincere word of apology to all the esteemed contributors to this volume. I appreciate their patience and the spirit of camaraderie. In short, these are the thoughts which had sowed the seeds of this *festschrift* a few years ago.

Social Development: Youth, CSR, NGOs and Gandhi

This volume has received encouraging responses and contributions from scholars of social work discipline. Except for a few contributors, most scholars knew Professor Navale and were associated with him in one or the other multi-dimensional state, national or international level engagements. They shared inspiring professional relationship of collegiality, mutual respect and personal regards. These contribution-chapters are tributes to Professor Navale's life-long work done on the Gandhian principles of social intervention with youth, community, NGOs, government and semi-government policy forums and industry. Thematically speaking, the papers have focused on areas of 'GO – NGO' collaboration, women empowerment, role of youth, NSS, CSR, tribal empowerment and Gandhian approach to concerns of social work. Now, let us have a synoptic glimpse into the narratives of each paper and get introduced to the world of interesting debates on the ideas, institutions, individuals and actions.

This volume is organized along the following major questions and concerns:

1. How is the youth defined? What is the history of youth engagement in self as well as social development? What are the realistic assessments of the promises and potential of the country's much trumpeted and celebrated demographic dividend, namely the youth, towards contributing to economic and social development. What are the challenges faced by the youth in the wake of liberalization, privatization and globalization of country's economies and the markets? How does the youth perceive and react to the reduced and retreated role of the state from the spheres of social and economic development? Does the youth continue to be the prime mover of social transformation? What role can youth play in combating such challenges in health development field as counselling and caring for PLHA? How to reduce or eliminate the risk behaviour of the young victims of HIV/AIDS?
2. What are the historical and contemporary narratives on voluntary sector in India? What are, if any, the shifts in the role, activities, contribution, patterns and potential of the non-governmental organizations? What is their relationship with the two other powerful institutions of market and the state? Has the relevance of voluntary sector increased or decreased? What has caused either the increase or the decrease?
3. What are the existing and emerging perspectives on corporate social responsibility (CSR)? How is the CSR phenomenon relevant to and serve the social work interest? What are the

empirical evidences of CSR-practice? How have the Indian and MNC corporate entities responded to it? How does CSR contribute to the spheres of social and community development which are being gradually vacated by the retreating state? What lessons can be drawn from its growth and activities?

4. Why do Gandhi's ideas, thoughts, experiments, social action strategies, social reform activities, social reconstruction projects like *nayi buniyadi talim* (new basic training), non-violence, faith in inherent goodness of man, trusteeship, community-building, *sarvodaya*, man-making, rural development, women upliftment, universalist outlook, humanitarian values, pro-poor concerns, anti-exploitation campaigns, cleanliness crusades and a host of many other similar things continue to draw attention of social work and social science academics? It seems Gandhism and social work practice has umbilical cord like relationship. Some scholars have laboured hard to uphold and establish its contemporary relevance in various thematic fields of concern to this *festschrift*.

Youth as Prime Mover of Social Change

Youth of any community, society, region or a country is an indispensable asset for organizing a variety of socio-economically transformative campaigns, actions and activities. The biggest example of this process before us is that of Mahatma Gandhi. He organized Indians in South Africa and launched a non-violent movement with the help of the youth. He not only galvanized and energized the youth of his home region but also of the entire country. This is true of many countries in the world. The youth has always been an unfailing vanguard of the suffering masses for either initiating, sustaining or successfully steering the reformative or revolutionary movements, actions, struggles, agitations or protests against unjust practices and exploitative conditions. The world history is full of such examples. In Russia, it was Lenin; Hitler in Germany; Mao in China; Che Guevara in Cuba and Latin America; Nelson Mandela in South Africa and recently the American President Barack Hussein Obama in the USA and Narendra Modi in India– all were successful in rallying the youth of their respective countries for a course corrective efforts as they perceived it and as the context of their times demanded it. This attribute of the youth makes it a 'ready to take a plunge resource' of any society, community or country.

If we browse through the pages of world history of youth mobilization, involvement, participation and action, we find a very rich and hope building material in front of us. Every period of crisis in every history has afforded an excellent scope for constructive rebuilding and regeneration of any society of whatever type and characteristics. Youth has been at the centre of such vortexes of major transformations. Youth, indeed, symbolizes energy, empathy, power, courage, sacrifice, dreams, hopes, aspirations for the self and for the downtrodden and acts as a transformative change agent.

Closer home, if we look in our own country and in the state of Gujarat (before and after its formation in May 1960), we find that we have a rich history of big and small reformative, transformative and rot-removing efforts by youth. Most of them have been well documented, whereas others have remained unrecorded. The contribution of those youth who were the part of the nationalist freedom movement are well archived but the youth of certain sections of society such as the tribal or dalits remains to be paid due attention. Mahatma Gandhi's engagement with youth brought about unprecedented social changes during the freedom struggle. He made a multi-pronged deployment of the youth to achieve such lofty goals as political freedom, rural reconstruction, social reforms, ushering of democratic values of fraternity, equality and justice. Historically, this was unparallel.

After about a decade of India's Independence, the Bombay State was plunged into the demand for bifurcation of the state into Maharashtra and Gujarat. At the centre of this demand in Gujarat was the leadership of Indulal Yagnik and his power to appeal and mobilize the youth of the Gujarat part of the bilingual state. He persisted with his demand for separate state of Mahagujarat for about 5–6 years during 1956–60 on the core support of the state's middle class, urban youth. The credit for the birth of the state of Gujarat should substantively and clearly go to the account of its youth. Second major political system cleansing exercise took shape in form of the *Navnirman* Movement of 1970s. A leader from another part of the country, namely, Jay Prakash Narain, advocate of Total Revolution, inspired the youth of the state to crusade against the corrupt and anti-poor rule of the Congress. At the centre of this youth movement was the rise of food prices and the subsequent rise in the hostel food bills of students of Morbi Engineering College in Saurashtra and L.D. Engineering College in Ahmedabad. It was then perceived by the youth of the state that the hoarders, traders, black marketers and the politicians were acting in collusion and the people were suffering. They launched a successful protest movement and pulled down the corrupt state government. It must be noted here that the years in the decades of 1960s and 1970s were the years of not only state or regional level youth unease, unrests, protests, agitations and action-oriented movements but also of national and global levels.

These are the shining examples of somewhat macro and higher level of youth engagement in corrective and reformist or revolutionary political processes. However, there is still a level of youth engagement which is right down our nose and has remained insufficiently noticed and appreciated. It can be described as belonging to the domain of institutionalized mobilization and engagement of the youth for social transformation through social reconstruction by direct action. One of the several positive outcomes of the post-Independence phase of our collective life as a nation is the spread of education. Today, it is for everyone to see the quantum jump that this phenomenon has taken. Colleges and universities have increased and expanded multi-fold. A sizable but mobile part of the population, in form of the youth, is today housed in these colleges and the universities of the country. The raw and unharnessed energy of these youth needed to be positively used in nation-building and rural as well as urban reconstruction. A nation-wide programme in the form of National Service Scheme (NSS) was, hence, launched in the country, specifically to engage the college/university youth into the task of nation-building and rural reconstruction.

Professor Anil S. Navale, among others, was at the forefront in founding and grounding this programme in the state of Gujarat. In the early 1970s, the college and university youth was galvanized and mobilized into action on a hitherto unprecedented scale. In Baroda, Professor Navale was at the centre of mobilizing the youth of the M.S. University of Baroda and the teachers too for starting and spreading the NSS message as well as the activities. He would personally go to each faculty of the university, to the numerous departments of the faculties and move from one class room to the next class room to inform, mobilize and appeal to the students to join the NSS. To the legitimate credit of Professor Navale, the students' response was so overwhelming that apart from the students of generic courses in arts and commerce faculties, the serious and career-oriented students of professional courses like law, science, polytechnic, engineering and medical faculties of the M.S. University got attracted to a variety of NSS activities.

His drive, in fact, can be described as a sort of a revolution in mobilization and engaging of the university youth into extensive community and national social service. Such a large-scaled phenomenon was never before witnessed in the history of the university. Subsequently, the good work of NSS in the home city, university and the state took Professor Navale to newer organizational heights across the country and beyond. Professor Navale's contribution to youth mobilization and engagement for nation-building and rural reconstruction along Gandhian ideas, thought, practices and method has remained insufficiently noticed, acknowledged and appreciated. A civilized, educated, modern and critically appreciative intellectual community of social work scholars, practitioners, teachers and professionals cannot neglect to look into and comment on such seminal and profound contributions to the enrichment of the discipline as done by Professor Navale.

NSS and the Youth: Genesis, Rise and Decline

The importance of all-round development and engagement of youth in our society is somewhat of a recent phenomenon. But my association with youth dates back to 1979 when I joined the National Service Scheme (NSS) programme as Field Organizer in the M.S. University of Baroda, my *alma mater*. This massive national initiative was launched in 1969 by the Ministry of Youth Affairs and Sports, Government of India (Government of India 1969). I was privileged to be associated with it. My job in the NSS at the MSU-Baroda was to work as a link between the less privileged rural youth and the privileged urban youth who were fortunate to receive higher education by entering into the colleges and the universities. This was primarily done through continuous but different field exposures. This served dual purpose. The university urban youth got an opportunity for rural community service and, thereby, achieving self-development. The rural youth, in turn, got an opportunity to meet their urban counterparts and interact with them. The rural reconstruction activities were planned in such a way that both mutually benefited. The activities were conducted on group or collective as well as on one-to-one basis. Thereby, I observed that they gained direct learning through interactions and got indirect insights into each other's world view by making observations.

As an NSS Field Organizer, I too was professionally and academically rewarded immensely. I observed that the experiences and insights gathered from it were of a mixed type. Some were good and some were not so good. The main drawback was the inherent organizational tendency to pick up those activities which were subjectively, contextually and affordably available as well as possible to organize – given the limits of the field conditions and sociological profile of the area. They may not always be normatively, ideally and objectively of a desired type. Thus, the seeds of academic concerns, professional, research and extension involvement in youth activities were sown during the early part of my career. This valuable work experience with the youth at the NSS lay at the back of my mind in conceiving this particular project. It was an excellent opportunity to understand the youth, their aspirations, imaginations, interests and potential for self-development, general social development and sustainable development. I have been a witness to so many youth activity campaigns conducted under the auspices of NSS.

Hence, I have come to conclude that given proper guidance, direction, encouragement and freedom of idea and action, the youth is capable to achieve miracles. Reflecting on these experiences of past involvement with the youth, a fresh volley of questions pertaining to youth began to spring in my mind, such as: who are youth, what are their aspirations, what are the realities they are surrounded with, what problems they face today, how they can be helped in resolving them, what can promote their self-development, how can their energies be channelized in a concerted, planned and well-directed manner for theirs as well as overall societal development. The entire volume is devoted to this comprehensive list of questions to be answered in part or as a whole depending on the respective author's own orientation, inclination and interest. In other words, the answers to quite a few of these questions will be found in various seminal contributions received for the volume from the eminent scholars and academicians.

I, however, wish to attempt an answer to the questions as to who are the youth and what are their socio-economic conditions and wellness aspirations. In my humble understanding, youth is a highly motivated and enthusiastic person. It is an important but formative phase in human life-cycle. As it happens in most other sociological and demographical cases, there is no one age-based definition of youth. Different societies, organizations, agencies, and countries have defined youth contextually and subjectively. So it is good to begin with recommendatory definition of somewhat universal character and then it would be useful to examine the country specific definition of youth. As defined by the United Nations, all persons covered in the age group of 15–24 years are defined as youth. The Indian National Policy document of 2003 widened the net and covered all those in the age band of 13–35 years and defined them as youth. Subsequently in 2014, the concerned Ministry of Government of India modified the age group band covering youth and fixed it at 15–29 years for more focused and concerted emphasis on designing various youth welfare initiatives (Government of India 2014).

Apart from the Census-type, a particular age group-based definition of youth, decided at the top policy echelons of the country, there are various socio-economic and cultural dimensions concerning the youth regarding which I got valuable opportunity to have a close look and deep peep into the lives of rural and urban youth through the window of the NSS activities. I observed that the youth is like the spectrum of a rainbow. It is a multi-coloured social phenomenon. Each colour can be seen independent of others as well as a part of the whole spectrum. I felt that the destiny of the youth is rooted in their wider social milieu and in the prospects of life opportunities made available to them by society, state and the economy/market.

I also noticed that the most rural and urban youth from difficult economic conditions and background have grown up into youth while securing the livelihood for the otherwise struggling family. Shouldering the entire or part responsibility of one's family leaves little time for education in school, college or university (which are invariably located in towns or cities away from the village). The needs and the desires of the youth in general are not adequately met or fulfilled, except for a small well to do and privileged sections of youth in rural as well as urban areas. In developing countries, most youth are born in the midst of difficult poverty conditions and grow up in challenging circumstances. Hence, making an attempt to answer the rest of the associated questions raised earlier becomes pertinent and relevant proposition.

In 2012, the world leaders met in Rio de Janeiro with fifty thousand concerned individuals and representatives from all major sectors and sections of society such as academia, business, policy-makers, law, civil society organizations, etc. to pursue the global goal of achieving sustainable development (Hongbo 2013). Rio was an extension of the concerns voiced and agreed upon in Earth summit of 1992. The Millennium Development Goals, launched by the United Nations about 13–14 years ago, have been actively pursued by the world leaders in organizing the fight against poverty, providing all access to basic health, education and gender equality. These goals are relentlessly pursued through collective public efforts, voluntary commitments and memberships among and within the countries. The objective of reducing the global poverty conditions for achieving full human development as well as upholding the human dignity by generating huge wealth through sustained incomes and just equitable distribution of world resources is a laudable millennium goal, covering youth as well as the other age categories in a society.

Vyas's following words have echoed the same concern somewhat more poignantly when he argued that:

> To leave out one third of the population behind in our quest for higher growth, cannot be justified by any canon of ethics. It is also bad economics as *sustainable growth*, even in terms of GDP will remain elusive with such high burden of marginalized households. It is possible to make a marked improvement in our efforts to eradicate poverty, if ... an environment is created where a set of values are shared, mutual obligations are respected, and commitment to given tasks is considered sacrosanct (2013: 29).

In this context, the economic status of Indian youth too needs to be synoptically appraised. It is reported that only 2 per cent of India's youth is imparted vocational training. The figure of 7 per cent for the entire working age group having received such training is not quite encouraging for the country (Varma 2013: 7).

Another shocking revelation has come from the data of the National Crime Record Bureau. It is reported that 41 per cent of the suicide victims were under the age of 30 years (*Times of India* 2013: 2), which actually pertains to the youth category. This is an extremely worrisome development. There could be several reasons for such a high rate of suicides among the youth – such as market or liberalized economy-induced stiff competition for jobs, fear of retention or loss of the job under new conditions of 'hire and fire', partial or non-payment of wages or salaries for the work done, perennially lurking financial hardships, various typically age-related conditions like failures in examinations, loosely formed and inexperienced, impulsive handling of intimate personal relationships, family problems, adventures and irrational decisions. In short, this shows that there is an urgent need for massive institutional intervention of various NGOs and community-based organizations to rekindle the hope of good life among the youth and provide them with life-shaping and man-making opportunities.

One more distressing fact regarding the contemporary conditions of youth in India has emerged from the UNESCO Report's findings (Rajan 2013) on the current trends in internal migration of youth in India. From a total youth population of 274 million, 92 million youth migrate internally in India. According to 2002 Census of India, one out of every three youth was an internal migrant (Rajan 2013). But this picture changes when we look up the 1993 and 2007–08 data sets generated by NSSO. According to it, the number of young internal migrants to total migrants has increased from 67 to 75 per cent. From a total population of 326 million internal migrants, almost 33 per cent are youth in the age group of 15–29 years age. There is no doubt about the economic contribution made by such a vast mobile labour population, but the younger migrants among them suffer from serious losses of opportunities in benefitting from the processes and outcome of human capital formation. They encounter serious challenges in consistently getting education, access to skill formation and training as well as adequate and suitable employment. It is also revealed by the studies (Rajan 2013) that despite politico-electorally the much celebrated 'demographic dividend', utilizing of the potential of the youth is not reflected in the policies and measures concerning migration and labour force. Hence, the National Youth Policy of 2012 has focused on this neglected demographic segment of youth as a target.

Despite this renewed policy intervention and focus, it is felt that some of the major issues pertaining to young migrants have remained unattended. In order to rectify this situation; the youth needs to be made part of formal labour force by adopting a strategy to give them the benefits of education, training and employment (as mentioned earlier just above). Labour reforms are urgently needed. Other associated aspects like age, gender, marital status of the migrant youth too must be paid more research and policy attention.

Rise and decline of an empire in history and of an institution, a welfare scheme or a development programme in a democratic society are considered as a part of collective life. In this *festschrift*, the rise of NSS is narrated and celebrated with exhaustive details of its genesis, growth, challenges and achievements. It seems, as in history so in present, the golden age of NSS in India has come to an end with a little hope of its meaningful revival and return to old glory. Today, the NSS is alive only in its 10–15 per cent originally conceived potential and basked glory of the past years. This has serious political implications too. The perfectly democratic politics of the country has made a paradigm shift. In the first six decades of the Independence, the emphasis was on enforcing democratic values as committed in the Constitution of India through a variety of initiatives and mechanisms.

In early years of the second decade of new century, we are witnessing major shifts from centrist politics to politics of the right. The forces and institutions of religio-cultural right are impatient to take over, expand and dominate these hitherto condemned 'left-liberal-secular' institutions like NSS, universities, trade organizations, youth bodies, women's organizations, civil liberties protection groups, professional and sports associations, media groups, etc. for advancing their 'doubtful' democratic agenda, albeit at times through democratic, legal and constitutional means and at other times manipulative means. Recent NSS activities are infiltrated by the RSS and programmes are so designed to suit their agenda. In an all Gujarat event of celebrating the NSS Day on 24 September 2014 at Patan in North Gujarat University, one of the several competitions organized (apparently to bring out the talent in the young students) was 'the singing competition'. The student of Baroda NSS got the third prize which was a media news event along with the entire list of the office-bearers of the NSS. In an event, recently hosted by NSS at Baroda, the city regional chief of RSS (among others from Vivekanand Kendra, former NSS office bearers, etc.) addressed the NSS gatherings of the students.

These developments are mentioned only to point out the trivialization of NSS objectives at the hub and home of NSS in Gujarat, namely, the M. S. University of Baroda. Agreed that singing and dancing is a new commercially driven market and media induced craze among the young, but the moot issue is about falling prey to it by NSS. In such an ideological vacuum, lack of imagination and normative void in the NSS administration, the religio-cultural and political bodies like RSS, VHP, ABVP will naturally find it as an attractive site for expanding and deepening their ideology and agenda through harmless-looking youth activities. This, at the moment, seems to be the *fait accompli* of the NSS and the country. Whether this endangers the consolidation of constitutionally ordained democratic functioning of first six decades of the Republic of India is for the future to tell (but for concerned academicians to imagine and fear).

Industry and the CSR

The other powerful and lingering dimension of Professor Navale's contribution and legacy lies in building, nurturing, sustaining and expanding the 'university-industry' interface which was initiated many years before the birth of today's much debated and discussed phenomenon of corporate social responsibility (CSR). The scale of this individually initiated interface in terms of the money sourced and spent, geographic area of rural and urban centres covered, various activities done, and results achieved or fruits yielded were far lesser and fewer than the scale of its contemporary variant in form of the CSR. But the inspiration and guidance sought from Gandhian ideas and vision, spirit of community and national service invoked, sheer energy generated and deployed and unflinching commitment ploughed by Navale was no less note-worthy and significant. The career profile of Professor Navale presented at the end of the volume bears a great testimony to these micro narratives of activities and events, claims and facts discussed here.

Apart from the focus on youth predicament, engagement and empowerment by some essayists, a few scholars have made enormous contribution to this felicitation volume by devoting themselves to deciphering the normative, empirical and policy dimensions of corporate social responsibility (CSR). The moot issue in the debate is whether industry's social responsibility should be statutorily defined and enforced by the state/government actions or it has to be a matter of self-realization and purely voluntary action on the part of the industry. The major argument in favour of policy decision on CSR and its enforcement by the state is that the random and unregulated 'chequebook philanthropy' (Venkatesan 2014: 6) done by the corporate houses is not enough. Its impact on social sector remains uneven, skewed and chequered.

The new Companies Act, 2013, has made it compulsory for some 16,000 registered companies in India to comply and contribute to social development through CSR mechanism. The assumption is that if these companies contribute a 2 per cent of their annual profits, the social sector in India can have at its disposal a gigantic sum of ₹ 20,000 crores as an organized corpus (Venkatesan 2014: 6). Needless to state, this policy step has potential to change the face of social sector in India. Interestingly, this has also opened up an enormous and unprecedented scope for the new, young, talented graduates – passing out from the best schools of social work, development studies centres and other social science research institutes in the country and abroad – to engage in the mammoth task of building and strengthening the Indian social sector. In the same way, this development widens the scope for the teachers, researchers, professionals and practitioners of social work to offer innovative and research-based consultancy services on CSR-fund deployment to the desiring corporate houses.

This development has two aspects. One, it has released unprecedented prospects for supporting social sector activities. Secondly, it has also opened up its underbelly. The track record of NGO sector in India has remained a mixed bag. There are about 30 lakh NGOs in India. Several cases of malpractices, wastage and frauds with regard to the NGO funds are intermittently reported. An NGO initiative, in most cases, is an extremely small scale localized, miniature type of an individually motivated and executed as well as corrective or ameliorative effort. Despite being honest and committed many do not have wherewithal, capacity or potential for replication and expansion even if large funds are made available.

On the other hand, there are shining examples of CSR being put to impressive and transformative, progressive and corrective use. Of course, how to spend and on what to spend CSR funding by a particular participant industry is its own prerogative. There are several areas to be selected and focused on keeping in view an industry's own product mix, location, etc. New NGOs can be formed or the existing and proven ones can be roped in with suitable modifications in the contents of intervention. The NGOs working in the areas of human rights, environment, governance, indigenous art forms or hand-made products can be patronized, reformated and re-channelled by infusing necessary CSR funds. Venkatesan (2014) has listed following instances as evidence of this mutually beneficial interactive process of give and take:

1. Microsoft Corporation launched an innovative project on digital literacy which benefitted 40 million children.
2. Hindustan Unilever Limited's CSR initiative in rural markets procured revenue growth rewarding *Shaktiamma* rural distribution model.

According to him, the innovation of CSR is not to be viewed as an 'onerous imposition' or an unwanted burden by the state, but it should be seen as an opportunity for building valuable corporate image.

There are two big corporate houses, namely, Reliance (Mukesh Ambani) and Tata, who have spent huge amounts for CSR through their preferred instrumentalities. For instance, in 2013–14, the Reliance Foundation spent 3.24 per cent of Reliance Industries' net profit for supporting many CSR activities (Pandey 2014: 11). Such a huge amount of ₹ 712 crores as CSR budget to the Foundation was sector-wise spent judiciously on health (59%), rural development (23%), education (11%) and remainder on other activities (7%). Similarly, the largest Indian corporate conglomerate, Tata Group topped the list with CSR spending of ₹ 1,000 crores in the year 2013–14. It is very heartening to learn that in about a decade's period Tata Trusts and Group have spent ₹ 8,000 crores on CSR activities (Zachariah and Singh 2014: 11). The sectors focused for CSR spend by the Tata Group are skill-formation, health and education. There are several others like Aditya Birla Group, who spent ₹ 200 crores through Aditya Birla Centre for Community Initiative and Rural Development as CSR allocation in 2013–14 which is higher than ₹ 150 crores in 2012–13. In sum, under the new regulatory requirements, about 8,000 companies in India will be obligated to spend an estimated mandatory sum of about ₹ 15,000–20,000 crores which is going to be outlaid as CSR budget corpus. This undoubtedly brightens up the future of social sector in India (Zachariah and Singh 2014: 11).

However, our hopes of favourable outcome from CSR efforts must be reigned in as there always shall be a gap between the normative and the empirical. Compliance to new CSR laws and requirements is emerging as a critical and thorny issue. It is adversely affecting the relations between the industry and the government. There is an evidence of veiled threat from the government to penalize the non-compliant and erring industry on CSR. The government is reported to be drawing up plans to penalize those industries and companies which are found to have not spent money as their CSR obligations. Originally, the Companies Act required the industries to spend money on social development but if they could not do so then the board of directors of the erring industry are to offer some explanation. This provision in the law has recently created a situation of confusion, uncertainty and mutual ill-will. Government is in two minds. One view in the government, which is dominant, favours stringent CSR compliance by the companies. According to it, a company's failures over two-three years shall invite penalties.

The industry and the media sources resent this. Both have argued that making profit itself is the evidence of having shouldered the CSR as creating employment and providing livelihood is a huge contribution to social development. Putting money as wages, salaries and income in the hands of the workers actually amounts to enabling them to socially develop as there will be spending on clothing, education, health, nutrition, better housing, recreation, etc. Income generation and thereby, wealth creation is also found to be leading to partial saving which in turn comes back to either public or private investment. This economic cycle itself is a contribution by industry to CSR. Another point of corporate resentment is regarding the handing over by the government and political leaders the shopping list like directives for spending CSR money in this or that area of social development. It is rightly feared that bureaucratic stringency over rule enforcement for CSR compliance will increase distrust between the two. Some believe and have argued that the CSR process must be made more hassle-free, simple, easy and suspicion-free so that the intended goals of social development can be achieved without any conflict, coercion, compulsion and distrust.

The NGOs

Globally and nationally, an enormous literature of varied range exists on non-governmental organizations. Their theoretical potential for social transformation, actual working and contribution to social development and relevance are some of its sub-themes of perennial critical interest to the community of social scientists and particularly to social workers. The following observation by Shah and Chaturvedi is one specimen-like example of this assumption:

> No local community and action group can function in isolation from, and independently of, the larger social, economic and political system and the dominant ideology of the state and the nation. This has particularly to be taken into account by a reformist group ... which aims at rural (or any such other) development without radically disturbing the existing framework of political economy of the country and the state. However, we do not regard a voluntary agency as a mere instrument of the larger system with no capacity of its own to do innovative work. A voluntary agency (is) allow(s)(ed) some scope and (given) some elbow room for innovation in selecting its programmes and to carry them out efficiently. Therein lies the significance of a voluntary agency ... (1983: 122).

Sheth and Sethi (1999: 155–181) too have done an excellent analysis of the NGO sector in India by examining and narrating the historical context and contemporary discourse. They had succinctly observed that:

> Notwithstanding the phenomenal growth of the NGO sector in recent years, it has received surprisingly scanty attention from academic researchers and social analysts ... the phenomenon continues to be approached from the narrow standpoint of respective disciplines, ignoring its overall structural location and transformative potential; ... (T)he phenomenon itself has changed, expanded and diversified ... (T)he very conceptual apparatus developed by these disciplines is inadequate for grasping the radically changed reality (1999: 156).

It is also an interesting fact that failure of the long-dragged state efforts and free market initiatives could not make any change in the poverty conditions in the country. The deepening poverty and growing inequalities could not be tackled. This generated among the people a sense of desperation, distrust and frustration with the political system. The poor and marginalized people began losing faith in the politicians, development bureaucracy, political parties and local government bodies. It is in these conditions that the non-governmental organizations found fertile ground and congenial climate to emerge and occupy the vacated official political space. These are the larger systemic and structural concerns which are undoubtedly valid and relevant, but the profession and practice of social work views this phenomenon from different perspective. It is more oriented to the sort of attending to distressed SOS social calling. It is an engagement of rushing at the spur of the moments and getting swung into immediate action. Many social situations, confronting the social work practice, do not have the luxury of passing through the prolonged multi-stage processes of decision-making as well as exhaustively debating and weighing policy-making options. The editor's contribution to this volume (i.e. Chapter 5) has thrown sufficient light and clarified these issues adequately.

Reviewing Relevance of Gandhi in Social Development

Gandhi's ideas, thoughts, experiments, social reform activities and social reconstruction projects like *nayi buniyadi talim* (new basic training), non-violence, faith in inherent goodness of man, trusteeship, community-building, *sarvodaya*, man-making, rural development, women upliftment, universal, humanitarian values, pro-poor concerns, anti-exploitation campaigns, cleanliness crusades and a host of many other such things organically attracted the scholars of social work. The practice or praxis parts of Gandhism hold deep interest among social workers. It sometimes seems that Gandhi's relevance to social work practice is a continuing phenomenon and an eternal source of inspiration and aspiration for social service. It must be pointed out that some scholars do have differing position on Gandhi's relevance. Many find legacy of Gandhian institutions as defunct, counterproductive and redundant. Iyengar's following words have captured the decline and hope for their resurgence clearly:

> Gandhi left us in 1948. Today, 66 years since, many of the institutions he established and those by his followers after his death appear in peril. Their core seems to have weakened, reflecting both poverty of thought and rigidity in practice. There is limited availability of committed persons who can manage the institutions with confidence and vigour as resources have dried up. The state, in the rare cases where it extends support, tries either to co-opt or otherwise views the institutions in adversarial terms. In general, broad social support for Gandhian ideas and work, with the exception of benign social service, is almost non-existent.
>
> The two generations post Gandhi are more or less ignorant about ... his life and times, and his thought and practice ... (P)aradoxically, in recent times Gandhian thought is experiencing a revival the world over. In the midst of rising direct and structural violence in every society, there is a serious effort to revisit Gandhi's thought ... (M)any look towards the Gandhian institutions in India (i.e. all those institutions that were founded during the lifetime of Gandhi to carry out constructive programmes by him for rebuilding rural India ...) for serious experiments, learning and sharing. However, these institutions themselves disappoint ... We need to understand why these institutions seem to be in crisis (and find out) what ails the Gandhian institutions (2014: 45).

Some rigidly pursued Gandhian practices of compulsory nature have become an irresolvable dilemma. For instance, some students of Gujarat Vidyapeeth, the only university founded by Gandhi, recently went on a strike against the authorities for not allowing the use of mobile phones on the campus. The Gandhian Vice Chancellor's self-denial of mobile phone use did not inspire the students to emulate and internalize the values of *aparigraha* (non-consumption). The power of Gandhian values is failing in restraining the rural students from temptation to indulge in the consumerism bombarded by the media marketing operations. Pramod Kapoor has made an interesting assessment of Gandhi. He says:

> Gandhi is viewed and reviewed, analysed and interpreted in a different manner every decade or so ... Gandhi appeared to me more as an intriguing man than a *mahatma*. As I read more, I found that I would at times agree, disagree or even be indifferent, but I found it hard to disengage from the life and times I was witnessing through the books and papers that I pursed (2014: 69).

The Contributions to the Volume

In all, we were committed 23 contributions, but finally could receive 17 valuable chapters for this volume. The thematic order of their presentation has undergone some change in response to and compulsions of various editorial concerns.

This volume begins by first presenting the seminal contribution by Sudarshan Iyengar. The chapter, *Government and Non-Government Organizations' Collaboration for Socio-economic Development in India: Some Issues*, has the potential to set the tone for the emergence of a vision of a new contemporary society. It summarizes the changing relationships between the three prominent institutions impacting the life as a whole, namely, the state, civil society and the market. The primacy accorded to the concerns and objectives of the nation-building in the initial decades of Independence began to shift towards building an egalitarian and humane society. This cannot happen without radical social transformation. The all pervasive and dominant institutions of the state could not succeed in this task despite trying from 1950s to 1970s. The socialist path and pattern of development did not yield rapid economic growth and, hence, the state began to retreat. It opened up the so far controlled and regulated economy. Private sector and market forces took charge. Economic policies were changed. An era of LPG commenced. The mirage of temporary economic growth became possible but the national goal of social equity suffered. During this tumultuous period in India's social, economic and political life, the institutions of civil society remained vibrant and committed to the empowerment of the weaker and the marginalized sections across the country. The manifestation of civil society occurred in form of emergence of robust NGO sector. Weakened government of a retreating state needed legitimacy and facade of doing development for the poor and the needy.

Iyengar has rightly argued that India's freedom struggle under Gandhi had nurtured voluntary activities. Many original initiatives in form of social reform movements, labour movements, women's movements, dalit empowerment, etc. took place then and grew later. The NGOs still enjoy greater trust and access to marginalized and unreached sections of the society that the state fails to secure. Iyengar has argued that there is a fundamental difference between the state perspective and that of the NGOs, rooted in religious and civil society assertions. Good part of the writing is devoted to discuss and analyse these two perspectives in detail and map their respective potential for social change. Thus, voluntarism is critically viewed from Gandhian, governmental and civil society perspectives. Towards the close of the article, interesting suggestions are offered by the author with regard to strengthening the partnership between these three agencies. The shortcomings are suggested to be removed. However, the onward march of the free market is weakening the state and this is likely to impact the relationship among all the three institutions. Like state, the NGOs too may fall in line drawn by the marauding free market.

As was amply seen in the contribution by Iyengar, in his very succinctly written chapter A.S. Kohli too has focused on the NGOs. In his chapter, *Administration of NGOs in Changing Socio-economic Scenario: Dimensions and Issues,* he has chosen to concentrate on one of the several significant aspects of the NGOs, namely, administering them in a rapidly and substantially changing socio-economic scenario and copping with the resultant issues. Kohli has argued that the NGOs have come to play important role in social and human development. However, their management and administration as a sector is not effective. The NGO sector in India is stated to be facing several complex challenges which are sketched here briefly. In order to meet these challenges, Kohli has suggested and designed a training course for the NGO functionaries by outlining its major components.

The country's top five-six schools of social work are well known for their standing commitment to the country that whenever, whichever part of the country is struck with any natural or man-made disaster, the teams of volunteers from these schools have gone extra mile beyond the *classrooms* in reaching the sites and victims of disasters and mobilized relief resources and, thereby, organized the rescue, relief and a little later resettlement and rehabilitation operations. The TISS, Mumbai, rushed to Latur earthquake for the triple-R (rescue, relief, resettlement) work. The Baroda School went to Panchanpur, Gaya district in Bihar, to work in the relief camps set up for the Bangladeshi refugees who were pushed out from their country by the Pakistani Army in early 1970s. Similarly, when Machhu Dam burst loose in Morbi, Saurashtra (Gujarat), in August 1980, causing a flash flood, the Baroda School took up the triple-R work. The Delhi School came down to Kutch, Gujarat, for the same mission as to organize rescue, relief and resettlement work. This is a glorious tradition upheld by the Schools of social work in India.

The contribution, titled *Youth Volunteerism in Managing Disasters: Learning through Action,* by Sanjai Bhatt is a landmark testimony to this remarkable *parampara*. It opens the discussion by dwelling on the issues of semantics and praxis of volunteerism. Bhatt argues that the societal existence, well-being and volunteerism are inseparable. He explains that volunteerism has a long history. It reinvents itself as the nature of call for intervention from society, state and market continue to change in every one or two decades. Volunteerism is neither labour donation (*shramdaan*) nor charity. It is a process of social capital formation. It is a process of igniting and keeping the 'human spirit' aflame as a light of hope for all those in distress anywhere in country. The UDAI Project (University for Development and Integrated Learning) originated as a Delhi School of Social Work and Delhi University's response to the victims of: (i) earthquake in Gujarat in 2001; (ii) Kosi river flood in Bihar, and (iii) the Sikkim earthquake. It planned and executed the interventions of short and longer durations. The article contains a detailed narrative of triple-R initiatives and activities undertaken and useful lessons learned in the process. The net outcome of the UDAI Project is reported to be very enriching, rewarding and hope-sustaining experience on both the sides of the effort, i.e. the disaster victims and the university volunteers

The editor's chapter, titled *State, Voluntary Sector and Social Development in India: A Synoptic Assessment of their Interface,* assumes that state and society are chief actors or agents of social development. In order to assess as to how they both have fared and interfaced on the issue of social development, the exercise has taken recourse to examining the available and relevant secondary literature. The changing role of NGOs and the state is discussed on the basis of the views of some experts. This estimation and examination is done by analysing various perceptions about the role of state and voluntary sector vis-à-vis the just provisioning and distribution of certain basic public goods. The contribution reveals interesting dynamics. It found that often in some cases social development is attempted without understanding the proper meaning of it. It is further observed that this has sometimes caused duplication of efforts as some programmes, schemes; projects, etc. get repeated by different agencies involved in social development. Sometimes, a particular target group receives excessive attention. In sum, a synoptic assessment is made of the meaning, role, limitations and potential of these two important institutions of social development – chiefly on the basis of expert and popular perceptions.

C. Thomas Abraham's poetically and somewhat dramatically composed and commenced chapter, *Volunteerism in an Age of Globalization,* is actually grounded on substantive issues. It is about designing the architecture of voluntary societal care on collective basis for those who need it and cannot individually secure it like the children, women and elderly. It is focused on mechanics of individual efforts and collective responsibility without going into any of the ideological frameworks. The author does not compromise on freedom and equality as central principles of organizing good society. The free market model thrives on by placing a huge premium on individual enterprise, initiative and effort. It rewards accordingly. However, the moot issue raised in this essay is regarding the care of those who fail or partially succeed to comply with the demands of the free market economy which is being increasingly promoted by globalization. The author has suggested 'volunteerism' as a solution to this problem of excessively encouraged 'individualism' at the cost of collective care and collective good. Once again, the youth has emerged as a beacon of hope, as the student and non-student youth in urban and rural areas are already engaged in community service. Various international youth initiatives are examined in the process. The essay concludes on a positive note that globalization has also strengthened volunteerism as well as exposed it to new challenges.

The theme of women's empowerment has acquired considerable salience and currency in development discourse. Their potential and role is sufficiently emphasized. Several strategies are designed and the experiments conducted. R.D. Sampath Kumar has examined the effectiveness of the strategy of the Self-Help Groups in his chapter, *Empowering Women through Self-Help Groups.* He has argued that SHG intervention is globally recognized as an effective tool for alleviating poverty and, thereby, improving the overall socio-economic conditions of the needy. The normative and conceptual understandings of the processes of empowerment are empirically tested with a scientific methodology by conducting a case study of Andhra Pradesh. Interesting findings are drawn from this exercise and reported briefly. Women's empowerment occurred in terms of development of leadership qualities, skills and economic independence. Its impact on fellow SHG-members, families, children and community are reported to be manifold. The biggest yield of this exercise is that the SHGs in Andhra Pradesh have begun to get gradually federated and institutionalized. Micro-finance for self-help, development and support has emerged as a huge domain, attracting the private enterprises in the state.

R.B.S. Verma's essay on *Youth for Sustainable Development*, as indicated in the title, views youth as '... a vital and vibrant resource' for bringing about social transformation by engaging them in various interventions for change and development. Youth is rightly viewed as a vast potential of human resource waiting to be tapped. Verma has tried to construct a normative perspective and attempted to prepare an index to measure youth potential for achieving sustainable development. This is done first by clarifying the conceptual meaning of the term 'youth' by exploring three formulations. Then, contents of sustainable development, drawn from the United Nations Division, are alphabetically listed. Underlying principles and premises of sustainable development are enumerated on the basis of secondary sources. The possible dimensions and advantages for youth involvement in sustainable development are then discussed and listed vide each area of possible intervention – such as community education, rural and urban development initiatives, population education, enforcement of already enacted legislations, eco-development, health and nutrition.

Youth seems to be the most sought-after and dependable segment of any societal demography. That almost all major non-governmental, some governmental and voluntary developmental campaigns of progressive nature are either conceived and/or planned for implementation, keeping the youth in focus. Global warming and climate change is one such new challenge before us. Responses from the existing institutional and organized structures to these twin phenomena are either lacklustre or insufficient. Mital Petiwale's chapter, *Challenges of Climate Change and the Role of Youth*, sets out to examine the challenges posed by climate change and discuss the potential and prospects of the role of youth in meeting them. A normatively conceived programmatic exercise is then done to chalk out the strategies for engaging the youth through a set of Ten Commandments which have turned out to be the hallmark of social work profession. Petiwale has drawn from and made critical use of positive initiatives from the publication of The United Nation's *World Youth Report* (2010). The writer has rightly pinned the hopes and optimism for a better climate change management on 'strength perspective'.

The National Service Scheme, well-known as NSS, has been India's one of the most prestigious schemes for mobilizing the youth and engaging it in the gigantic task of nation-building through social and community service in rural, urban and tribal areas of the country. It is implemented through the nationwide network of colleges and the universities across the country. Ever since its genesis in 1969, it has not looked back. Its gradual expansion and spread is the testimony of its importance. Such a countrywide initiative cannot be expected to have smooth sailing throughout its course. Challenges came up to it but they were deftly faced and suitable course corrections were done. H.S. Suresh has dealt with this theme in his chapter on *National Service Scheme in Higher Education: Some Critical Observations.* In his opening section, he presents a strong case for viewing the nation, the youth and the NSS together as a conceptual and empirical framework. The historical origin, philosophy and objectives of the NSS are explained. The NSS is thickly connected with the educational infrastructure and, hence, ancient and modern educational structures and processes are detailed in the subsequent part. Thirdly, Suresh attempts to list the achievements and benefits of NSS to the students and the community. Final section has presented and discussed the challenges faced by the NSS. It simultaneously reviews the continuously changing macro and micro conditions in the country which have a serious bearing on the performance, relevance and continuity of the NSS.

In an age when business and corporate/industrial houses have been dominant economic actors, their impact on human life has grown manifold. They derived dominance and legitimacy from their phenomenal quest and success in creating wealth for the people, community, society and the nation. Their influence has grown so much that they have left the state and civil society behind. The latter too look up to the market and economic-financial actors for their contribution and supporting various welfare initiatives by the state and the NGOs. Surendra Singh argues in his chapter, *Corporate Social*

Responsibility: Some Major Dimensions, that the corporations are to be viewed as the citizens of a country with a set of civic duties and responsibilities to be discharged as common individual citizens do. A part of their economic power must engage with processes and activities undertaken to enhance collective social power.

Singh assumes that a voluntary tripartite balance of power among the three has potential to go a long way in enhancing the overall quality of life of the people. Singh appreciates the initiatives in this direction coming from them as the National Association of Accounts Committee Report; Part III (1977) has outlined the areas for social intervention by the business entities. Every business or an industry is accountable to its stakeholders. Now, under the normative rubric of corporate social responsibility (CSR), this accountability extends to its employees, share holders, consumers, society, community, environment and government. The essay discusses the objectives of the CSR, various approaches to CSR and outlines its scope. It has attempted to construct a conceptual framework of corporate citizenship and regulatory mechanism of CSR. The essay has effectively covered Indian scenario on CSR and various issues, problems faced and concludes on normative notes on CSR.

It welcomingly seems that Y.S. Siddegowda and Jagadish B. have taken upon from where Surendra Singh's essay ended. In their chapter, *Social Development through Corporate Social Responsibility: A Case Study of Karnataka*, they have first briefly explained significance, semantic and mechanics of CSR. Then they have described key initiatives and various frameworks guiding the process. Detailed listing of the impact of CSR is done by giving empirical data. The Karnataka case of social development through CSR is stimulating and encouraging. Such giant corporate houses as Infosys, Wipro and MphasiS have advanced the cause of CSR in a manner that it will set an example for others to emulate. The essay concludes with a big list of suggestions for improving on CSR concerns, commitments and strategies.

The chapter by Koteswara Raju Penmetsa, *Empowering the Indigenous Groups through Peoples' Institutions: A Case of Social Transformation of Tribes in Andhra Pradesh,* breaks fresh ground by examining the role of people's institutions in empowering the tribes. It can be indisputably stated that tribes in many regions of the country have lagged behind. In tribal society, the people's institutions must be community-oriented so that development initiatives can be more effectively channelled towards social transformation. The *Maa Thota* programme (with *wadi* or sustainable livelihood as a central focus) envisages such a development of tribal society which is in harmony with its ecologically rooted economy, livelihood traditions and cultural practices. The state agencies and NGOs are assumed to be having primary responsibilities of mentoring these processes. The new developmental interventions like regenerative ecology, soil conservation, rain water harvesting and developing orchards can be receptively interwoven into tribal cultural and economic ethos.

New managerial and organizational skills need to be gradually transferred to the tribal people's institutions. In order to place this entire concern and the process in a framework, Penmetsa has devised a three-pronged relevant *Maa Thota* project structure. This is quite an innovative approach as it has *Gram Siris, Samutu, Vikasspreraks* as mediating, facilitating, emancipating and enabling arms of the *Maa Theta* project. The distinct feature of this contribution lies in its concern over withdrawal policy as a part of the interventionist initiatives. Once human and social capital formation takes place, a gradual withdrawal strategy must be activated by the completion of third year of the project. The project staff can be phased out, leaving the reigns in the hands of the project beneficiaries. Penmetsa has profiled an interesting and creative mission of '...empowering the indigenous groups through their own institutions'.

A definite pattern has by now emerged with regard to community participation in all those developmental issue-areas where state or governmental efforts are either absent or found to be falling short. Apart from community involvement in forest management, health provisioning, environmental protection, policing, social reforms, awareness campaigns, water management, numerous income-generating developmental initiatives, education is another issue-area in which community participation has a long history of intervention. Community and education have a symbiotic relationship. That is to say, nourishing the other leads to self-nourishment. The modern history of education at all levels – be it primary, secondary, college or university – owes a great deal to the non-governmental initiatives and support. Some remnants of this history are present in our midst as caste or community named hostels or educational institutions of yester years are still working in dilapidated structures. The community funding has received booster doze after greater privatization of education and retreat of the state. Many private universities are opened across the country carrying name and prestige of successful corporate conglomerates like Reliance, Wipro, Adani, Nirma, Jindal, etc. Education is once again being pushed away from public domain and placed in private care. Ambani-Birla Report, 2000 on its restructuration was the harbinger of this new trend. Only problem with this paradigm shift in education management and administration is that it leaves out many from its coverage as their income levels limit their access to new private temples of lower and higher education.

The chapter by D.P. Singh and Ritu Mor, *Communitization of School Education for Development: Analysing Role of Village Education Committees in Punjab*, has raised pertinent questions and has tried to capture these symbiotic processes and offer researched explanations about its outcome. They have examined these contemporary trends at the foundational level of school education. After scripting a rich thematic background to the issue, they have constructed a case narrative on the role of state and community in administering and managing school education in Punjab. The state of Punjab has tried to provide access to education to all needy communities as a part of its wider social commitments. It has successfully roped in communities in this initiative. Creation, composition and functioning of Village Education Committees are empirically investigated. An interesting and impressive set of findings of the study on such aspects as enrollment, school results, dropout rate, meetings, infrastructure and incentives to students are reported and discussed critically.

The chapter by Sangeeta Sharma Dhaor, *Risk Behaviour of PLHA and Social Development in India*, is somewhat unique. Apparently it seems to be concerned with an out of frame theme than the concerns addressed by this *festschrift*. But it is not so. It is very much a part of the thematic framework as it too addresses the question of youth, though in a different setting. HIV/AIDS is such an infliction that it devastates the victims. PLHA (People Living with HIV/AIDS) too must be viewed as a victim community in need of utmost attention, care, support and sensitive handling by the institutions of the state and society. Sharma Dhaor has made a brilliant attempt to probe and peep into the sensitivities of the PLHA. Their socio-economic conditions and sexual habits as well as behaviour are statistically analysed and meticulously profiled with the help of primary quantitative data. The qualitative deficit is eliminated by using focused group discussion with select PLHA which gives us good idea about the depth of hurt, anger, frustration and basal desire for revenge with one and all who are encountered. Health care of such a special category of the needy as the PLHA as a core component of social development strategy is well brought out.

Gandhi's work and life has proved to be the most treasured legacy of Indian freedom movement. During his lifetime and after, Gandhi has left a deep imprint on the Indian psyche. The world of Indian academia is particularly influenced by Gandhian philosophy. From among the several subjects taught and researched in Indian universities, the professional discipline of social work has monopolized over Gandhian legacy of philosophy, ideas and actions. So many scholars of social work have again and again visited and re-visited Gandhi in the hope of finding a remedy to many hitherto not known issues or looking forward to confirming the present day practice of social work by reflecting them in the Gandhian mirror. Approaching Gandhi again and again in search of renewed relevance of his ideas and practices is on increase. Mahajan P. Mani and Sreepriya C.K. in their chapter, *Gandhian Philosophy, Social Welfare and Social Development: Social Work Perspective,* have taken a revisit to Gandhi and tried to find out and discuss its renewed worth in organizing contemporary initiatives for social welfare and development of the needy sections of society.

The central focus of their chapter is to '... get into the Gandhian concept of welfare and development.' The semantics and philosophy of both these terms are firstly clarified by them. They have admirably attempted to extract the richness of Gandhian concept of social work. It encompasses, they have argued, the entire spectrum of human and social life by covering '... humanity, spirituality, morality, compassion, political freedom, role of state and government and cooperation .... The Gandhian philosophy of social work is not an individual problem – oriented, ameliorative but community-oriented process of rural development' which is guided by a set of certain cardinal values. Gandhi has offered two methods to achieve this philosophical goals – one, service to humanity, and the second, overall upliftment of mankind. Constructive programmes and *sarvodaya* movements are other means of Gandhi's methods and techniques. The contribution has, indeed, very well detailed and highlighted the minor programmatic components of Gandhian praxis in these two categories of action. They conclude by critiquing today's practices of social work from Gandhian perspective as not being holistic but being segmental like the medical profession caught in complex web of specializations and super specializations.

The chapter by Jayshree B. Thakore and Ram Kumar Balyan, *Impact of Gandhian Philosophy on Human Resource Management*, is an innovative attempt to explore the philosophical teachings of Mahatma Gandhi, the principles he followed and advocated. This the authors have done by composing a synoptic biographical sketch of Gandhi's life and work. The next part is composed to ascertain and list the major ideas and principles preached and practiced by him. The authors have particularly focused on those concepts in Gandhian philosophy which are related to human resource development and its management. The stress is given on enriching the concept of HRM. Commonalities in two diverse practices are to be identified and are suggested to be further suitably applied. The human capacities are to be sympathetically but correctly mapped and developed by adopting proper methods and approaches. These are then to be used for productive gains for the self and the others. The authors have mostly depended on and approached the Gandhian philosophy from a normative orientation, but their concern about its contemporary relevance and potential impact on HRM practices makes it empirically interesting.

In his chapter, *Gandhian Approach to Rural Development*, Mahajan P. Mani discusses the Gandhian concept, theory and practice of development. It particularly discusses the relevance of development as it stands today by attempting to examine broad concepts of development in terms of theory and practice. In order to fill the gap for development at a more personal and small scale, some teachings of Gandhi are examined for the possibility of incorporating them into mainstream development concepts. Gandhi's ideas of justice, equality, employment, politics, industrialization, personal contribution, non-violence and trusteeship are examined. It can be viewed that Gandhian thought has a lot to contribute to development in general because it gives attention to the individual, making them the centre of development. Mani concludes his essay by stating that the Gandhian theories may appear to be supplementary but are '...vital to the creation of a silent but substantive transformation...' in our understanding of issues of contemporary development.

The four major themes of social development in India, namely, youth, NGOs, CSR and Gandhi around which this *festschrift* is organized and compiled, apparently look (in some cases) inchoate and disjointed. But if viewed closely and microscopically, one would be immediately able to see the interconnectivity of relevance to social work discipline. As the frontiers of social work discipline have expanded over the time, new concerns and themes too have emerged and developed. CSR and HRM are developments relatively of recent times. However, their place in the discipline is getting consolidated as their roots are deepening. Youth, NSS and NGO is an integrated domain with periodically inter-linked and sometimes de-linked connectivity. Interest in Gandhian ideas, principles, strategies and ethics continued more so at normative and semantic than at empirical and policy levels. There is some kind of nostalgic and utopian sensitivity with the memory of Gandhi's work – more so in western India due to attached historicity and familiar geography associated with his name.

The question of relevance of social work learning, teaching and practising shall perennially remain unsettled as in all such other cases. Therefore, continuous or periodic, recasting and redrawing of disciplinary lines for greater clarity, focus and purpose of our collective and individual effort shall be rewarding and useful. It is a normal feeling and behaviour that whenever on the brink of major transformation and shift, doubts and uncertainty arise. Search for reassurance, re-routing, relocating and research begins. Through the respective individual endeavour, the chapters in this volume have made an admirable effort to analyse, interpret, understand and explain the fading, out-going and departing or emerging, arriving, and unfolding dynamics in the main field of social work and sub-fields of social development. This *festschrift* has aimed at making modest contribution on a few traditional and modern components of the discipline of social work in general and changing nature of various aspects of social development in particular.

References

Bajpai, Kanti P. and Shukul, H.C. (eds). 1995. *Interpreting World Politics: Essays for A.P. Rana*, New Delhi: Sage Publications.

Baviskar, B.S. and Patel, Tulsi. (eds). 2010. *Understanding Indian Society: Essays for A.M. Shah*, New Delhi: Orient Blackswan.

Baxi, Upendra and Parekh, Bhikhu C. (eds). 1995. *Crisis and Change in Contemporary India*, New Delhi: Sage Publications.

Brass, Tom. 2003. 'Book Reviews', *The Journal of Peasant Studies*, 30 (2), pp. 220–225.

Desai, Murli. (ed.). 2000. 'Social Work Education: In Felicitation of Prof. Armaity S. Desai', *The Indian Journal of Social Work*, Special Issue, 61 (2), April.

Government of India. 1969. *National Service Scheme Manual*, New Delhi: Ministry of Youth Affairs and Sports.

____. 2014. *National Youth Policy–2014*, New Delhi: Ministry of Youth Affairs and Sports.

Hongbo, Wu. 2013. 'Next Steps to the Future We Want', *UNNEWS* (Monthly Newsletter of the UN Information Centre, New Delhi), X (7), July.

Iyengar, Sudarshan. 2014. 'What Ails Gandhian Institutions?', *Seminar*, 662, October, pp. 45–49.

Kapoor, Pramod. 2014. 'My Experiment with Gandhi', *Seminar*, 662, October, pp. 68–73.

Pandey, Piyush. 2014. 'Rel Foundation Spends ` 712 cr on CSR in FY14', *The Times of India* (Ahmedabad Edition), 24 June, p. 11.

Parekh, Bhikhu. 1995. 'Raojibhai Patel (Mota): An Appreciation', in Upendra Baxi and Bhikhu C. Parekh (eds), *Crisis and Change in Contemporary India: Essays in Honour of Raojibhai Patel*, New Delhi: Sage Publications.

Patel, Chhaya. (ed.). 1999. *Social Work Practice: Religio-Philosophical Foundations: Essays in Honour of Professor Indira Patel*, Jaipur and New Delhi: Rawat Publications (Reprinted in 2009).

Patel, Sujata, Bagchi, Jasodhara and Raj, Krishna. (eds). 2002. *Thinking Social Science in India: Essays in Honour of Alice Thorner*, New Delhi: Sage Publications.

Rajan, S. Irudaya. 2013. 'Internal Migration and Youth in India: Main Features, Trends and Emerging Challenges', Discussion Paper, An unpublished UNESCO sponsored study conducted at Centre for Development Studies, Kerala.

Shah, A.M., Baviskar, B.S. and Ramaswamy, E.A. (eds). 1996–1998. *Social Structure and Change*, Vols I–V (Volumes in Honour of M.N. Srinivas), New Delhi: Sage Publications.

Shah, Ghanshyam and Chaturvedi, H.R. 1983. *Gandhian Approach to Rural Development: The Valod Experiment*, Delhi: Ajanta Books International.

Shah, Ghanshyam. (ed.). 1990. *Capitalistic Development: Critical Essays (Felicitation Volume in Honour of Prof. A.R. Desai)*, Bombay: Popular Prakashan.

____. 1997. *Social Transformation in India: Essays in Honour of Professor I.P. Desai*, Vols I and II, Jaipur and New Delhi: Rawat Publications.

Shah, Ghanshyam, Rutten, Mario and Streefkerk, Hein. (eds). 2002. *Development and Deprivation in Gujarat: In Honour of Jan Breman*, New Delhi: Sage Publications.

Sheth, D.L. and Nandy, Ashish. (eds). 1996. *The Multiverse of Democracy: Essays in Honour of Rajni Kothari*, New Delhi: Sage Publications.

Sheth, D.L. and Sethi, Harsh. 1999. 'The NGO Sector in India: Historical Context and Current Discourse', in Chhaya Patel (ed.), *Social Work Practice: Religio-Philosophical Foundations: Essays in Honour of*

Professor Indira Patel, Jaipur and New Delhi: Rawat Publications (Reprinted in 2009).

The Times of India (Ahmedabad Edition). 2013. 27 June, p. 2.

The United Nations, 2010. *World Youth Report: Youth and Climate Change*. New York.

Varma, Subodh. 2013. 'Only 2 Per Cent of India's Youth have Vocational Training', *The Times of India* (Ahmedabad Edition), 14 June, p. 7.

Venkatesan, Ravi. 2014. 'Making CSR Really Matter', *The Economic Times* (Ahmedabad Edition), 31 March, p. 6.

Vyas, Vijay Shankar. 2013. *Reaching the Unreached: To Make Poverty Alleviation Programmes More Effective*, I.P. Desai Memorial Lecture 23, Surat: Centre for Social Studies.

Zachariah, Reeba and Singh, Namrata. 2014. 'Tatas Spent' 1k cr on CSR Activities in FY14', *The Economic Times* (Ahmedabad Edition), 17 July, p. 11.

CHAPTER 2

Government and Non-Government Organizations' Collaboration for Socio-economic Development in India: Some Issues

SUDARSHAN IYENGAR

In 1998, three prominent social scientists edited a book entitled *Social Change through Voluntary action* (Dantwala et al. 1998). They were trying to address the question whether voluntary action can be a potent instrument for bringing about social transformation. Implicit in this question is the premise that by social transformation it was meant building an egalitarian and humane society. Government through its policy statements does not explicitly state these values any longer although, during the era of centralized planning in India, the State was committed towards a democratic and socialist society. With major changes in economic policies from 1991 onwards, economic progress is being pitched at the top of the agenda. Economic growth is accorded higher priority than growth with equity. The dominant role of the state is being given up in favour of private and market initiatives.

When the theme of growth with equity was vigorously pursued between 1960 and 1985, there was an attempt to shift the development paradigm from 'top-down', 'centre driven' to 'bottom-up', 'participatory'. Decentralized district level development had become a popular theme from Fourth Five Year Plan onwards. V.N. Gadgil was a committed votary of the same. With the commanding heights of the economy under the control of the state, the district and the rural development programmes even under the decentralized bottom-up mode could not have yielded desired results, because the contradiction was so apparent. This has been brought out well in a study undertaken in the 1980s (Dholakia and Iyengar 1998). Interestingly, the period also coincides with the involvement of the voluntary agencies and NGOs (Non-Government Organizations) as active partners in rural development programmes. The Gandhian tradition had continued to live for some decades even after Independence. A somewhat detailed account is available for Gujarat and for India in a number of studies focused on various aspects of NGO involvement in development (Bhatt 1989, 1995; Shah and Chaturvedi 1983; Shah 1990; Iyengar and Shah 1998, 1998a, 1998b, 2000, 2001 and also published in 2002).

What is interesting, however, is that the government has been keen on inviting NGOs for collaborating with the GOs (Government Organizations) in the efforts for economic development[1]. Whether such an invitation and expectation is arising out of respect for the values that the NGOs are supposed to carry with them, or is it because governments have realized that they cannot deliver social development alone needs examination. As is known, India has a tradition of voluntary efforts for development of the marginalized sections of the population. When the tradition was introduced with force in the middle of freedom struggle, the social and political ethos was high. Presently, according to Dantwala, Visaria and Sethi, 'there has been a glaring deterioration in the social and political ethos in India' (Dantwala et al. 1998: 9). There appears to be a fundamental difference in perspectives, the one of the religion and civil society and second is of the government, which wants NGOs[2] to collaborate in its development programmes. In this chapter, an attempt is made to discuss the two differing perspectives and examine the prospects for social change under both. In section two, the two perspectives are analysed, and in section three, role of government in promoting and facilitating the NGOs work are discussed.

Voluntarism in a Religious Perspective

An individual or group of individuals in a civil society undertakes voluntary activities for social good. In Indian society undertaking such social or public good activities have a component of spirituality. A student of divine truth, known as *paramarthi* seeks *moksha* – a salvation of the *atman*-soul and for that he has to perform *paramartha*-doing good to others or in other words doing public good. *Paramartha* is to be done without *swartha* – selfishness. Losing self-interest is the best way of taking the self to the exalted heights of *paramartha* and, thus, obtaining *moksha*. Thus, there is a strong religious foundation in the voluntary act of performing public good in the Indian public life. Religious philosophies of various hues have deep impressions in the sphere of such activities. It is a moot point whether the life moved following these tenets in the Indian society from the Vedic times onwards. But the ideals have continued to survive. However, there have been changes in this approach after the Indian society was exposed to the western philosophy, thinking and culture about two centuries ago. I shall deal with that in the course of my discussion later. Presently, let me pursue with the genesis of voluntarism in India a little further.

At a very fundamental level there is no difference between voluntary work and work for self in the Hindu philosophy. It is the *karma* that has to be performed. *Karma* is duty and the duty is to be performed with devotion. If we take recourse to Swami Vivekananda's thoughts, religion has three parts: philosophy, mythology and rituals. Philosophy is basic for every religion. Mythology is developed to explain and illustrate religion with the help of legendary lives of great men and women in the form of stories, fables and folklore. Ritual gives the philosophy a concrete form so that everyone may grasp it well and practice. Swami Vivekananda says that ritual is concretized philosophy. The ritual is *karma*. By *karma* or duty with devotion is meant helping others or doing good to the world. Apparently, this is to help others but really to help one self. The world is there with or without you. Hence, to think we can do good to the world is a false notion. We want to do good to others because we want to improve our self. We should be thankful to those who help us in improving our self or allowing us to do *karma*.

The philosophical foundations of the Hindu religion, thus, do not make any distinction between voluntary work and personal work. The day-to-day disposition of the *grahastha* is also philosophised in such a way that the *paramartha* is emphasized. The famous *Ishawasya Upanishad's* first hymn says '*Ishwasyam idam sarvam yatkincha jagatyam jagat, ten tyakten bhunjitha ma gudha kasyasvim dhanam'*. However, the symbolism or the ritual could not hold the society for long to continue with the duty with devotion or karma for doing good to others. New rituals became necessary and from time to time spiritual and religious leaders introduced them. Three moral values got introduced in the process – *karuna* (compassion), *daya* (mercy) and *dana* (charity). Gautam Buddha, the founder of Buddhism and Mahavira, who founded Jainism, reinforced compassion and mercy in the form of *Jiva daya* effectively. Kings and monarchs patronized charity and the traders in every society institutionalized it.

The values did not change much even during the Muslim and Mughal regimes. Islam preached *khairaat* (charity). A devout Muslim was to keep aside a fixed part of daily income to be donated for public good. Charity and donations had complete religious and social approval. The state also along with the business leaders and rich in the society donated for building *sarais* (inns), *dharamshalas* (inns) and other community structures used as common utilities. A devout Hindu or a Muslim found solace in helping the poor. The three values – *karuna, daya* and *dana* or *khairaat* – thus became cornerstones of voluntary activities in civil societies in India for almost two or three thousand years. A good Christian is also basically a volunteer in a society and is guided by the principle of love thy neighbour. Thus, most religions do not make any difference in the substance of voluntary spirit in an individual and expects to serve one's own interest by serving the interests of others.

Voluntarism in Civil Society Perspective in India

It is obvious that the voluntary activity in India has religious base, but over a period of time there has been substantial change in it especially from the beginning of the twentieth century. People of Gujarat and Rajasthan are known for their entrepreneurship. Interestingly, both the states are drought-prone. Niggardly nature turns even the human species into hardy varieties and cultivates in them a ruggedness to survive in the most arduous circumstances. People from this region have also been migrating in search of greener pastures. From the second half of the nineteenth century, Gujaratis from North Gujarat, Saurashtra and Kutch started migrating to Ahmedabad, Vadodara, Surat, and Mumbai and other parts of Maharashtra in the west, Chennai and Bangalore in the south and Calcutta in the east. It was mainly a rural-urban migration.

They earned, saved and improved their economic conditions. Their socio-cultural linkages with their native villages continued.

Most of those who prospered became philanthropists. Their first welfare acts resulted in the construction of water huts, parks, gardens and benches for resting in public places. These philanthropic acts elevated the social status of the donors, satisfied their spiritual urges and were consistent with the religious dogmas of promoting well-being in the society. The Bombay Public Trust Act, 1950 and the Society Registration Act of 1860 were indicators that a need for legalizing social organizations was felt much before the economic development activities were taken up by the voluntary organizations in the country.

With improved social awareness and the legal framework, the voluntary activities covered health and education hospitals, dispensaries, school buildings and health education trusts. In the villages, individuals and small family trusts undertook such voluntary activities of building social and physical infrastructure. In the towns and cities, more organized forms undertook these voluntary acts. The institution of *mahajan,* involving trading and business leaders and members, assumed the responsibility of public good in the towns and cities. The basic value was of *jiva daya* – the concern for living being as such. Charity and donation of part of the income earned for social good was the basic driving force of the institution. Towns and cities in India witnessed voluntary activities by the *mahajans.* Migrations also led to the formation of caste based associations. A spate of voluntary activities supported by donations also was witnessed in urban India. Caste *dharmashalas,* hostels, community halls and other common facilities were built and managed by these associations. Some of them such Parsi Panchayat also had a strong component of supporting poor students with scholarships to pursue higher studies within the country and abroad. Other voluntary associations of the educated elite were also formed. The Indian National Congress, registered in 1885, was one such organization that eventually turned into a political party that has dominated mainstream politics since registered. However, the political organizations are kept out of the scope of the present discussion.

Mahatma Gandhi's Perspective on Voluntarism

Towards the beginning of the twentieth century, Mahatma Gandhi brought about significant changes in the concept of voluntarism in the Indian civil society. The Father of the Nation and the chief architect of the freedom struggle of the country, Mahatma Gandhi, added a very significant dimension to the already existing *jiva daya* and philanthropic traditions. It was his idea of creative and constructive voluntarism for human development. Gandhiji's influence began from 1920s and in the last 80 years the voluntary movement in the country continues to be under his influence.

Gandhiji entered the political scene in India in a decisive way and began having a major impact. Along with the major political agenda of freeing the country from the British, he also had clear views about the socio-economic development of the Indian society. In 1909, he had already penned *Hind Swaraj*, depicting in it the India of his imagination and understanding. More important was his strategy to fight the British. The political movement that he led mobilized a large number of youth full of idealism and commitment for overthrowing foreign rule. This youth force, after spells of intense political activity, had time and energy during peaceful periods. They had to be usefully channelled. Gandhiji gave a call to the youth to take up rural reconstruction. Hardly any other political leader elsewhere has been able to combine political protest and social reconstruction, as Gandhiji was able to do. He effortlessly combined the drafting of ultimatums to the Viceroy, cleaning toilets and tending goats to maintain sound health. Gandhiji's call for constructive work for development changed the tenor of voluntary activity in the country completely.

Between 1925 and 1947, a large number of young persons came under his spell, spread themselves in different interior parts of India and initiated social reconstruction. As a result, even now there are a substantial number of active NGOs that had begun their activities under the influence of Gandhian thought. Their relevance and effectiveness will be examined later. During the pre-Independence days, the business class and urban based entrepreneurs provided the necessary financial support to most of these organizations. Interestingly, the institution of *mahajan* also came forward to support the Gandhian voluntarism. Until the Independence of India, most of these organizations floated on a tide of high idealism. The period could be described as the golden period of voluntary work in societal reconstruction. The British Government had hardly any programmes for rural development. Activities that were taken up by the volunteers of the freedom struggle became very visible and important. Urban youth led by idealism entered and settled in remote rural areas. They took up activities relating to *khadi* and village industries, basic education, women's education and amelioration of the backward castes by working against untouchability. *Khadi* and village industries and basic education took roots in Gujarat and elsewhere and a large number of organizations came up in different parts of the country.

Mahatma Gandhi had a unique appeal. His concept of voluntarism was novel. Interestingly, during his time India was also going through some kind of renaissance. Swami Vivekananda's teachings and call for social service had an appeal for many. On the religious front, Swami Dayanand Saraswati with his *Arya Samaj* had brought about Hindu revivalism. Christian Missionaries had already made inroads in many parts of the country. They were creating a network of educational institutions that trained Indians in the western schools of thought. Yet Gandhi had great appeal. It may be recognized, however, that the political atmosphere during the time was charged. Commitment to cause was significant and the cause was concrete. Gandhiji's approach towards social good also had an element of spirituality cutting across different religions. He candidly admitted Christianity's influence on his thinking and action and recognized Islam as one of the important religions of India and sang prayers from the Holy *Koran*. He was religious in his approach in which he accepted *bhakti* (devotion) and prayer as the tenets that gave spiritual strength to an individual. His insistence for truth and non-violence gave immense moral courage to fight injustice of any kind. His agenda to reconstruct the society by taking up educational programmes and developmental activities, including the economic programmes such as spinning on *charkha* and producing *khadi*, brought pragmatism and this worldly concerns that bothered common people. He identified and recognized moral values in public life and upheld them.

Gandhiji went beyond the concept of service that was the dominant discourse that governed the voluntary spirit and action in India before and during his times. Swami Vivekananda, who interpreted the spirituality and the duty of human being towards other human beings drastically different from other spiritual and religious leaders, also largely confined to the service of the poor. He revived the concept of duty with devotion – *karma,* and placed it above compassion, mercy and charity. The voluntary activities had got restricted to help the poor by way of charity and building common physical infrastructure in villages and towns. Swami Vivekananda brought the entire gamut of voluntary activities into the vortex of service of the poor by getting involved physically as well. Charity alone was not enough. A volunteer had to work for the betterment and upliftment of the poor and sick in the society. He called them *Daridra*

Narayan. Those who were in the service of the poor (*Daridra*) were in the service of God (*Narayan*).

Gandhiji brought toilet, compost, *charkha* and goat. He knew and declared that the real independence of India will be achieved when we are able to remove poverty and provide dignified livelihood for every citizen in the country. India will be free when the society gets rid of its social evils such as discrimination based on castes. He, thus, had an economic, social and of course a political agenda. The agenda had to be implemented with the help of spiritual values. All this together generated mass appeal.

There is perhaps yet another factor that led to greater acceptance of Gandhian voluntarism. Gandhiji was quintessentially a *grahastha* – a householder. He had a family and he went through all the motions of a family man. He went to South Africa to earn a living and support his family and took up a normal profession. He was no *sadhu* or a *sanyasi* who had left the world in search of god or attainment of *moksha*. For lay persons the family man's profile of Gandhi may also have had some appeal. Since he practiced first what he preached, Gandhiji may have inspired the *grahasthas* in the Indian society. He was one among many although distinctly different. If he could take up the voluntary work, others could and did.

Voluntarism in India after Independence and Influence from the West

I am not resorting to a very detailed and rigorous analysis of the Western traditions in voluntarism here because of both lack of space and my own inadequacy. However, I shall make some observations. Religion has had a basic impact on the voluntary work in Western world too. A true Christian has been defined. Some of the basic values in pursuing voluntary work have been the spirits of service, to be useful to others and to be helpful to others. The dominant political discourse that has evolved over time and come to stay has been that of liberal secular democracy. Individual freedom and liberty has been upheld as the most basic fundamental value. State's distance from religion is clearly recognized and emphasized. And democratic form of government has been appreciated most. Respect for individual freedom has made way for the functioning of market to deal with economic problems.

In an ideal situation, when all components and institutions of the liberal secular democracies work smoothly, the scope for voluntary work becomes extremely narrow. It is reduced to humanitarian services towards the weak and the sick. The real world situation is different from the ideal. Hence, a political space has been recognized for the voluntary initiatives. It is that of a monitor who can cry foul. The voluntarism in the West, thus, includes developing critique of the mainstream and in some cases demonstrating alternatives. It has influenced voluntarism in India in the post-Independence era and more so in the post–1970 period. Besides the Western value based voluntary activity, efforts to support development initiatives in the developing countries with the help of NGOs also emerged in the 1980s and 1990s. The government in the developed countries promoted NGOs in their respective countries, which in turn supported the NGOs in the developed countries. This arrangement was part of the North-South global partnership efforts. This point will be discussed again later.

Voluntarism in the post-Independence India has changed in many ways. Some initiatives resemble the West and some do not. With India winning Independence, the perspective underwent a fundamental change. Struggle for freedom from the foreign rule was no longer on the agenda. Economic development and social reconstruction were the tasks ahead for the government. The development paradigm that was accepted by the Indian State and the mainstream politics did not coincide with Gandhian economic thought. India was faced with high rising population, low food production and high unemployment. Modernization implied industrialization. Development and the expansion of capitalism were shunned and the country got wedded to a socialistic pattern of development. Promotion of a mixed economy and development through centralized planning became the main strategy.

India after Independence also witnessed another fundamental difference relating to patronization of voluntary efforts. The benefactors who belonged to the business and entrepreneurial class shifted their attention to mainstream economies and the flow of financial support to Gandhian activities slowed considerably. Further, the proposed government programmes required relatively large funds that could not come from the private sector. The *mahajans* and caste associations limited their support to the service sector only. Voluntary initiatives for development and reconstruction, thus, came to be patronized largely by the state. Interestingly, most Gandhian voluntary workers and organizations became largely dependent on the state for their survival. Most of the voluntary organizations, thus, turned into delivery organizations that tried to deliver honestly what governments thought were right things for the people. This type of situation remained till about 1970.

The year 1970 may be considered a watershed for the voluntary agencies in India. Significant changes took place in politics. An era of populist politics had begun. According to the well-known political scientist Rajni Kothari, the populist politics manifested in two ways. Some young ruling party leaders agitated over party policies and management, tried to break away from the party hierarchy and establish rapport with people directly. They also pitched their leadership claims at higher levels. They took recourse to populist politics and gave the slogan of *garibi hatao*. It is well known that in 1971, Indira Gandhi's ruling Congress Party won the Lok Sabha elections with a thumping majority. Discontinuing the privy purses of the erstwhile *maharajas* and nationalization of the banks were two actions that were taken to announce the pro-people politics. The second manifestation came in the form of grass-roots movements. These movements were initiated to mobilize people around issues relating to caste, gender, regional development opportunities and environment. A large majority of them remained non-political and non-governmental.

It took about 30 years after Independence to fully realize that the government was not able to improve the conditions of the weaker sections through its programmes. The Gandhian organizations reacted only when emergency was declared. However, even after restoration of democracy in 1977, most Gandhian organizations were content with playing the delivery role and did not find it necessary to question the objectives. During late 1980s and 1990s, when the controversy raged over Sardar Sarovar Project (SSP) on river Narmada, Gandhian organizations got divided into two camps. For the first time, some Gandhian organizations came out loudly challenging the development paradigm and dubbed this government project as anti-people. Interestingly, most of them had been implementing a number of government programmes without ever seriously questioning the framework within which the government had designed its interventions.

The dependence of the voluntary organizations on the Indian State for financial support also increased in the 1970s. As a consequence of the populist or pro-people politics, the Indian State further consolidated its power by intervening in several economic development activities. Most of the rural development and urban support programmes were funded only by the Government. Finance for voluntary organizations from the non-government sector was limited largely to charity. It became difficult for them to undertake any constructive work without state finances. The characteristics of the voluntary organizations changed. First, most of them became typical delivery organizations implementing government schemes and programmes. Second, some of them built large empires with the state funding. Only a few continued to pursue their own goals with limited support from civil society.

The post–1970 period also witnessed an increase in foreign aid for development. The Governmental and Non-Government Organizations (GO & NGOs) from developed countries brought with them huge amounts of monetary assistance. The communication medium also changed from regional languages to English. Commitment was no longer the value. Professionalism entered and market rate of remuneration to the workers of the voluntary organizations began. Volunteers got exposure to foreign countries especially Europe and America. Their value system underwent some change. A representative of one of the major foreign funding organization had remarked that the GO & NGOs pursued the government policies and, thus, introduced donor government's biases in the programmes. The professional approach was a good garb in which to conceal the donor country's agenda. The issue is controversial even now.

In short, voluntary activities in India have been widely diversified. So much so that the term voluntary has been replaced by non-governmental and voluntary institutions are popularly known as NGOs. It should be understood that the context has changed. Human misery and suffering is not the only context in which the whole voluntary service with or without religious values is being delivered. Secondly, and perhaps more significantly, volunteerism in the context of socio-economic development of a liberal secular democratic society assumes political character. How far the state and the government are able to appreciate this is the issue that calls for examination. In this context let us now review the government's perspective on voluntary organizations.

Government's Perspective on Volunteerism

Government has two components, the political structure and the bureaucratic structure. Both generally do not clearly display perspective, but have perceptions about voluntary organizations and its role and we have to decipher perspective from them. As is known, the dominant development discourse in India has been that of building a society that has both economic growth and distributive justice. The vehicle selected for the purpose was the state. The development model that came to be known as the Nehruvian model accorded priority and power to the governments in planning and implementing economic development programmes.

Fifty years down the line a lot of criticism has come up on this approach and it has been argued by several scholars that the model was non-starter (Ahluwalia and Little 1998). However, even in the present times when the famous globalization, privatization and liberalization have been the tenets for economic development, the political structure is not completely comfortable with it and tends to realign forces and strategies in a way in which the role of the state is not diluted. The basic premise, if one surmises, has been that of the state being a 'provider'. In this paradigm, voluntary efforts and initiatives do not have any place. The political organs in and outside legislature are assumed to be equipped to 'cry foul', i.e. be an objective critic of the government if it went against people. Thus, the role of the voluntary organizations is implicitly subsumed by the political organizations. Bureaucratic structure is slightly different in this regard. There are some individuals at all levels, i.e. very senior and junior levels, who think that the objective referee in the form of voluntary individuals and organizations is an integral part of a democratic society. But, by and large as bureaucracy, the response is to follow the line of the political party in power. And party in power seldom approves the role of the voluntary organizations. But, the political parties continue to feel the need for non-government organizations in the areas in which the bureaucratic structure fails to deliver effectively.

Over a period of time, the political parties have realized that there is a need for relatively honest brokers and service delivery people. Inefficient and corrupt bureaucracy is no longer the vehicle for delivering well-intended programmes for the people. Further, even in the Nehruvian model, Gandhian thinking based rural development work was assumed to be undertaken by the voluntary organizations. Most of the rural development and social welfare programmes of the government required a vehicle other than the bureaucracy and, thus, the State and its various governments provided financial support to the voluntary organizations. Most voluntary organizations turned into NGOs. The non-profit, relatively honest carriers of the government programmes came to be known as NGOs. In the last decade or so with the introduction of the micro watershed programme in rural development, the financial allocation increased substantially. The political parties saw immense opportunity to please their political agents at the district and lower levels and states such as Gujarat witnessed sudden mushrooming of the NGOs overnight. This mixture of non-party NGOs and party NGOs has led to a new confusion in the perceptions on either side about the NGOs and its role.

Implementing schemes and projects funded by the governments or by the national and international donor organizations gave rise to some new features and problems among the NGOs. As stated earlier, NGOs had to professionalize and appoint well-paid professionals to deliver. Handling of finance and the project related requirements changed the lifestyles of the workers. Accountability shifted from people to government department of the donor, both could be manipulated. Corruption in financial terms in values entered and spread fast. In many areas the corrupting influences were subtle. As a result, the government and political parties today view NGOs as necessary evils and partners in the process. Bureaucracy at most echelons perceive NGOs as people taking credit on government resources! According to a large majority among bureaucracy, NGOs work on small scale, spend more money and get more credit and they work in large areas with stringent resources and draw flak. They have also of late started seeing NGOs as local support units of political parties. Thus, by and large, the political apparatus and the bureaucracy both share perspectives, which do not recognize the political space the voluntary individuals and organizations should have in a democratic society. In effect, the role of the civil society is negated under the present scheme of things in the political and government arenas.

Role of Government in Promoting NGOs

Before any expectations are raised about government promoting and facilitating the NGOs for socio-economic development in the country, one needs to fairly clearly lay down the roles of both the agencies in pursuing the goal of development of the country. Government is yet to undergo a complete paradigm shift. From being a 'provider' the government should turn into a 'facilitator'. Individual and group initiatives in socio-economic activities have not only to be encouraged, but also government should create space for it. People have to participate actively. In fact, people have to come together and plan for their communities, villages, blocks and districts. The governments have to provide technical, technological and human expertise in the exercise undertaken by people. At critical places, the governments have to provide financial support for capital and recurring capital needs. Latter is the role of a facilitator. The political ethos has to imbibe and internalize the paradigm shift.

The voluntarism in the society has to respond then accordingly. Many scholars have debated the role and relevance of voluntary initiatives in a developing country like India. It is fairly well recognized that the state cannot succeed completely in alleviating the status of disadvantaged groups. In fact, even when the state assumed almost total control over the commanding heights of the economy during the planning era, it could not effectively deal a blow to poverty and unemployment problems. Social problems and tensions also could not be resolved to anyone's complete satisfaction. Even when the interventions are conceived on a pro-people paradigm, they very soon get caught in the web of vested interests. Since 1991, the country has made a major decision to shift to market-derived growth and development. The shift may or may not help the poorest of the poor in the society. There are problems such as lack of requisite skills to utilize opportunities that may become available as a result of the operation of market forces, and lack of proper educational and health facilities in remote rural areas, where most of the poor live to acquire changing skills required in the market.

According to Rajni Kothari, the Indian State, the politicians, the government, the NGOs, investigative journalism, public interest litigants, Naxalites and other aggressive activists have failed to improve the status of the downtrodden. He pinned hope on the poor and the unorganized themselves and thought that if at all leadership arose from among them their lot would improve. However, he was not totally certain and hopeful about the long term future of the poor organizing themselves because there were a lot of questions on the type and nature of group formations that might take place. He is not at all comfortable with the present NGO-related scenario. He says, '...this new constellation of 'voluntary' effort, encompassing funding agencies and international NGOs, units within government bureaucracies and the Planning Commission meant to assist national and local NGOs, provides a completely new model of both joining-in and containing, co-opting and corrupting the large mass of genuine, grass-roots based activist efforts. Whether this NGO model of volunteerism will further accentuate the great divides between the haves and the have-nots, or ameliorate the condition of the latter, is still an open question' (Kothari 1998).

According to another development scholar Anil Bhatt, there has been proliferation, competition, conflict and rivalry among voluntary groups. Secondly, there are a few adverse effects of professionalism also. The spirit of volunteerism is going down yielding to commercialization. All these trends, according to Bhatt (1995), do not augur well for NGOs and their credibility is at stake. Yet another scholar Indira Hirway too is worried about the present trend among the NGOs. Hirway's concerns relate to the emerging lifestyle and work style of NGOs consequent upon receipt of international funding (Hirway 2002).

Activist and volunteer Dr Anil Patel, who is also a physician and community health expert, feels that volunteers in the voluntary agencies (and not paid workers in NGOs) are a class by themselves because they were sensitive to the cause of the poor and the downtrodden and are above mundane self-interest. They have at times to wake up a confrontational approach towards the government when the latter is engaged blatantly in anti-people activities. Responding to a dominant theme for some activists, of capturing power to make governments more accountable and responsive to the people at large, Dr Patel held that in a democratic framework, the voluntary agencies' function should be to check the power, of the state. In the game of power political organizations quickly lose their capacity to make a correct assessment of the situation at the ground level. Voluntary agencies by their continuous and effective presence ensure a realistic assessment. He echoes the role of the monitor who can cry foul.

Both reform and revolution have to be on the agenda of the voluntarism. Helping the poor and who are in misery and pain will continue to attract the noble citizens in any society. No society should discount the Mother Teresa on the earth. *Karuna* and *Jiva daya* will continue to drive some volunteers in every society whether there is any societal support or not. However, volunteerism will have to enter in the political process as well as it did once during the freedom struggle under the leadership of Gandhiji. One may lament at the lack of such a leadership at the present juncture, but that should deter us from the course that needs to be chartered.

If the above perspectives are shared perspectives then the role of the government in promoting and facilitating voluntary organizations can be delineated somewhat clearly. In case of true volunteers and voluntary organizations, the government has to be tolerant and responsive. Transparency and right to information will have to be respected and all types of information should flow freely. The state should facilitate institutions that record, voice and debate healthy and constructive criticism without colouring voluntary agencies with political shades.

In the process of planning and implementing variety of socio-economic development programmes, there would be a large contingent of NGOs. They will have to be supported with finance. Resource mobilization from within the country and outside should be encouraged. While it is necessary that the credentials of the supporters are examined in the larger interest of the state and the people, unnecessary harassment and political victimization should not be done. The government should encourage and support capacity building and professionalization of the NGOs.

The Panchayati Raj Institutions (PRIs) should not be pitched against the NGOs as competitors. The complementarities of the two have to be recognized and encouraged. The people, NGOs and PRIs have to work as partners for change.

Liberalization and the opening up of the economy have brought a major change in the policy thrust of the country. There has been a conscious decision to reduce the role of the state, to remove unnecessary controls and regulations and to professionalize the public sector. When the power of the state ebbs, market forces become the alternative power centres. Under ideal conditions, the market can operate efficiently and ensure rational allocation of resources and distribute incomes equitably. However, as usual, the question is not about the rules of the game but the issue is one of the needs for umpires and neutrality of them. The revolution is not violent or bloody. It is the strength of the volunteers to organize people and call foul. Despite reduction in its role, the state may still play truant. The need for refereeing is there too. However, in becoming umpires and in refereeing the volunteers, a set of values must be upheld under all circumstances. Deep commitment to cause, devotion, honesty and transparency in all dealings would be absolutely essential. All actions will have to emanate from people.

Notes

1. At least Central Government has been very keen and very recently the Prime Minister of India, in his first address to the Nation in July 2004,

invited NGOs to extend helping hand to partner development efforts of the government.

2. Voluntary efforts and NGOs are apparently used interchangeably in the literature. But I have made a distinction between the two. All voluntary agencies can be also called NGOs, but all NGOs cannot be called voluntary agencies. For details refer to Iyengar (2001).

References

Ahluwalia, Isher Judge and Little, I.M.D. (eds). 1998. *India's Economic Reforms and Development: Essays for Manmohan Singh*, New Delhi: Oxford University Press.

Bhatt, Anil. 1989. *Development and Social Justice: Micro-action by Weaker Sections*, New Delhi: Sage Publications.

____. 1995. 'Voluntary Action in India', *Economic and Political Weekly*, XXX (16), 22 April.

Dantwala, M.L., Visaria, Pravin and Sethi, Harsh. (eds). 1998. *Social Change through Voluntary Action*, New Delhi: Sage Publications.

Dholakia, Ravindra and Iyengar, Sudarshan. 1998. *Planning for Rural Development: Issues and Case Studies*, Bombay: Himalaya Publishing Co.

Hirway, Indira. 2002. 'Contemporary Challenges before Voluntary Agencies', in Sudarshan Iyengar and Digant Oza (eds), *Gujarat: A Balance Sheet* (in Gujarati), Mumbai: Navbharat Sahitya Mandir.

Iyengar, Sudarshan and Shah, Anil. 1998. 'The Contribution of NGOs to Development: Some Issues and a Case Study', in M.L. Dantwala et al. (eds), *Social Change through Voluntary Action*, New Delhi: Sage Publications, pp. 92–112.

Iyengar, Sudarshan. 1998a. 'Voluntary Initiatives for Tribal Development in Gujarat', *The Journal of Entrepreneurship*, 7 (2), pp. 211–235.

____. 1998b. 'Voluntary Initiatives for Tribal Development in Gujarat', in Vidyut Joshi (ed.), *Tribal Situation in India: Issues in Development*, Jaipur and New Delhi: Rawat Publications.

____. 2000. 'Role of Non-Governmental Organizations in Development of Gujarat', *Economic and Political Weekly*, XXXV (35-36). Also published in Hirway, Indira et al. (eds). 2002. *Dynamics of Development in Gujarat*, New Delhi: Concept (Published for CFDA, Ahmedabad).

____. 2001. 'Karma as Dharma', *Humanscape*, February.

Kothari, Rajni. 1998. *Communalism in Indian Politics*, Ahmedabad: Rainbow Publishers.

Shah, Ghanshyam and Chaturvedi, H.R. 1983. *Gandhian Approach to Rural Development*, New Delhi: Ajanta Publications.

Shah, Ghanshyam. 1990. *Social Movement in India: A Review of Literature*, New Delhi: Sage Publications.

CHAPTER 3

Administration of NGOs in Changing Socio-economic Scenario: Dimensions and Issues

A.S. KOHLI

The practice of social work has its roots in charity, philanthropy and relief for the poor. Presently, it involves a very wide and broad spectrum of activities to cater to social, economic, physical or mental needs of human beings. The socio-political systems of the ancient world of Rome and Greece, the institution of family, village and caste, etc. in India and other western countries, contained a variety of services, which came under the blanket terms of 'social services', which used to include any kind of charitable or philanthropic activities. The term 'welfare services' were used to denote a large variety of services rendered to the more vulnerable groups like the physically handicapped and other special groups like women, children and aged (Friedlander 1964). In the Indian situation, community based welfare programmes, like organizing a health check-up camp or distribution of meals and cloth to poor, have been in existence from ancient times. Various religious communities on humanitarian lines organized social service and welfare activities to help and protect their members (Thudipura 2007).

Slowly and gradually these sporadic and haphazard welfare (faith based) activities were metamorphosed into stable and structured organizations. These organizations then came to be known as voluntary or Non-Government Organization; the programmes of assisting people were then organized on these levels.

1. Remedial services includes general social services for the needy people
2. Humanitarian services were inspired by the dire need of people
3. Preventive Services tried to provide safety measures to meet the problems of individuals and groups.

However, NGOs were locally rooted and were flexible in their approach to reach and or assist people.

In the Indian context, there was a strong belief after Independence that it was the state, which should assume the primary role in all areas of development. The state was seen as an instrument of liberation from inhibiting shackles of traditions as well as instrument of equalitarianism in areas of growing inequality and injustice. NGOs have become especially prominent in the last two decades. They have been taking initiative in diverse areas be it the field of education, providing drinking water, organizing forest management groups or thrift societies for working women. NGOs are supposed to take the lead and are emerging as the key player of social transformation (Jacob 2006: 41).

The Indian State was initially indifferent, if not hostile, towards encouraging NGOs in the sphere of development, although charity and relief organizations were tolerated to a certain extent. This climate changed after the mid-1980s. First, in the Seventh Five Year Plan (1985–90) and later in the Eighth Five Year Plan (1992–97), the government openly welcomed and encouraged participation of NGOs in the development sphere. Recently, the state has sanctioned about 1.5–2 billion annually for NGO funding, which is a substantial amount (Patel 1998).

The rise of NGOs is one of the central processes in the sphere of development since the 1980s. This period also coincides with the demise of developmentalism as a project of the nation-state and the rise of post-developmentalist neo-liberal political economy (or what has also been described as market triumphalism). In what is often characterized as a move from inefficient states to efficient markets, NGOs hold a distinctive mediating position (Sheth and Sethi 1999).

There are many definitions of NGOs. The voluntary sector includes non-governmental, non-profit organizations. They may be engaged in a variety of activities: implementing grass-roots/ sustainable development, promoting human rights and social justice, protesting against environmental degradation and many other similar tasks. Some activists resent and reject the term NGO and instead designate themselves as social action groups, political action groups or social movements (see Kothari 1993). Anna Hazare's village development group at Ralegaon Siddhi in Maharashtra and Ela R. Bhatt's Self-Employed Women's Association (SEWA) in Gujarat are both identified as NGOs, but are very different from each other in terms of size, membership, funding, approaches, strategies and outcomes. These differences only show that one should be very careful while making statements about NGOs. However, several are found to be extending a red carpet welcome to internal scrutiny of their working and performing by the funding bodies or their commissioned investigating/evaluative agencies.

NGOs though claim to believe in openness and transparency; many of them are not open to scrutiny by outsiders. Those who have achieved a degree of success and fame are often hostile to any objective studies by outsiders not approved by them.

The NGO sector in India is characterized by tremendous diversity and heterogeneity (Sheth and Sethi 1999). Ignoring this diversity, unfounded generalizations are often put forward and unfair comments and criticisms are offered by academics, media and researchers somewhat in haste and impatience. It must be, however, realized that the NGOs differ from one another in size, funding and functions; in the levels at which they operate; and in organizational structures, goals and membership. There are over 14,000 NGOs registered under the Foreign Contributions Regulation Act. In all, there may be over 3,00,000 NGOs in India.

Administration of NGOs in Changing Scenarios

Given the profound implications of the NGO involvement, there is a greater need to examine the changing relations among NGOs, state agencies, multi-lateral and bilateral funding organization. In current developmental scenario, when the scope of NGOs is diversifying, they no longer are the simple organizations. The NGOs have transformed themselves into complex organizations. As such, the management of NGOs is not a simple state of affairs. It has not only to organize funds for running development projects but also ensure that the programmes bring the desired change in people's life.

The administration of NGOs requires both organizing and managing resources (e.g. people) in a way that the project is completed within defined scope, quality, time and cost constraints.

Therefore, it becomes imperative for organizations to optimize allocation of resources and integrate it with inputs to meet predefined objectives.

A traditional phased approach by the NGO identifies a sequence of steps in the development of a project:

1. project initiation stage
2. project planning or design stage
3. project execution of production stage
4. project monitoring and controlling systems
5. project completion stage

There has been a pragmatic shift in managing developmental projects as the task of the person engaged in formulation of projects not only means planning and completing projects but also sustaining the projects. The projects are appraised by the funding organizations regarding the social, economic and technical feasibility to sanction grant followed by continuous monitoring and evaluating at each stage of the project for judicious utilization of resources and capacity building of the people concerned.

It is recognized that developmental organizations not only require flow of capital for undertaking projects in different fields but also make investment in developing human capabilities. Without capacity building for managing institutions, learning legal-rational procedures for decision-making and accounting raising questions and suggesting alternatives, development will not be socially sustainable. Further, NGOs are considered more accountable, responsive and committed to bringing social change. Many international organizations which were earlier working through national governments now prefer to work through NGOs in implementing some of their project. So the arrangement of funds may not be a major problem but it calls for accountability in the utilization of the resources with funders as well as those people for whom funds have been provided. Foreign donor agencies have evolved a good system of monitoring the expenditure of the funds given to particular receiving agencies.

Challenges for Management of NGOs

The voluntary sector in India, comprising mostly of NGOs due to shrinking role of the state are increasingly taking up newer challenges. The sector is actively intervening in areas like poverty reduction, rural development, livelihoods, health, education, urban improvement, natural resources management, etc. (Khasgiwala and

Navale 2005). The growing complexity of its work and size is accompanied by increasing funding from various bi/multilateral sources, as well as other foreign institutional donors. A need is, thus, emerging for better management of human and other resources as well as programmes and projects by the NGOs. New techniques of project management training and designing development project, appraisal, monitoring and evaluation, human resource management, etc. have come up over the last few years (Ramachandran 1998).

The training course may be designed to equip managers and functionaries in NGOs with requisite skills to carry out their functions effectively. The content of such course may specifically focus on the following:

1. Challenges thrown up by the WTO (World Trade Organization) and GATT (General Agreement on Trade and Tariffs)
2. Civil society and people's movements, specially the rights-based approach
3. Project management, Project cycle approach, Logical framework analysis, etc.
4. Basic concepts of management, human resource management, organizational behaviour, organizational development, conflict, organzational change, etc.
5. Legal and policy environment, including registration, statutory returns, FCRA, Income tax audit, etc.
6. Fund raising and donor management
7. Managerial accounting, foreign currency accounting, procurement of goods and services, specifications, etc.
8. Training and development, training need assessment, evaluation and impact analysis
9. Project appraisal, baseline and endline, monitoring and evaluation and outcome mapping

NGOs have been acting as catalyst agents in the way of development and lots of changes have been done to empower the masses so that they could live their lives and seek their betterment. In spite of providing all these supports to the people (so that they could come in the mainstream), the NGOs are facing challenges which are impending the development process and thwarting change in the existing pattern.

Some of the problems which NGOs face include:

1. *Lack of Information Related to Availability of Programmes:* Very few government departments have a 'user friendly system' of

information dissemination or documentation related to the number of programmes available, who are eligible to apply and how one should proceed.

2. *No Scope for Pre-project Orientation:* An important component regarding awareness among its staff about project-objectives budget and their own responsibilities is not sufficiently built in project proposal. This results in obvious problems during implementation phase of the project.
3. *No Scope for Continuation of Project in Any Form:* Budget provisions come to an end abruptly and the project activities have a similar end. A method of integrating the phasing out of the project into another government programme or scheme usually does not exist. In cases of merit, this can be considered as an innovative, accommodative and ameliorative measure in the wider interests of the targeted beneficiaries.
4 *Lack of Administrative and Financial Flexibility:* Directives for administering the project should be clearly laid out for obvious reasons. However, when poor salary grades are fixed for academically/professionally qualified staff, it becomes difficult to find suitable candidates for various posts. Further, instructions for utilization of the budget have to be strictly adhered to and there is no flexibility to transfer funds from one head to another. These budgetary bureaucratic rigidities should be paid some attention towards incorporating necessary flexibility.
5. *Insufficient Overhead/Administrative Costs:* NGOs find it very restrictive and difficult to manage within the small amount permitted under these heads.

Summing up the Argument

The NGOs play a pivotal role in the social and human development. They not only organize welfare service but are now considered as partners of development and change. However, the effective administration and management of NGO sector calls for continuous improvement as a timely and adequate response to the changes in socio-economic and political scenario. The capacity building of NGO sector is as important as the empowerment of community.

The NGOs have been around for quite some time and they are likely to grow in the foreseeable future as the retreat of the state in social sector continues on variety of justifications. Although the NGO sector as a whole has been studied by country's outstanding social scientists and researchers from such disciplines as economics, sociology, and political science, more systematic studies are required to say anything with confidence about them. In the absence of such studies, our understanding of the issues facing NGOs will remain vague, superficial and hazy. Sociologists of organizations, political sociologists and sociologists of development and professional social workers all need to pay serious attention to them. Such a cumulative effort will enable us not only to understand NGOs better but also to appreciate their contribution to development and social changes in a far more rewarding manner than is the case at present.

References

Baviskar, B.S. 2005. 'Non-governmental Organizations and Civil Society in India', in Jaya Ram (ed.), *On Civil Society: Issues and Perspectives*, New Delhi: Sage Publications.

Bhatt, Ela R. 1998. 'Empowering the Poor through Micro-Finance: The SEWA Bank', in M.L. Dantwala, Harsh Sethi and Pravin Visaria (eds), *Social Change through Voluntary Action*, New Delhi: Sage Publications.

Friedlander, W.A. 1964. *Concepts and Methods of Social Work*, New Delhi: Prentice-Hall of India.

Hirway, Indira. 1995. 'Selective Development and Widening Disparities in Gujarat', *Economic and Political Weekly*, 30 (41-42), pp. 14–21.

Jacob, K.K. 2006. 'Social Work: A Christian Perspective', *Contemporary Social Work*, XXIII, April.

Khasgiwala, A. and Navale, A.S. (eds). 2005. 'Corporate Sector for Social Development: Issues and Challenges', *Social Work Review*, Special Issue on NGOs, Faculty of Social Work, The M.S. University of Baroda, Baroda.

Kothari, Smitu. 1993. 'Movements and Redefinition of Democracy', in Philip Oldenburg (ed.), *India Briefing*, Boulder: Westview Press.

Patel, Rohini. 1998. 'Voluntary Organization in India: Motivations and Roles', in M.L. Dantwala, Harsh Sethi and Pravin Visaria (eds), *Social Change through Voluntary Action*, New Delhi: Sage Publications.

Ramachandran, Vimala. 1998. 'Voluntary Organizations: Professional Agency or Sub-Contractor', in M.L. Dantwala, Harsh Sethi and Pravin Visaria (eds), *Social Change through Voluntary Action*, New Delhi: Sage Publications.

Sheth, D.L. and Sethi, Harsh. 1999. 'The NGO Sector in India: Historical Context and Current Discourse', in Chhaya Patel (ed.), *Social Work Practice: Religio-Philosophical Foundations*, Jaipur and New Delhi: Rawat Publications.

Thudipura, Jacob. 2007. *Urban Community Development*, Jaipur and New Delhi: Rawat Publications.

CHAPTER 4

Youth Volunteerism in Managing Disasters: Learning through Action

SANJAI BHATT

Volunteerism: Semantics and Praxis

Volunteerism has a long history in our country. Our societal existence and volunteerism are inseparable. The need and nature of individuals, community and society have changed from time to time but the functions of the voluntary organizations have remained the same, i.e. the continuous betterment of human beings and the society. During its long journey, volunteerism has created many opportunities and added many dimensions. All religions provided explicit support to the growth of volunteerism. It is an evolved social process institutionalized over a period of time through various religious, ethical and political traditions. Volunteerism had appeared in different forms in different times at different places differently and distinctively.

As a corner stone to any civil society, volunteerism contributes to more cohesive societies by building trust and reciprocity among citizens. While the demand of good governance has generated more scope for volunteering and voluntary action on one hand, the issues emerging from the ongoing process of globalization has questioned the spirit of mutual help and cooperation. Globalization has led to gradual withdrawal of the state from social sector due to which there is a growing need for more services on a voluntary basis. Today, wide-scale poverty, unemployment and illiteracy necessitate volunteering and voluntary actions on a large scale. Similarly, natural calamities like floods, cyclone, earthquake, frequent wars and the ensuring destruction lend urgency to the need for volunteerism and voluntary action (Mathur 2000). At all levels – local to international – efforts are being made to inculcate, develop and promote volunteerism in all fields, such as social, economic, cultural, humanitarian, peace building, etc.

The government has promoted youth volunteerism through its various programmes and schemes but it is unfortunately the issue of volunteers' promotion and development that is not receiving the same attention. It has taken a back seat in the wake of increasing consumerism whereas the context of volunteerism and voluntary actions is fast changing. The voluntary efforts often face the lack of acknowledgement, recognition and public celebration. On the other hand, the environment for volunteerism is expanding especially in the backdrop of increasing economic inequalities, socio-ethnic conflicts and cultural discrepancies. According to the report of UN Secretary General on the follow-up to the implementation of the International Year of Volunteers, 2001, 'opportunities for citizens to be engaged through voluntary action at the local level and have their action at the local level recorded and recognized are steadily expanding. Acceptance is spreading for the idea that all people have a right to development and that active participation through volunteerism is one important avenue for exercising that right. New communication technologies make it ever more possible to build contacts and support networks among individual volunteers and organization that involve volunteers on a local, regional and global basis'. Due to faster demographic and technological changes, the social structure and social relationships are changing at fast pace which is playing an important role in the changing discourses in the notion of volunteering. This also offers new challenges and opportunities to volunteering in contemporary societies of India.

Though volunteering is a state of mind and phenomenon for all ages, the volunteering is generally seen linked with youth. It may be due to characteristics of different age groups. Young persons in comparison to other age groups are full of energy, creativity, adventure and idealism. Young people look at the world through multiple lenses. It is important to understand that youth do take volunteerism because of variety of reasons such as personal pleasure, praise, appreciation, creativity, experimentation, ideas, idealism but not always for purse. The government has also initiated a variety of programmes and schemes for young persons. Programmes such as

National Cadet Corps (NCC), National Social Service (NSS), Nehru Yuvak Kendra (NYK) are all illustrations of promotion of volunteerism through various government programmes. There is a misconception in the contemporary context that the volunteers are only those who contribute to the well-being of other by giving their time, talent or energy free after a day's work. By this definition, only those in the middle and upper-middle classes of society are seen to be volunteering. But volunteering continues to be a wide spread phenomenon in our rural and tribal areas. Among the very poor, the practices of helping others, helping community, helping public are widespread.

These programmes of volunteering are suffering with government apathy, bureaucratic attitude, red-tapeism, delays and *Statisms*. Over the past five decades, the rise of the nation-state, the power of the central government and the totalitarian role of the state in development has created a mind-set among all our people, where dependence on state, state services and programme has become widespread. As a result, self-help practices, initiatives to assist other on one's own choice and volition, contributing of one's energies and resources to the well-being of the community are getting increasingly eroded, if already not happened. Therefore, the first challenge facing volunteering today is to overcome the statist mind-set and rekindle in the people the spirit of self-help and collective well-being (Tandon 2005: 24). Most of these government programmes are incurring major portion of their budget (nearly 60% to 70%) on sustaining infrastructure of these programmes/schemes instead of spending on actual services. Resultantly, these programmes suffer with qualitative outputs/initiatives and express their achievements in quantitative fashions which do not represent the ground realities.

Further, the conception of these schemes is based on faulty premises. Volunteers are seen as an instrument of *doing something* not matured enough to take initiative, decisions. Volunteering is a typical programme of involving students/youth in constructive activities but what does the word *constructive* constitutes and means depend on instructors' perception. Promotion and development of volunteerism cannot be and should not be seen as a programme but as a mission or a mass movement. It cannot be limited to a select few, privileged few or visible few. Volunteerism should be viewed as an essential constituent of effective citizenry and citizenship which is yet to be adequately recognized. All volunteering programmes are *prescriptive* hence does not provide any space for participation in decision-making. Another faulty premise is that volunteerism is designed for those who are not gainfully employed thereby it targets youth first and housewives or retired persons in subsequent categories for volunteering.

Tandon (2005) has aptly remarked that the volunteering today is facing increasing formalization of Voluntary Development Organization and NGOs. As a result, paid staffs with necessary professional qualifications are being attracted towards social development efforts and programmes, many a times at the cost of volunteers. Formal institutions make it difficult for individuals to contribute their own energies and talents in an informal and flexible manner. The formalization of volunteer programmes, including those like NSS have also led to stagnation in the creativity of volunteers. Formal United Nations Volunteers Programme also does not encourage ordinary citizens to make their own limited but important contribution based on their talents and motivations. There is a need to find creative ways by which the energies capacities of one billion Indians could be mobilized as volunteers (Tandon 2005).

There are certain myths and misconceptions as well as stereotypes as far as volunteering is concerned. Volunteering is not related to doing a particular prescribed amount of work but investing one's energy in meaningful work; it is not spending time but quality and productive time; it is not just an activity but more an effective response towards beneficiary. Similarly, it is neither *shramdaan* (labour donation), nor merely *charity*, it must respond to people's actual needs or to create some social goods or social capital (Midgley 1995). Volunteers are now making it possible to learn about and to respond to the conditions of others in distant areas. Hence, it is an act of solidarity to support distant other in emergent and hard situation.

While an ordinary educated Indian thinks that youth are more attracted towards modern style of living and have nothing to do with volunteering are totally wrong as there is a widespread public sentiment to support those who are affected by natural calamities like cyclone, earthquakes, floods or man-made disasters like communal violence, accidents, environmental disasters or terrorism across the country in the recent past. This can be seen as a new upsurge of the human spirit in India. The UDAI (University for Development and Integrated Learning) Projects at three different locations: (i) in Kutch, Gujarat, (ii) later on during Kosi flood in Bihar, and (iii) in Sikkim earthquake-affected regions, stand as testimony of volunteering by student youth of Delhi University which is country's premier centre of higher learning in the capital.

UDAI (University for Development and Integrated Learning) Project

The wider community of Delhi University shared deep concern with the fate of the victims of earthquake in various parts of Gujarat state in January 2001. As a response to this catastrophe, a core committee was formed and was in turn asked to formulate an action plan by way of developing and executing short and long-term intervention in Gujarat. We underscored the need to respond to the call of social worker's concern for the disaster-affected people. This involved going beyond the traps and temptations of the ideology of individualism and required transcending the culture of self-centred materialism in an era of free market. This has pervaded all spheres of life in general. As a result of this consultative process, following a scientific line, it was decided to conduct a need assessment in the affected area. The team broadly identified six different areas of Gujarat for selecting the proposed area of operation. These areas were Nilpar in Rapar Taluka (sub-division), Kanthkot and Motichirai in Bhachau Taluka, Radhanpur in Patan Taluka, Meglalpar in Maliya Miana Taluka and Dhrangadhra in Surendranagar Taluka. These sites were visited to broadly assess the extent of damage and the quantum of relief disbursed among village population.

The place and the partner agency for the rehabilitation work were decided by employing the SWOT (Strength, Weakness, Opportunity and Threat) analysis. Five organizations were scrutinized on these criteria and among them finally *Gram Swaraj Sangh* (GSS) of Nilpar was selected as the partner agency for the proposed rehabilitation project. GSS is a non-profit, non-political organization established in the year 1978, is a part of Kutch *Navnirman Abhiyan* meaning 'Kutch Reconstruction Initiative'. Firmly believing in the Gandhian philosophy of self-help, it has been working, since its inception, for the overall development in the Kutch region of the Gujarat state and has become the focal point for relief and rehabilitation activities in the Rapar Taluka and Bhachau Taluka. All its activities and interventions were based on a fundamental belief in self-help, confidence and capacity-building for enabling villagers to meet, plan, organize and implement their own rehabilitation and development process. *Gram Swaraj Sangh* facilitated this process with an overall aim of making the people independent and to strengthen their self-reliance (Thudipura 2007).

After need assessment, the detailed project was prepared and named as, *University for Development and Integrated Learning* (UDAI – which phonetically resembles to Hindi language word of the same pronunciation meaning 'rise'), with two broad objectives: (i) to be part of the rehabilitation process designed for earthquake affected people in few selected villages; and (ii) bringing experimental learning back to the university system by integrating the youth in disaster management and prevention.

Main Issues

Preliminary estimates suggested that the cost of damages were to the extent of ₹ 20,875 crores (US$ 4.5 Billion) to private and public properties. The nature, extent and magnitude of damages caused by the Bhuj earthquake were quite high. Before starting the main work, a one-week field trip was made. People were consulted and the main issues emerging out from this exploratory exercise were as follows:

- Distribution of relief materials was not proper. There were villages which refused to take relief. It was highlighted that the Muslims and Harijans were the worst affected and they were discriminated even in relief.
- Most of the relief materials had been sent to Kutch area and moderately affected areas like Rajkot and Surendranagar were neglected.
- Insights about functioning of various voluntary organizations working in the earthquake affected area, especially federations like *Janpath* and Kutch *Navnirman Abhiyan.*
- The role of university students, NSS and NCC in the rehabilitation work.
- The possibilities of relocation of villages.

Professor Jitendra Desai, Vice Chancellor (Gujarat Vidyapeeth) also suggested that all the universities in Gujarat should get together along with Delhi University to create a Joint Action by Universities for Rural Reconstruction and Rehabilitation (JAURRR) and work in a cluster of villages. He also stressed that these universities could jointly act as a social group. However, it could not materialize due to varied reasons.

The Gujarat earthquake presented an unfortunate opportunity to the people to learn how to understand and manage such a tragic event.

This kind of a disaster raises many questions, concerns and such issues that require all the people to seriously look into established theories and models of work related with disaster management and rehabilitation and compare all possible options. It was with this perspective and considering the situation analysis, need assessment and the observations of study teams that a plan of action at two levels at the field and at the university level was proposed. The rehabilitation project was to be a joint venture of the Delhi University and the *Gram Swaraj Sangh*. The project was to make a humble attempt to contribute in the following fields namely, housing, education, health, psycho-social support, employment generation, environment and legal awareness.

Modus Operandi of the UDAI Project

The project was planned for catering to the above objectives in their respective areas of intervention for 1,250 to 1,500 families in the chosen area with the partner agency. It was proposed to set up Village Reconstruction Centre (VRC) covering not more than 250 families in a village or its hamlets. This happens to be the average number of families in a village in Gujarat, especially in sparsely populated desert areas of the state. In all, six such VRCs were set up. It was planned that some student volunteers and one village level worker from the partner agency would man each VRC. The composition of such a group was to be multi-disciplinary. These centres were planned to be the focal points imparting public awareness for different fields of activities mentioned above to ensure total community participation it was planned to create a participatory structure in the form of Village Reconstruction Group (VRG).

VRG was to be the main decision-making body to decide the future plan of action in the field on a weekly or monthly basis. Seeing the social divisions in the rural society along caste and religious lines it was decided to give representation to people from all the sections in the constitution of these groups. Considering one representative from 25 families, the group at a time was to be constituted by around fifteen members. It was the considered view of the planners of the participatory approach and structures that respecting the knowledge, wisdom and freedom of people would be more effective strategy to achieve the aims and objectives of the project. The project activities were planned to be volunteer based (Kumar 2002). A programme coordinator at the university level was to be responsible for smooth implementation of the project and a programme organizer at the field level to take care of logistics and liaison with partner agency.

The project was planned to ensure continuous presence of volunteers in the field on rotation basis in a batch size of a minimum of 15 volunteers at a time. It was expected to benefit a total of 450 volunteers with the experience of rehabilitation work. It benefitted 256 student volunteers and 60 teachers in 26 batches keeping a three-day overlapping period, requiring the new batch to take charge and be familiar with their responsibilities ahead of the past batch. The total financial requirements of this project were worked out in detail with the partner agency and it was expected to be in the tune of around ₹ 50 lakhs. Nearly 60 per cent of the needed money was to be raised by different activities and as contribution and grants from other agencies. We could complete the project by spending ₹ 9 lakhs on volunteers excluding the cost on programme activities.

Activities at the University Level

The Kutch region in Gujarat is home to draught, cyclone and earthquake. It falls in seismic zone V, seismically the most vulnerable area of India. The needs of the inhabitants of this region, especially in the field of housing, education, employment generation and trauma counselling were appreciated by the study team. The rehabilitation programme undertaken by the UDAI consisted of several (post-seismic disaster rehabilitation programme) activities aiming to fulfil all these needs. Though, it is only the aspect of public education which is being presented with emphasis herewith. These activities tried to expose the local population of the three villages to the needed knowledge in the above-mentioned fields by creative means of communication and presentation of viewpoints.

The university coordinated various activities of the project with its partner agency in the field through the volunteer teachers and students participating in the rehabilitation project. A short orientation programme focusing on basic information and skills required for the project was organized for each batch of selected volunteers. Necessary inputs were provided to the orientation programme by including new information in different phases of the project on the basis of the feedback received from the field.

For generating and sustaining interest of university community in the project for its entire duration following measures were taken:

- Wide publicity to the project through appropriate means in the university departments, colleges, offices and student hostels.
- Small fund raising and volunteer registration drives.

- Mobilizing non-teaching staff during the examinations.
- Seeking the services of the faculty members for the project with the facility of duty leave for this purpose.
- Involving National Service Scheme (NSS) volunteers for disaster preparedness by giving first-aid kits and emergency response training.
- Rotation of the autumn and winter break in different colleges and departments in consultation with authorities concerned for facilitating the year-round participation of teachers and students in the programme.

Activities Undertaken at Project Site

This project was to be implemented in five villages namely, Kalyanpur, Ratneshwar, Selari, Sangramsur, and Sonapur in Rapar Tehsil, Bhuj District. The five villages, thus, identified for carrying out a focused work in next one year, were chosen for long-term intervention, after extensive consultation with partner agency. The following activities were mainly undertaken in these villages:

Table 4.1

Profile of the Activities Undertaken at the Village

1.	Organizing recreational and educational activities for children at the village level
2.	Mobilizing and organizing youth through games and discussion sessions in different villages
3.	Generating awareness regarding balanced and appropriate diet and physiotherapy
4.	Conducting awareness programmes for villages about the rehabilitation packages announced by the government
5.	Awareness generation and training in construction of seismic resistant housing structures to villages and masons
6.	Organizing villagers to form village councils/associations for redressal of legal issues, including claims for compensation and other entitlements
7.	Construction of temporary shelters for stay of Delhi University volunteers during the tenure of the project
8.	Developing an eco-garden by planting and maintaining trees at the centre
9.	Supervision of ongoing construction work in coordination with workers of Kutch *Navnirman Abhiyan*

Volunteerism – At the Core of the Project

The project UDAI had stressed that batches of 15–20 volunteers from teaching, non-teaching and student members of Delhi University would undertake UDAI activities in the field for one year. Each batch would stay in the field for a minimum of 15 days. The travel and food expenses were taken care by the project UDAI. The schedule of the batches going to field was prepared in a manner to ensure continuity and handing over of responsibilities to the next incoming batch. Before leaving for field, every batch underwent a three-day orientation and training course, conducted at the Delhi School of Social Work, with resource persons from within and outside the department. We also taught 100 words of Gujarati language to our volunteers and gave a five page primer for reference. Thus, volunteerism was the main essence of UDAI project, involving university community in different ways. Volunteers were encouraged:

- To generate awareness of the project, its relevance, aims and objectives.
- To organize a '*Remembering Gujarat Earthquake*' programme on 26th of each month by holding seminar, exhibition, debate, show, publicizing project activities, selling stickers with UDAI related slogans, competitions for slogan writing, project logo, writing essay, etc.
- To motivate student unions/associations/groups of departments/colleges/hostels of the university in organizing innovative programmes for generating support for UDAI project.
- To help in fund raising and volunteer registration drive.
- To conduct research and documentation of the UDAI activities, and to provide constructive suggestions of project activities.

The First Batch of Volunteers

The work was started in the field by the first batch sent under UDAI. It covered the following tasks:

Public Health: Health camps were organized and involvement of medical students was sought to facilitate future work.

Rural Housing: It was suggested to enforce SRH (Safe Rural Housing) measures as per the socio-economic position of families and generated levels of awareness about the packages announced by the government.

Water Management: Campaigns were initiated aiming to cope with water shortages and involvement of watershed management personnel was sought for future efforts in this direction.

Employment: Frequent markets for *Bharatiya* Kala products (embroidery art works) were held by women folks. Besides, in order to check migration of youth, vocational training was imparted.

Education: Adult education was started and attention was paid to starting a library.

Ecology: Tree plantation was done and recycling of garbage was started. On arrival of next batch, the tasks were handed over to them. The first batch oriented the second batch with the ground realities for three days after which they came back to Delhi.

Other Activities

The students observed and learnt several group dynamics such as emergence of leadership, importance of democratic functioning through real life exposure and working collectively as a team. They were also involved in the construction of permanent shelters for the volunteers of UDAI project, information collection during visit to villages, need assessment and prioritization of needs. The volunteers also prepared village profiles of all the three villages through PRA (Participatory Research Appraisal) techniques (Kothari 1990). Surveys and participatory methods were employed to collect data about geographic location, demographic stratification, caste composition, village infrastructure, economic status, occupational pattern, impacts of earthquake, relief measures, and compensation received.

The Subsequent Batches

The next batch continued the work started by first batch and also began some new activities like income generation programme, yoga exercises, formation of youth clubs, etc. Some functional problems were also faced during work, like communication, transport and difficulty in dividing small groups for three villages. Problems specific to these three villages were identified and efforts were made to overcome these handicaps with the cooperation of official authorities. This created a better understanding between villagers and authorities. Supply of fodder emerged as a major problem and was brought to the notice of concerned officials. It was also suggested that UDAI volunteers should be dropped from the scope of supervising the construction work and this should be done by the GSS, the partner agency.

The next batch also continued the work and initiated some additional work like arranging trekking tour, athletic meet at schools, cleaning of dwelling units, constructing an 80 mtr approach road, *shramdaan*, etc. It also raised certain problems like, absence of a lady volunteer disrupting the adult education programme as most beneficiaries were women, smaller size of batches, lack of proper and factual orientation to rural life, gender disparity within batches, etc. In order to rectify these lacunas amendments were made in forthcoming batches. After this batch, the next group consisted of 26 volunteers with two resource persons. In addition to continuing the work started earlier, it started a Self-Help Group (SHG) and *Mahila Mandal* in Selari village, imparted vocational training, organized 'Inter-class Cultural Fest' in Selari, training of seismic resistant houses, awareness about harms of plastic and 'say no to plastic' campaign, construction of a temple in Selari, held *Kisan Vikas Shibir* in Selari and conducted a technical survey of the three villages.

For the smoother day-to-day functioning, volunteers formed four groups to decentralize their tasks and responsibilities – Food Committee, Living Arrangement Committee, Work Plan Committee, and Discipline Committee – each committee having a convener and co-convener. A daily briefing was done in the morning to chalk out the work plan for the day, conducted by the coordinator at 7 a.m. Review meeting was done every evening after dinner by convener and co-convener at 8 p.m. All the responsibilities were held in rotation, thereby giving each of them a chance to assume leadership roles.

Tasks Accomplished Under the UDAI Project

A complete range of various tasks accomplished under the UDAI project is summarized as follows:

Education: The schools for boys and girls were started in five villages. Following were its key elements:

- Enrollment drive campaign
- Recreational activities with children
- Basic health education
- Promotion of parent's participation in school

Rural Housing: Following critical areas were addressed under this component:

- Awareness generation and training in earthquake and cyclone-resistant construction and retrofitting to villages and masons

- Supervision of ongoing construction work, started as a response to the earthquake

Public Health: Attention was paid to the following:

- Medical camps and follow-up of earthquake affected persons and families
- Identification of major health problems and psycho-social support needs
- Awareness generation about hygiene, sanitation and reproductive health
- Malaria prevention
- Networking with public health centres
- Counselling and psycho-social support services

Income Generation Programmes: Special attention was paid to women in this category:

- Initiation of Self-Help Groups, especially among women
- Exploring market options for *Bharatiya kala* (embroidery art work)
- Organizing *Kisan Vikas Mela* (Farmer's camps)

Legal Aid: It dealt with the problems related to compensation to victims:

- Identification of families having problems in getting compensation.
- Legal awareness and guidance with regard to compensation packages and procedures

Environmental Conservation: The elementary tasks were undertaken:

- Plantation drive in monsoon
- Environmental awareness raising
- Imparted water conservation technique by volunteers of Delhi College of Engineering students

Net Outcome of the UDAI Project

The UDAI project has succeeded in attaining the following:

1. Community building and rehabilitation of target groups/villages
2. Management of services under the project and otherwise in an organized manner
3. Bringing university closer to its third objective, extension, and thereby society

4. Developing Delhi University as a partner of caring community
5. Helpful to develop short-term/long-term academic/training course in disaster management
6. Opening new vistas for real life education and learning

Experiences

The UDAI project has provided multiple learning opportunities to volunteers in form of acquisition of skills, learning to be the resource persons and group leaders, as well as deriving benefits of an enriched university student life.

The university has generated vast human and financial resources to begin rehabilitation work in Selari with a commitment for a year. This project has also been unique because it was completely voluntary. At the end of three months, 76 students in six batches have volunteered and participated in this project by visiting and working in Gujarat for a period of 15 days. Likewise, 14 resource persons (teachers, staff and research scholars) have volunteered for making the field trips to Gujarat.

Learning

The UDAI Project has undeniably been a tremendous opportunity for learning with regard to the volunteers and resource persons, who visited Gujarat. However, importantly benefits of the learning accrue not only to the student volunteers and resource persons but need to be seen in the context of the university at large as well as at the level of villages in Kutch where the project has been based. Many teachers and student volunteers of Delhi University have participated as resource persons in the different Orientation Programmes held for the batches prior to their visit. Likewise, the staffs of the Department of Social Work have contributed their time and energy immensely to ensure the smooth functioning of the project. Resource persons from other universities like Jamia Millia Islamia have shared their experience of the earthquake-affected areas and participated in the Orientation Programme.

Volunteer's Learning

All the volunteers and batches have been encouraged to record their experiences in Gujarat. In addition, there have been a number of formal and informal interactions with different batches that have encouraged a sharing of experiences. An attempt is made below to discuss the learning of these volunteers based on their written and verbal reports.

Acquisition of Knowledge by Volunteers

Each of the six orientation programmes have oriented student volunteers to develop an understanding with regard to the area of disaster. The learning specifically has been with reference to:

1. *Disaster*
   (i) Types of disaster
   (ii) Problems related to disaster
   (Iii) Effects of disaster in relation to housing, property, education, family life, etc.
2. *Knowledge of Life and Living Conditions in Earthquake Affected Areas (EAA)*: The volunteers have gained an understanding and appreciation of:
   (i) the life and living conditions of the victims/people of the Kutch following the earthquake
   (ii) the coping mechanisms adopted by them
   (iii) the problems faced by them
   (iv) the role of such factors as individual and community resilience
3. *Obtaining Useful Insights into the Role of Government and Different Voluntary Organizations*: The students have developed an understanding of the roles played by different agencies in the rehabilitation of the people affected by the earthquake. They have had some appreciation of problems related to relief and rehabilitation work, issues related to networking and problems in service delivery.
4. *Learning to Understand the Need and Problems of Community*: The exposure of volunteers to different villages in Kutch has helped them to understand the needs expressed by the community. Immediate and long term needs have been expressed by the people of Kalyanpar, Sangramsar and Selari. The volunteers have used different methods, including the PRA method, to arrive at the conceptualization of these needs and understanding the problems faced by the people. This has significantly helped in their abilities to conceptualize plans and prioritize the problems and needs that require attention immediately and develop strategies wherever possible to address these.

Acquisition of Skills by Volunteers

The fortnight long exposure in Kutch has provided a tremendous opportunity to develop some skills and build on existing skills.

1. *Skills Related to Living in Rural Areas*: For many of the volunteers this project has been a unique opportunity to build on their skills. Several of them have expressed that despite the orientation and their knowledge of what lies in store for them in Kutch, the actual life in Kutch came as a surprise. This project has helped the volunteers build skills to function in an area where basic amenities are not available. The girls of the first few batches were privileged to use the toilets and bathing facilities at the school campus in Selari as the school principal (Mr Khimji Bhai Raiyani) was gracious enough to allow them the use of these. However, the boys in these batches had to use open fields and bathe in a stagnant water tank which they did very unhesitatingly despite the fact that it was neither easy to adjust nor hygienic to believe. In addition, due to the sheer physical nature of the work involved, many of the volunteers developed blisters and boils. There were hardly any complaints from these batches regarding the problems they faced although many of them expressed that this was so because they were so cognizant of the realities in Kutch and would feel ashamed to complain about minor problems.

   The skill building also extended to their learning of the local language. The Orientation Programme of all batches did have at least two sessions of language learning where they were equipped with basic phrases that they would require in the field. However, a fortnight in the field gave them the opportunity to further enhance these skills.

2. *Skills Related to Group Living:* Almost all batches have reported as to how unique learning opportunity this entire project has been, especially with regard to group living. This project has given all the volunteers an opportunity to relate to others in the context of a group and learn the importance of group work and appreciate the skills required for group living. The volunteers of batch-I and batch-IV were all drawn from one department with resource persons too predominantly drawn from the same department. The other batches (Batch II, III, V and VI) were mixed batches comprising students from various departments/colleges. Despite these variations, the major learning reported by

students of all batches has been with regard to their: (i) skills related to group living, (ii) skills related to rapport building and rapport maintenance among themselves, (iii) sharing resources that are precious, (iv) adjustment and learning to handle intersectional conflicts, and (v) learning to relate to each other. In addition to this, batches that had volunteers from more than one department/college report that they have learnt to appreciate and accommodate each other's views and develop an inter-disciplinary perspective. The learning of many of these students has gone beyond the narrow confines of the discipline that they belong to and, as many student volunteers put it, the experience of being part of UDAI project has been a learning beyond classrooms.

3. *Skills Related to Working with Individuals:* Student volunteers across batches and disciplines have reported the unique learning with regard to working with individuals in the selected village. Many of the batches have been encouraged to write down their personal reflections of the trip and they have written about the satisfaction of being able to work with community members and being able to make a difference.
4. *Skills Related to Working in a Team:* The student volunteers have expressed their gratitude to Delhi University for this opportunity as they have learnt to think and function as a team. They were always conscious of their role as representatives of Delhi University and their batch as a link with the other batches. Some report that they have learnt to be objective with regard to work performance, the importance of appreciation and 'giving a pat on the back' and the importance of co-operative and coordinated work. Importantly they have learnt to sacrifice or compromise individual objective for the sake of group or collective objectives.

Resource Persons' Learning

As all resource persons too have volunteered their time to visit Gujarat as part of UDAI project, much of the learning mentioned above applies to them as well. In addition, as group leaders the learning has been with regard to group management skills, organizational skills, learning to handle intra-group conflict, learning to boost group morale and keep the team spirit alive where necessary and to manage individual and group problems. The most important aspect of their learning, however, has been with regard to handling finance, planning work and budgeting for the days spent in Gujarat in keeping with the UDAI project requirement.

Benefits and Learning at the Level of the University

The experience of running this project has clearly yielded the following benefits:

- A clear appreciation by the university for the kind of role it can play with regard to its participation in disaster management. This being the first such organized venture, it was not without initial hesitations and doubts. However, the university was able to demonstrate how it can play an active role in rehabilitation work. It has moved from merely generating financial resources to playing an emphatic and active role in rehabilitation work.
- The university has been able to motivate so many volunteers from among the university community to join the UDAI project thereby sensitizing large groups to think how they can play a more decisive role with regard to rehabilitation work. However, it needs to be said that our work in further motivating the large university community needs to be stepped up so as to involve larger numbers.
- The vast academic and field expertise of the university has been made available to plan, implement and participate in this project.
- The implementation of UDAI project has certainly provided many learning opportunities and added to our body of experiential learning.

Points to be Kept in Consideration in Future Projects

This project required better networking among ourselves and involvement of various colleges and departments who have hitherto not been as actively involved. Following suggestions are made on the basis of the experiences gained in UDAI Project:

- A specific term course of orientation for all students in the university community needs to be designed and conducted. The purpose of this course is to acquaint the student community about the different kinds of disasters; effect of disasters and the role each plays in prevention, motivation, relief and rehabilitation work.
- Formulation of a cell (clearing house) for information related to disasters.

- The university should generate and have minimum resources available and be able to establish linkages with other agencies for joining rehabilitation efforts.

Benefits of the UDAI Project

The quick benefits can be seen at both levels community and university. A brief list of benefits accrued to the community is given as under:

1. *Asset Building:* Consistent with the discussion held in May 2001 between the partner agencies (GSS, Nilpar and Delhi University), the volunteers of the six batches have been able to construct five shelters. Two of these are being used by the UDAI project for stay of volunteers and three are functioning as classrooms in the school at Selari). In addition some toilets have been constructed and in one of the batches construction of road was done.
2. *Education:* This has been one of the thrust areas of the project and as the summaries of the report of different batches reveal almost all batches have worked in these areas. Awareness has been generated on many issues related to housing by volunteers but a more concrete contribution has been made with regard to beginning and/or facilitating adult education classes, women's education and children education in the three selected villages.
3. *Employment Generation:* A humble beginning has been made with regard to generating employment for the victims/persons in the community. Three persons have been employed by the project itself. We do hope that subsequent batches will be able to expand on this. One batch has also reported that they began the process for vocational training in women. Another batch has explored marketing options for the hand-embroidered (*Bharatiya kala*) clothes of the local women.
4. *Contributing to Social Harmony:* The UDAI project volunteers have been cognizant and aware of the socio-economic fabric of the local communities in the villages. They have respected the norms and culture of these people and have, through conscious method, avoided disturbing the homeostasis of the community. However, despite rigid caste and class barriers prevalent in the community, the volunteers have attempted to make in-roads into the community unifying different groups through their involvement in various cultural and recreational activities.

UDAI has become a brand name. After successful completion of the project, we were educating wider communities on disaster management. A dozen publications, reports were published benefitting academic and research community. We have initiated UDAI-II to provide relief and rehabilitation of flood affected villages in Supaul, Madhepura and Saharsa districts of Bihar. This time, we added relief collection centre at the department and collected relief material worth ₹ 10 million. Learning from past experiences and turning our efforts for longer duration, we have created a band of 40 volunteers as a community based organization called *UDAI Sahayatri* (UDAI Co travellers). We are in final phase of hand holding after 36 months of ongoing intervention with support of Delhi University. Now we are also in negotiation with the state government while finalizing a programme for earthquake victims especially children in Sikkim which may be called as launching UDAI –III (UDAI for Sikkim). The spirit of volunteerism and knowhow from professional social workers are creating a new approach in community based volunteers-led disaster response.

References

Kothari, C.R. 1990. *Research Methodology*, New Delhi: Vista Prakashan.

Kumar, Somesh. 2002. *Methods of Community Participation*, New Delhi: Sage Publications.

Mathur, Hari Mohan. 2000. 'Involuntary Resettlement and Voluntary Organizations: A View from India', IV International Conference (Unpublished), Trinity College, Dublin, Ireland.

Midgley, James. 1995. *Social Development: The Development Perspective in Social Welfare*, London and New Delhi: Sage Publications.

Tandon, Rajesh. 2005. 'Volunteerism in India Today', *Yojana*, 45, December.

The United Nations. 2001. *Role of Voluntarism in the Promotion of Social Development*, Published by The UN Secretary General during the International Year of Volunteers, 23 February.

Thudipura, Jacob Z. 2007. *Urban Community Development*, New Delhi: Rawat Publications.

CHAPTER 5

State, Voluntary Sector and Social Development in India: A Synoptic Assessment of their Interface

CHHAYA PATEL

Different features characterize different periods, epochs or stages of human history as mark of prominence and distinctiveness. The contemporary period can be easily characterized as an era of struggles for transformation through socio-economic development. From local to global levels, numerous mechanisms in form of various state and society run agencies, institutions and bodies are engaged in pursuing one or the other developmental goal. Development is a new *mantra*, a catch-all concept, on every agenda. All societies, countries are chasing this mirage like dream, ideal and vision. Compared to the countries of the developed world, the developing or non-developed countries are particularly impatient and wary to grapple with this concept. They are confronting it as a big challenge. Various attempts are made to conceptualize the ideal, vision and philosophy of development (Giddens 2001):

The chief actors or players in development domain are as follows:

1. Local, state and national governments as public bodies.
2. Voluntary sector organizations and agencies are viewed as societal institutions.
3. Numerous international non-governmental donor agencies like ILO, UNICEF, WHO, Action-Aid, the United Way, World Bank, Ford Foundation and so on. The role of the international bodies has not been always free from controversies as shown by Karat-Sethi debate (Karat 1984; Sethi 1985).

Two distinct sub-themes or branches of development have emerged in last few years in form of social development and economic development. Often they are referred to as socio-economic development as one semantic expression. Therefore, it is quite correct to state that the agenda of social development is a monolithic enterprise and calls for multi-angular, multi-dimensional and multi-lateral initiatives and interventions. In this chapter, it is attempted to raise and answer as well as discuss the following issues and the questions:

1. To conceptualize what is social development and then to examine as to who are the chief actors.
2. To find out as to what they have done about social development.
3. To ascertain on the basis of the available and relevant secondary literature the extent to which they have succeeded in achieving the goals of social development.
4. To estimate and examine various perceptions about the role of state and voluntary sector vis-à-vis the just distribution of public goods which can be the legitimate part of social and economic development.
5. To list and discuss the major lessons which can be drawn from this exploratory exercise of macro level but synoptic appraisal.

According to our assumptions as well as understanding, state and society are chief actors or agents of social development. How they both have fared and interfaced on the issue of social development, various quantified perceptions about their respective roles, and what major lessons can be drawn is the focal theme of this contribution.

Major Arguments

One argument that is prominently doing rounds is that social development is tried to be achieved without understanding the proper meaning of it (Kulkarni 1978; Jacob 1992; Midgley 1995). This is argued to have resulted in duplication of efforts, programmes, schemes, projects, etc., excessive attention to a particular target group, uninformed contents of development and hardly any prioritization (Gore 1973; Kothari 1987; Nandedkar 1987; Kumar 1997; World Development Report 1997). It is, therefore, important to retrieve, recapitulate and re-state the meaning of social development for better understanding of their interface between the state and society or in other words, voluntary sector.

Second argument that has powerfully emerged is that the role of state is on a decline and about to get over (Chatterjee 1994; Ludden

2005; Reddy 2005). The state is on a retreat from the social sector. It has failed to achieve the goals of speedy socio-economic development and social justice. In fact, it went about it in such a way that it antagonized the two other constituents of human society, namely, civil society and the market to the extent of self-defeat. The state failure widened the borders and expanded the horizons of the role, intervention and participation by the civil society and the market. Liberalization fuelled these processes and restructured the role of state and civil society in achieving the goals of social development. Yet, a paradoxical situation exists regarding this. Some experts prefer only regulatory role for state whereas others want the state to actively participate in the economic and social sphere. Survey data also shows conflicting pictures.

Globalization of economy has further questioned the role of state and society and intensified the debate. Whether the weakening of the state is good or bad and what consequences, it can have on overall development of society has emerged as a moot point. Some are questioning the potential of state to provide good governance and balanced social development. In order to inform the discussion on these arguments, what now follows is a semantic clarification and assessment of operationalization of the three major concepts used in the title of this chapter, i.e. state, voluntary sector and social development.

Meaning, Role and Limitations: An Assessment

It must be recalled that the state claims and holds public sphere as its pre-eminent domain. Its emergence, evolution and continuing existence show that the political institution of state is an irreversible reality. Its powers of policy making and functions of governance can vary from one to another country. Its nature too can vary but its existence cannot vary, even in the midst of such slogans as 'third space', 'borderless world', 'retreat of state', 'globalized society', or 'triumph of market processes, forces and institutions'. Despite all these developments, the presence of state as a supreme and sovereign domain of power and pre-eminence remains unchanged. State is, thus, an interventionist, regulatory mechanism. Its role is yet to be subjected to any such recessive or reductionist terms in those societies where the goals of respectable or minimalist social development are yet to be achieved. Reallocation of resources towards this goal in those societies is possible only through the interventionist, regulatory and distributive agency of state (World Development Report 1997). The World Development Report or WDR (1997) states as follows:

> Building a more responsive state with reduced distance between government and the citizens and communities it is intended to involve four broad policy imperatives: (i) Ensuring broad based public discussion of key policy directions and priorities, (ii) Encouraging the direct participation of users and other beneficiaries in the design, implementation and monitoring of local public goods and services, (iii) Adopting a sectoral approach in priority areas, and (iv) To focus on mechanisms that build accountability and competition in government's relations with the communities.

The state in India is ideally placed in a balanced mode of not getting overloaded, over ambitious and at the same time addressing the concerns of equity, freedom, justice and good governance. Society, in India, has yet to come to terms with its internal contradictions of linguistic regionalism, ethnic diversities, caste, and sectarianism, cultural and economic unevenness and so on. Due to its lack of performance, the state had to withdraw from certain areas of governance but its role in achieving goals of social development is still very relevant. Society itself is a second major factor in social development. There are areas, aspects and target groups of prospective beneficiaries, which for various historical, cultural or social reasons remain unattended, uncovered and unnoticed. The histories of such types of glorious, shining examples are found as an evidence of pioneering initiative in the pre-policy or pre-state intervention for tribal and child development (Patel 1986; Patel 1990). Society and voluntary sector of society point finger towards those areas, which have escaped the attention of state's developmental initiatives, intervention and extension. The voluntary sector in India is credited for having rendered yeoman services to social and other development. (Shah and Iyengar 1998; Sheth and Sethi 1999; Bhatt 2005). It is equally discredited for becoming a parallel sector like any agency, office or department of government (Jani 2005).

In a scathing attack on civil society and NGO, Gauri Nath, in his article on: 'NGO *Ke Havale Vatan Saathio*' (translated in English as: 'Homeland in the Hands of NGO, Oh Countrymen') published in *Hans* on 7 July 2005, a monthly started by Munshi Premchand and currently edited by Rajendra Yadav (as narrated in Jani 2005), states as follows:

> Dishonesty is increasingly accepted and practiced as an established social value. In this type of civil society attempts are afoot to justify prostitution by covering all types of adultery, corrupt practices in the garb of modernity ... In such a time, who in reality is having a dream of creating an exploitation free society? Who wants to really contribute in a struggle for getting justice for all? .... There is no dearth of such NGOs who corner massive wealth by coining and raising false slogans. In Delhi, alone it is said, there are 25,000 NGOs. Today thousands of NGOs are busy counting dollars and pounds under the cover of progressive and pro-people postures.

Jani (2005: 3) further summarizes Gauri Nath's anguish that 'some honest activists work for welfare of common people in the beginning, but later on get addicted to the luxuries of bungalows and cars and start looting the same very people'. Undoubtedly, Jani has raised a very pertinent point in his article that:

> ... when the whole society and the system have become rotten, how can any one sector remain immune from it? When all sectors ranging from education, police and judiciary have been impacted by such rot, how can an NGO sector remain immune? (2005: 6).

No wonder then the birth of India Against Corruption movement had to happen. Efforts, campaigns, protests, agitations, persistence and leadership by Anna Hazare, Arvind Kejriwal, Shanti Bhushan, Prashant Bhushan, Manish Sisodiya, Kiran Bedi, Yogendra Yadav, and Medha Patkar, etc. yielded rich rewards in form of Lokpal law and the national office against corruption.

The case of Bihar is well known where one social worker registered three NGOs with a view to giving two of the three NGOs to his daughters in dowry and the third one was to be retained by him for his old age care. In Gujarat too, some such evidences have surfaced. Political workers have got the largesse in form of boarding schools and *Ashramshalas* covered under the category of NGO. More than social service, they are meant to earn easy-lazy income. Jani has, thus, made an interesting assessment of contemporary voluntary sector in India. However, Anil Bhatt strongly resents the half-baked and superficial attacks on voluntary sector and defends it as follows:

> It seems that it has become a fashion to skyrocket the deficiencies, decay and defaults of voluntary organizations. Till now, political leaders and the bureaucrats rarely missed an opportunity to criticize the NGOs in an abusive language, but now the journalists, thinkers, social scientists and professional writers are competing with each other in condemning the NGOs (2005: 18).

Bhatt (2005: 18) concedes that, there are some valid points in criticism against the NGOs. But these criticisms have wholly missed the overall role of NGOs, the voluntary sector itself and its contribution. Bhatt (2005) argues that the growth and expansion of voluntary sector is mainly due to its growing credibility in the eyes of international-national donor agencies and the government's hope and trust in NGO's potential and capacity to enhance social development. Bhatt's sharp and pointed volley of questions and views is a timely reminder to us of the prevailing realistic situation. He asks as follows:

> It must be remembered that the NGO sector is also the product of country's centuries' old tradition of inefficiency! Which sector of the country is efficient? Governmental sector, cooperative sector, public institutions, judiciary and even the privately owned industries' history is also full of inefficiency .... It is not easy to achieve targeted results as per the prior plan, time and money budget in an unequal and exploited society where vested interests have tight grip, and where poor-deprived class also suffers from fear, doubts, traditions, customs which obstruct their development and progress (2005: 18).

Thus, if we view from all angles and dimensions of this phenomenon, the contribution of voluntary sector in social and economic development is noteworthy. Bhatt's worry and warning about the fate of NGOs is well-composed in his following words:

> The attacks, which are presently being made on NGOs, are the result of an exaggerated attitude of treating all NGOs alike, without any sense of right or wrong, and of certain shallow and professional intellectual's attitude of jumping into a running bandwagon. As a result, the politicians, bureaucrats and certain vested interests use such criticism to remove inconvenient NGOs .... It is worth noting by all that in today's time of all round fall and decline, if there is any ray of hope, it is the NGOs (2005: 20).

There cannot be any better, well-grounded, analytically balanced and realistic assessment of the contemporary voluntary sector scenario in India than the above quoted words of Bhatt. These words balance fear and hope, pessimism and optimism, idealism and realism, haste and patience, exaggeration and actual as well as keep the discourse grounded and rooted.

Empirical Evidence from National Survey

It must be ascertained from the critically evaluative discussion in previous section as to which actor – state or society – possesses potential of meeting the remaining or neglected challenges of social development. Experts, scholars, social scientists, social activists, policy-makers, advocacy activists and media seem to be favouring greater role for voluntary sector as the only ray of hope in an otherwise defunct, decadent, corrupt and retreating as well as shrinking state sector. But the popular mood, perception and response to this debate is completely opposite to intellectual or expert perception on the issue. The Political Scientists of American and Indian universities, namely University of California, Berkeley, Ohio State University of USA and Bangalore University of India conducted a national level survey research project on 'State and Society' in 2001–02. The questionnaire was prepared in 11 Indian languages and was canvassed in 18 states of India. The data analysed and presented in the Table 5.1 are based on the responses received from 8,388 respondents drawn from methodologically the most meticulous sample frame.

Table 5.1

Popular Perception of Responsibility in Solving Problems Relating to Public Goods (in%)

S. No.	*Public Goods*	*People and Community*	*Government*
1.	Electricity	3	93
2.	Roads	5	85
3.	Medical Facilities	6	84
4.	Education Facilities	7	82
5.	Ration Supply	9	85
6.	Drinking Water	9	80
7.	Crime	18	69
8.	Pollution	36	50
9.	Cleanliness	48	37

Source: Chhibber, Pradeep; Shastri, Sandeep and Sisson, Richards. 2004. 'Federal Arrangements and the Provision of Public Goods in India', *Asian Survey*, xliv (3), May–June, p. 346.

This research study (Chhibber et al. 2004) has reported startling results on popular perceptions about the role of state and society in social development with concrete evidences as presented in Table 5.1. It needs to be stated as a measure of the strength of the evidence cited here that the sample frame of this survey was immensely representative of the universe, i.e. the country, on all the usual indicators of sex, literacy, income, education, region, housing area, occupation and so on.

A question was asked to about 8,388 sampled respondents from all over the country as to what did they think about the responsibility of solving problems related to important public goods. Not only interesting but eye-opening and insightful responses are reported by the survey. On five civic and social infrastructure related public goods/indicators like electricity, roads, medical and educational facilities, ration supply and drinking water, over 80 per cent respondents perceive government as responsible for their supply and maintenance. This goes to show that state cannot be so easily wished away as in popular perception and expectation; it has a big role to play in developing countries. Let us take up another important indicator of housing in India as an aspect of social development and what we find is that housing is still a dream for so many homeless. As against the minimum requirement of 50 sq ft of space for an individual, in India, 50 per cent of the total population has just 25 sq ft of space. About 60 per cent of the residential dwellings in India have just one room.

This shows that the task of social development is far from over and continues to be the biggest challenge to both the sectors – the government as well as voluntary. Each parameter of social development such as family (in the sense of size and gender balance), education, health, water, electricity and roads is far from being in a satisfactory state and has its own story to tell. As Sanjay Lodha[1], recently observed that people's expectations from the political parties during electoral campaigns, or while running the state and government are taking new forms. First, they were limited to *roti, kapda, makaan* (i.e. food, clothing and shelter), then it expanded to *sadak, bijli, paani* (i.e. road, electricity and water). In the twenty-first century, they are expecting *swashtha, shiksha, rojgaar* (health, education and employment) through good, efficient, accountable and responsive governance.

The words or the terms of the expressions may change but essential popular expectations rotate around these public goods as shown in Table 5.1 and as discussed in the earlier paragraphs.

Major Lessons of Interface Analysis

A bird's eyeview-like appraisal exercise undertaken here has made it possible to draw several important lessons for correcting, revising and reformulating our impression, assumption, analysis, interpretation and understanding of the role of two major sectors, namely, governmental (or state) and voluntary sectors (or the NGOs), and the task before them vis-à-vis the massive challenge of social development in a country and society like ours. Various scenarios have emerged from this discussion in form of a rich yield.

First lesson of this interface is that the conflict and controversy regarding the role of state and society is not a case for either-this-or-that solution or choice. That is to say, it should not be the case wherein a choice has to be made for either the state or the society as an engine or sole agent of social development. Second lesson is that both have a role to play despite the whole array of criticisms against them ranging from being mild to harsh. There are several areas of social life which have remained uncovered by the state agencies. To many remotely located peripheral and marginalized people, state has yet to reach out in an adequate measure.

Third lesson is that the whole issue of state-society interface over social development has to be viewed as a continuum, a process more of collaboration and cooperation rather than mutually outdoing competition. It has to be seen more as a journey rather than a developmental destination to be reached purely in physical/quantitative terms. Fourthly, there are many sub-texts like sub-processes distinctly emerging from the main text of social development such as legitimacy of the state, humanization and democratization of socio-culturally differentiated society, popular participation, and conscientization of the weaker sections of the society who have missed on the price of cake that they rightfully deserve in form of any of the public goods or social development goods like water, housing, education, health, electricity, roads, etc.

Fifth lesson drawn is that the other equally concerned sector must fill the deficit of one and *vice versa*. That is to say: if the state effort towards any social development indicator is absent or falls short, the voluntary sector must either initiate it or take it up from where the state/government left. Similarly, the state must take it up from where the civil society, an NGO or voluntary sector leaves due to whatever structural, functional or systemic constraints. There can be and there are numerous reasons for one agency's initiating a developmental effort and leaving it at some point for various usual, possible reasons of inefficiency, economy, structural constraints, absence of political or social will, insufficient social capital, administrative handicaps, beneficiary resistance, procedural delay, resource crunch and so on. Apart from this, the reason of sheer scale, magnitude, depth and coverage of the area and beneficiaries in a particular social developmental initiative, there could be a negative reason for abandonment of it by an NGO, VA or voluntary sector, howsoever important it may be. It is herein that the government or state can take over for either an extension or replication of a success of a pilot-like effort. Evidences of this process are well documented in a vast and continuously growing literature on social development studies (Midgley 1995; Giddens 2001).

Sixth lesson is that there is a need for patience, restraint and professional care in judging the developmental enterprise and processes, initiated, mediated, or abandoned by either the state, civil society, NGO or voluntary sector. Seventh lesson to be drawn is that some corrective and punitive measures have to be put in place to take care of the conmen, swindlers, and bogus elements, politicized or criminalized elements shielded by the protective cover of state or society. Lastly, the WDR's (1997) loud message is to be well taken that there are 'costs of leaving things as they are,' suggesting that social development is not a unilateral enterprise to be steered by either one or the other sector in society – be it governmental or voluntary/non-governmental – but it is truly a multilateral and multi-actor enterprise. So, in conclusion it may be stated, as the WDR says, that social development cannot be left unattended and neglected.

Note

1. Dr Sanjay Lodha is Professor and Head, Department of Political Science, M.L. Sukhadia University, Udaipur, Rajasthan. These observations were made in his Keynote Address to a UGC sponsored National Seminar, organized at Nalini Arvind and T.V. Patel Arts College, Sardar Patel University, Vallabh Vidyanagar, Gujarat.

References

Bhatt, Anil. 2005. 'Attack on Voluntary Organizations', *Naya Marg* (in Gujarati), 20 (16), 28 October, pp. 18–20.

Chatterjee, Partha. 1994. 'Development Planning and the Indian State', in Terrence Byres (ed.), *The State, Development Planning and Liberalization in India*, New York: Oxford University Press.

Chhibber, Pradeep, Shastri, Sandeep and Sisson, Richard. 2004. 'Federal Arrangements and the Provision of Public Goods in India', *Asian Survey*, XLIV (3), May–June, pp. 339–352.

Giddens, Anthony. (ed.). 2001. *The Global Third Way Debate*, London: Polity Press.

Gore, M.S. 1973. *Some Aspects of Social Development*, Jaipur: Rawat Publications.

Jacob, K.K. (ed.). 1992. *Social Development Perspectives*, Udaipur and New Delhi: Himanshu Publications.

Jani, Indukumar. 2005. 'Which are the Correct Capital and Sphere of NGOs?', *Naya Marg* (in Gujarati), 28 (16), 16 August, pp. 3–7.

Karat, Prakash. 1984. 'Action Groups/Voluntary Organizations: Factor in Imperialist Strategy', *The Marxist*, 2 (2), pp. 19–54.

Kothari, Rajni. 1987. 'Voluntary Organizations in a Plural Society', *Indian Journal of Public Administration*, 33 (3), July–September, pp. 433–453.

Kulkarni, P.D. 1978. *Social Policy and Social Development in India*, Madras (now Chennai): Association of Schools of Social Work in India.

Kumar, Hajira. 1997. *Social Work, Social Development and Sustainable Development*, New Delhi: Regency Publications.

Ludden, David. 2005. 'Development Regimes in South Asia: History and the Governance Conundrum', *Economic and Political Weekly*, 10 September.

Midgley, James. 1995. *Social Development: The Developmental Perspective in Social Welfare*, London: Sage Publications.

Nandedkar, V.G. 1987. 'Voluntary Association: A Strategy in Development', *Indian Journal of Public Administration*, 33 (3), July–September, pp. 465–481.

Patel, Chhaya. 1990. 'Review of Child Welfare Policy and Implementation in Contemporary India', *Arthat* (in Gujarati), 9 (4), pp. 10–24.

Patel, Priyavadan. 1986. *Tribal Development in Gujarat*, Surat: Centre for Social Studies.

Reddy, Sanjay G. 2005. 'World Development Report: A Brief Review', *Economic and Political Weekly*, 15 October.

Sethi, Harsh. 1985. 'The Immoral "Other": Debate between Party and Non-Party Groups', *Economic and Political Weekly*, 20 (8), 28 February, pp. 378–380.

Shah, Anil C. and Iyengar, Sudarshan. 1998. 'The Contribution of the NGOs to Development: Some Issues and a Case Study', in M.L. Dantwala et al. (eds), *Social Change through Voluntary Action*, New Delhi: Sage Publications.

Sheth, D.L. and Sethi, Harsh. 1999. 'The NGO Sector in India: Historical Context and Current Discourse', in Chhaya Patel (ed.), *Social Work Practice: Religio-Philosophical Foundations*, Jaipur and New Delhi: Rawat Publications.

World Development Report. 1997. *The State in a Changing World: World Development Report*, New York: Oxford University Press.

CHAPTER 6

Volunteerism in an Age of Globalization

C. THOMAS ABRAHAM

Sometimes the folk wisdom, prudence and sermons contained in the fables (like *Hitopadesh, Panchtantra,* etc.) illuminate the complex realities of life in a far simpler, convincing and palatable way than any number of social theories or philosophical schools can do. The process of education should be made as digestible as possible. I begin my chapter with such a rich moral story which is full of traditional concerns and ancient wisdom.

Once upon a time, the goddesses decided to hold a competition, a kind of Olympics, among the nations of the world. This was not an ordinary race in which the distance was determined and the winner would be the runner who took the shortest time, but a contest to see which nation or a society, acting as a team, could move all its members forward. When the race was flagged off, one nation assumed that the race would not last long. It urged all its citizens to start running as quickly as possible. It was like every person was engaged with himself. Very soon the young children and the elderly were left behind, but none of the fast runners bothered to help them out because it would have slowed them down.

At first, those who were in front were exhilarated by their success (more or less like the proverbial race between the hare and the turtle in our fables). But as the race continued, some became tired or hurt and fell by the wayside requiring rest. Gradually all the runners became exhausted and sick, and there was no one to replace them. It became clear that this nation would not win the race and may soon be out of it.

Everyone's attention turned to a second competing nation, which adopted slightly different strategy. It sent all its young men out ahead to compete, but required all the women to come along behind, carrying the children, the sick and the elderly and also caring for the runners who needed help. The nation's leaders explained to the women that this was a natural and efficient arrangement from which everyone could benefit. They provided great incentives for men to run fast, and in return gave them the authority over the women. It somehow skipped from realizing that the men could run faster to win the race because they were backed by the hidden back stage energy of the women.

At first, this seemed to work but the women found that they could run just as fast as the men if they were not burdened with caring for the weak. They began to argue that the work they were doing – caring for the runners – was just as important as the running and deserved equal opportunity and reward. The men refused to make any changes, the nation began to waste a great deal of energy in arguing, bargaining and negotiating. Probably this was one of the earliest gender based feminist battles fought in the history of mankind! Gradually, it became clear that this nation, too, was losing the race as it lost the track of the goal on hand and got entangled into futile argumentative engagements.

So, attention turned to a third nation, which had started out moving quite slowly, though making steady progress. In this nation, everyone was required both to run and take care of those who could not run. Both men and women were given incentives to compete, to run as fast as possible, but the rules required them all to share in carrying the burden of care. Having agreed to the rules that rewarded both kinds of contribution to the collective effort, people were free to choose their own speed, to find a balance between individual effort and collective responsibility. This freedom and equality contributed to their solidarity. Of course, it was this nation that won the race (UNDP 1999: 78). All it conveys is that 'pulling together' in a balanced and judicious manner helps in achieving the target – be it the running of the proverbial race or any other such collective social endeavour.

In this era of globalization, everyone is required to run. Who will take care of those who cannot run? The growing interdependence of people's lives calls for shared values and shared commitments to the human development of all people. The *Human Development Report*

(UNDP 1999) has captured the essence of 'individual effort' and 'collective responsibility' on the one hand and freedom and equality on the other. This is, indeed, a very inspiring, encouraging, relevant and telling moral story. It provides a carefully crafted moral and normative framework to the overall argument of the chapter.

Viewing Volunteerism as an Act of Will

At the outset, we must understand what volunteerism is in order to make better and useful sense of non-governmental efforts and interventions. Volunteerism has been a part of every society and civilization. The spirit of volunteerism is inherent in all human beings. It is not something that is learned over the time, though social environment and social institutions play a vital role in facilitating the growth of this spirit in individuals. There is no voluntary organization which is a private limited company that says 'this is *our* voluntary organization and here only *we* volunteer'. Volunteerism is an act of will, and those who have it will find a way of doing it and a place to do it (Chaudhary 1971). If stated poetically, the places or the sites for taking up voluntary activity are as wide as the world and the ways of doing it are as many as the stars in the sky.

Let us take up the finest example and illuminate this point empirically. Muhammad Yunus (2007), founder of *Gramin* Bank, Bangladesh, and Nobel laureate in economics, once complained as follows:

> ... when I was arguing that helping a one-meal family to become a two-meal family, enabling women without a change of clothing to afford to buy a second piece of clothing, is a development miracle, I was ridiculed. This is not development, I was reminded sternly. Development is growth of economy, they said; growth will bring everything. We carried out our work as if we were engaged in some very undesirable activities. When UNDP's Human Development Report came out, we felt vindicated. We were no longer back-street operators; we felt we were in the mainstream. Today, paradigms are shifting, undoubtedly. As everywhere else, in volunteerism also, certain modes of intervention are described as outdated and irrelevant. Certain words have suddenly turned out to be discounted words. Welfare is one such word which was ill-treated until the Nobel laureate Amartya Sen reinstated the relevance of welfare economics.

Malcolm Muggeridge (1986), author of *Something Beautiful for God,* a biography of Mother Teresa, is said to have asked the Mother: 'Do you think by doing the type of charity you are engaged in, you can bring about sustainable social change?' Mother Teresa's answer was: 'God never asked me to change the society. He only asked me to do this' (i.e. compassionate charity and welfare) Volunteerism takes place in response to one's conscience, and in response to an inner call which one experiences. When someone says: 'God asked me to do it', some other will say 'this is the need of the hour and I am doing it'. One can safely say that every such voluntary initiative is a unique story of inspiration in itself, leading to the ultimate cause of social development.

Conceptual Inadequacy of NGO as Voluntary Organization

NGO (Non-Governmental Organization) is an internationally accepted, commonly used expression to describe Voluntary Organization (VO). Non-profit organization is another commonly used expression. These are, however, negative words. Volunteerism is a beautiful, positive word which deserves to be in greater vogue in these contexts. Describing Voluntary Organization by the name Non-Governmental Organization or non-profit organization is like defining a woman as a non-man. Calling it by the name non-profit organization is to admit that profit-organizations are mainstream and that non-profit is deviational (Sundar 1986).

When did volunteerism first appear in the form of organized institution? Some say it was in the 1920s as an antidote to the hate and horror caused by the World War I. The first VO, Service Civil International (SCI), was born in France. This was followed by the Red Cross Movement, the British Volunteer Programme, YMCA, YWCA, US Peace Corps, *Deutsche Entwinklungsdienst*, and the UN Volunteers.

The theme of the International Year of Volunteers (IYV) World Conference was 'Volunteers: Capital of the Millennium' and its four objectives were: Recognition, Facilitation, Networking and Promotion. In addition, IYV also aimed at focusing world attention on youth participation in voluntary service. Millions of students and non-student youth in urban and rural areas are already making major contributions to economy, solidarity, peace and stability through community service in partnership with other like-minded groups. They contribute their time, talents, skills, creativity and energy for human development and for a better social fabric.

Professionalism in Volunteering

Commonwealth Youth Programme (CYP) Asia Centre organized two 'International Consultations on Youth and Volunteerism' following the UN Proclamation of 2001 as the International Year of Volunteers. The first of these consultations took place at Delhi (March 2001) and the second at Kuala Lumpur (June 2001).

One word which was frequently used in the Kuala Lumpur Consultation (and which was conspicuous by its absence in Delhi Consultation) was *professionalism in volunteerism.* This is an interesting observation because it indicates how the countries in South East Asia have undergone the globalization and applied it in the third sector namely voluntary sector (Quereshi 1988). The image of an effective volunteer today is not that of 'an impulsive do-gooder', but a 'systematic mobilizer of good will for a worthwhile cause'. The spirit of volunteerism and the values underpinning volunteerism are the same in both cases, but at the operational level there is a paradigm shift. The former might burn himself out in volunteerism and might be hailed as a 'martyr' or ' superman' who might have inspired a few to follow his charismatic steps. The latter will be an equally committed visionary but he will lead to sustainable changes in society as well as make his organization sustainable through effective management.

Characteristics of Professional Volunteerism

Professionalism and volunteerism are not opposite to each other. Professional volunteerism will have the following characteristics:

1. It will be backed by a body of knowledge. This necessitates research and documentation. In the absence of this, we will not analyse our experience, nor learn from the past, nor learn from others.
2. It will be systematically managed. Principles of management have a place in developing appropriate volunteer management systems, in taking care of achievement motivation, team building, etc. in a voluntary organization.
3. Volunteerism has its own ethics of practice. These may be described as the professional ethics in volunteerism. Good intentions may not be a justification for doing things in certain ways. One example is the need for confidentiality in case work.
4. The backing of a professional organization is a requirement for maintaining quality and intellectual/operational collaboration in any field. 'None of us is as smart as all of us together', says a Japanese proverb.

If professionalism is a positive contribution which globalization has brought to volunteerism, there are a lot of other factors which are challenges to volunteerism. A reduction in attachment to religion and traditional communities, and an increase in individualism are some of the negative contributions of globalization. These go against traditional values such as *sarvodaya, anthyodaya, gotong royong, shramdaan, not-me-but-thou,* etc. which are the rock bases of volunteerism. In many countries, the entry of more men and women into the paid labour market in health care sector threatens to reduce the availability of volunteers, particularly in the care field. Corporatization of health care sector is growing at a fast speed. It will definitely have some adversarial impact on the overall aspects of social development of the Indian society.

References

Chaudhary, D. Paul. 1971. *Voluntary Social Welfare in India*, New Delhi: Sterling.

Muggeridge, Malcolm. 1986. *Something Beautiful for God*, New York: Harper and Row.

Quereshi, Moeen A. 1988. 'The World Bank and NGOs: New Approaches', *Lokayan Bulletin*, 6 (4).

Sundar, Pushpa. 1986. *Private Voluntary Agencies in India's Development: The Ford Foundation Experience*, Delhi: Ford Foundation.

UNDP. 1999. *Human Development Report*, New York: Oxford University Press.

Yunus, Muhammad. 2007. *Creating a World without Poverty: Social Business and the Future of Capitalism*, New York: Public Affairs.

CHAPTER 7

Empowering Women through Self-Help Groups

R.D. SAMPATH KUMAR

Women, though forming a significant segment of population, were and are being discriminated in many forms since ages. Formation of women Self-Help Groups (SHGs) realized many positive outcomes. A SHG is a small economically homogeneous affinity group of the rural poor voluntarily coming together to save small amount regularly, which are deposited in a common fund to meet members' emergency needs and to provide collateral free loans decided by the group (Jha 2000). They have been recognized as a useful tool to help the poor and as an alternative mechanism to meet the urgent credit needs of poor through thrift (Rao 2003). SHG is a media for the development of saving habit among the women (Rajamohan 2003). SHGs enhance the equality of status of women as participants, decision-makers and beneficiaries in the democratic, economic, social and cultural spheres of life (Jain 2003).

Conceptual Discussion

The basic principles of the SHGs are group approach, mutual trust, organization of small and manageable groups, group cohesiveness, spirit of thrift, demand based lending, collateral free, women friendly loan, peer group pressure in repayment, skill training, capacity building and empowerment (Lalitha 2007). The major strategies of women empowerment include social, economic, political and gender justice along with demographical justice (rural and urban). The Self-Help Groups have been instrumental in empowerment by enabling women to work together in a collective agency. The SHGs are necessary to overcome exploitation, create confidence for the economic self-reliance of the rural poor, particularly among women who are economically mostly invisible in the social structure. These groups enable them to come together for a common objective and gain strength from each other to deal with exploitation, which they are facing, in several forms. Self-Help Group intervention has been well-recognized world over as an effective tool for poverty alleviation and improving socio-economic conditions of rural poor.

Links between Self-Help Groups and women's empowerment are viewed as optimistic, limited by devise, cost effective in eliminating poverty, and a misplaced diversion of resources. Self-Help Groups programmes range from small scale self-help to large poverty-targeted banks. Women should overcome from economic insecurity and become independent to secure or earn money. The concept of SHG can help the women to come out of the poverty, thereby channelizing the empowerment process. The core of empowerment lies in the ability of a woman to control her own destiny (Malhotra et al. 2002; Kabeer 1999). According to Krishna (2003), empowerment means increasing the capacity of individuals or groups to make effective development and life choices and to transform these choices into desired actions and outcomes.

Development alone cannot bring peace and prosperity unless social justice and gender equality are ensured, which comes through women empowerment. The empowerment process starts from within but access to new ideas and information will come from external agents. With new consciousness and the strength of solidarity, women can assert their right to control resources and to participate equally in decision-making process. Ultimately, women's empowerment must become a force that is an organized mass movement which challenges and transforms existing power relations in society (Batliwala 1994). Empowerment requires involving women directly in planning and implementation of projects (Rao et al. 1991).

As Hall (1992) notes, economic subordination must be neutralized for women to be empowered. The economic component of empowerment requires that women be able to engage in productive activities that will allow them some degree of financial autonomy, no matter how small and hard to obtain at the beginning. Chen (1983) and Agarwal (1994) observe that through collective action, women members of gender sensitive and progressive NGOs or women's associations which focused on economic activities have also been able to challenge constricting social norms, such as female seclusion. Access to savings and credit can initiate or strengthen a series of interlinked and mutually reinforcing 'virtuous spirals' of empowerment (Mayoux 2000). The SHGs, through microcredit, have an important role to play in lessening the vulnerability of poor by creating assets, income and improved consumption levels. The SHGs also provide emergency assistance. The women are, thus, empowered and made confident. They have got control over assets. This has, in turn, increased their awareness and self-esteem (Zaman 2001).

These empowered women realize that they have the ability to earn their living and a right to exercise their choices, a sense of self-worth along with the power to control their own lives, both within and outside the home. When women move forward, along with them the family moves forward, the community/village moves and the nation moves forward. Economic strength is the basis of social, political and psychological power in the society.

Today, SHGs are widely recognized as the hubs for information dissemination within villages and entry points for financial institutions as well as consumer goods organizations. However, it must be stated that enough has not been done to deal with this highly illiterate population in terms of upgrading their skill sets or making them competent in dissemination of knowledge through intensive programmes. They have been playing significant roles both in the social and economic fronts. Many strategies and programmes have been designed and implemented for empowerment of women for improving their accessibility to credit. The SHG approach has proved successful not only in improving the economic conditions through income generation but in creating awareness about health and hygiene, sanitation and cleanliness, environmental protection, importance of education and better response for development schemes.

Entrepreneurship development and income generating activities are a feasible solution for empowering women. It generates income and also provides flexible working hours according to the needs of home makers. Economic independence is the need of the hour. Participation in income generating activities helps in the overall empowerment of women. Empowering women through education, new ideas, consciousness, mobilization and participatory approach can enable them to take their own decisions, make them self-reliant and self-confident.

Anatomy of SHG's Working: Case of Andhra Pradesh

A study of SHGs in Andhra Pradesh was taken up to find out the impact on members, children, families and communities as well with the following objectives.

Objectives

1. To study the socio-economic details of the respondents of SHGs.
2. To find out the effectiveness of operationalization of SHGs.
3. To examine the cost-benefit analysis and problems faced with regard to income generation programmes.
4. To analyse the impact of SHGs on the women, children, family and community.

Method and Sample

The names of selected districts of Andhra Pradesh, the total number of SHGs and the samples drawn from each district are given in Table 7.1.

Table 7.1

Selected District-Wise List of Total Number of Self-Help Groups and the Samples Drawn

S. No.	*Name of the District*	*Total Number of SHGs*	*Sample*
1.	Guntur	729	73
2.	Mehaboob Nagar	449	45
3.	Hyderabad Urban	269	27
4.	Vizianagaram	1,239	124
5.	Krishna	165	16
6.	Prakasam	2,378	238
7.	West Godavari	4,092	409
8.	Visakhapatnam	452	45
	Total	9,773	977

From a total number of 9,773 SHGs in eight districts of the state, a sample 10 per cent was taken by using systematic scientific sampling method. The study was conducted in eight districts of Andhra Pradesh state with the help of a schedule and by conducting focused group discussion. The SHGs promoted by World Vision India in the eight districts were taken up to realize the objectives mentioned earlier. A total number of 977 SHGs were sampled.

Limitations of the Study

The study was confined to those SHGs which were formed two years back or even earlier. This condition was stipulated as the study focused on impact of SHGs on members, families and communities.

The findings of the study cannot be widely generalized. However, some of the findings might have relevance and can be applied to other SHGs also.

Findings

The findings of this minor but relevant research exercise are discussed as follows:

Profile of the Sampled SHGs

Table 7.2

Criteria for Admission into an SHG

Criteria	*Per cent (n=977)*
Yes	74.5
No	25.5
Criteria followed*	
Should be a literate	0.7
Hail from local community	54.3
Above 18 years	34.3
Members from below poverty line	22.2
Own house	1.8
Different areas	1.3
Married women	9.9
Good behaviour	4.2
Women only	10.7
Regular savings	19.3
Ration card holder	5.3

* Multiple Responses.

It can be seen from Table 7.2 that about three-fourth (74.5%) of SHGs had evolved criteria for admission of members and the remaining (25.5%) did not evolve any criteria, whatsoever. As regards the criteria followed, the data revealed that women hailing from local community (54.3%) with 18 years of age (34.3%) and below poverty (22.2%) were the chief guidelines adopted.

As regards the number of members in the SHG, a majority of the respondents (64.3%) stated that they have less than 10 members in their group and another 30.3 per cent of the SHGs had members between 10 and 15. The average number of members of SHGs was 11, (mean value 11.4). The data reveals that more than two-fifth (45.7%) of the SHGs were existing since 15 years and beyond. Another 35.6 per cent of the SHGs were in existence between 10 and 15 years and a few (14.7%) were formed between 5–10 years.

Frequency and Place of Meetings

The frequency and place of meetings are duly reported in Table 7.3.

Table 7.3

Frequency and Place of Meetings

Frequency	*Per cent (n= 977)*
Weekly	5.8
Fortnightly	25.2
Monthly	65.6
Bi-Monthly	1.2
Quarterly	0.9
As and when	0.3
No meetings	1.0
Place of Meetings	
Church	2.6
Community hall	9.3
Members' houses	80.6
Panchayat office	2.4
School building	1.4
Temple	3.9
On the road or under a tree	2.3

A majority of the SHGs conduct meetings once in a month (65.6%) and another one-fourth of them meet once in 15 days. As regards the place of meetings, it was mostly organized in one of the member's houses (80.0%) though some use community halls (9.3%) or religious places: be it temple (3.9%) or church (2.6%).

More than half of the SHG's do not collect any membership fee (56%) to become a member of SHG and the rest collect it. Further, it can be seen that around three-fifth of the SHGs collect a monthly contribution of ₹ 50 and another one-fourth of the SHGs collect ₹ 100 a month (25.7%).

Half of the SHGs stated that around 10 members attend without fail whenever the meetings were held. In some cases it was more than 10 members (21.6%). The rest of the SHGs had attendance of less than 10 members (23.1%).

Maintenance of Accounts and Records

As regards the maintenance of accounts and records, the data reveal that they were mostly maintained by outsiders who were other than the members of SHGs. In some cases, presidents (26.6%), secretaries (17.6%) and members of SHGs (15.6%) maintain the account books and registers. Further, it is interesting to note that most of the SHGs were able to keep the records up to date (88.4%).

A majority of the SHGs do not find it difficult to maintain accounts and records (63.8%). The rest stated that they have difficulty in maintaining them. In some cases they could not find a person to prepare accounts and maintain records without charge. Further, illiteracy of members and inability to spare time by the members were the other reasons stated for this state of the affairs.

Income Generation Programmes (IGP): Training, Credit Off-take and Re-payment

A majority of SHG members (83.0%) did not undergo any training programme before launching income generation programme. The rest underwent training on income generation programmes. The data reveal that a majority of the SHG members (62.8%) received training on marketing skills and savings (14.8%) prior to launching of income generation activities, besides vocational skills. The data shows that most of the members took credit for only small ventures costing less than ₹ 25,000. In rare cases it exceeded more than ₹ 25,000. Further data reveals that a majority of the SHGs were able to repay the loans (86.4%). For those who could not repay the loans, the reasons were ill-health or lack of unity among members or lack of income, in that order.

Returns of Credit: Pitfalls and Losses

Out of 63 SHGs, only 42 SHGs reported that they could get returns and the remaining SHGs did not reveal their returns. Similarly, only 53

SHGs reported that they could get some profit. As can be seen from the data, more than two-fifth of the SHGs could get returns of ₹ 20,000 and more, whereas the net profit in majority of the cases was only less than ₹ 10,000. Around 10 SHGs could not get any profit, whatsoever. Evidently, the data indicates that a sizeable number of respondents were of the opinion that they lack business techniques (23.1%) and have poor public relations (4.8%) and disunity among members (3.7%). Interestingly, more than half of the respondents (52.5%) did not express any problem in running the affairs of SHGs.

The SHG members seem to have problems in marketing the products, though about half of others stated that they don't have any such problem. A sizeable number of members had stated that the reasons for inability to market were largely due to mis-utilization of loans (39.6%). Another significant number of members stated that their products don't have any demand (34.4%) and as such it resulted in poor profits (19.6%).

Impact

The impact seems to be multi fold. The respondents stated that they were empowered in many ways. They were able to inculcate fiscal self-discipline (21.0%) and economic self-confidence (23.0%). They could acquire leadership skills and improve their economic standards. Further, the respondents stated that their children were able to go to schools regularly (46.5%) and a few could send their children to English medium schools. They also opined that they were able to provide quality education to their children (35.1%) and some of those who had completed primary education were able to have higher education.

Sustenance of SHGs: Modes and Problems Faced

The opinions of members regarding sustenance of SHGs are presented in Table 7.4.

The respondents opined that proper savings (40.1%) and repayment (28.3%) would enable the SHGs to sustain in future. Further, all the members should be united (26.6%) and should have mutual understanding (17.1%). On the other hand, poor participation of members (17.8%), disunity (12.9%) and lack of leadership were the other reasons for dysfunction of SHGs.

Table 7.4

Sustenance of SHGs

Variable	*Per cent (n=977)**
Modes of sustenance	
Consistency in savings	40.1
Democratic leadership	14.8
Mutual understanding	17.1
With support of GO/NGO	15.2
Proper repayment	28.3
Economic development	5.4
Commitment	13.2
United effort	26.6
Compulsory attendance of members in the meetings	5.0
Problems in Sustenance	
Poor participation by members	17.8
Disunity	12.9
Corruption	6.9
No responsibility	11.7
Illiteracy of members	8.0
Lack of leadership	3.1

* Multiple Responses.

Discussion

Lower social class women have realized the need to protect by empowering themselves. SHG is one such instrument which can make them self-reliant to some extent. The study evidently reveals that women from local communities formed into associations vis-à-vis SHGs with a minimum number of ten. Conditionalities such as admission, participation, contribution and frequency of meetings were stipulated by some SHGs. The study indicates that a majority of the SHGs were in existence since more than 10 years and above. The members seem to be very punctual to the meetings, highly participative and regular in payments whether it is monthly contribution or loan. Though these groups were able to maintain accounts and registers up to date, a sizeable number of others were found to be having problems. It is largely because of illiteracy of members or inability to find a person to maintain records without charge. A representative from Indira Kanthi Patham assisted to a majority of the SHGs in maintenance of accounts and registers.

Promotion of income generation programmes on individual basis constitutes 37 per cent out of the total sample of 977 SHGs. These members took loan from different sources and started small ventures such as dairy, petty business, tailoring, etc. Most of them invested less than ₹ 25,000 as capital. A majority of them were able to repay loans (86.4%) and others could not repay due to ill-health and in some cases lack of demand for the product.

The impact on members, children, families and community seem to be multi fold. These members were able to instil self-discipline and find that they were empowered in terms of leadership, skills and economic independence. The members could realize the strength of farming as a group and work unitedly. They were able to provide schooling to their wards and a sizeable members stated that they could provide quality education and some children could take up higher education studies. The impact of families resulted in economic development besides peace and harmony in the family. The women could exert greater say in the decision-making process of the family. The impact of communities had greater significance with these women participating in community development processes. One-fourth of these women could take lead role along with local leaders in initiating developmental programmes. They realized the importance of education, health, hygiene and awareness about local problems. Interestingly, they could find solutions to many of the problems. The increased participation resulted in unity and work for the development of the community. The participation of women in Panchayat Raj/Municipality institutions is very limited as 15 per cent of them could only participate in the political process. However, more than two-fifth of the women had the opportunity to participate in the local self-governments. Thus, women are now forging ahead on all fronts. The SHGs are now getting federated and institutionalized. Government has initiated a number of projects for their target population and every effort should be made to sustain these groups with positive interventions.

References

Agarwal, Bina. 1994. *A Field of One's Own: Gender and Land Rights in South Asia*, Cambridge: Cambridge University Press.

Batliwala, S. 1994. 'The Meaning of Women's Empowerment: New Concepts from Action', in G. Sen, A. Germain and L.C. Chen (eds), *Population Policies Reconsidered: Health, Empowerment and Rights*, Boston: Harvard University Press.

Chen, M.A. 1983. *A Quiet Revolution: Women in Transition in Rural Bangladesh*, Cambridge: Schenkman.

Hall, Margaret. 1992. *Women and Empowerment: Strategies for Increasing Autonomy*, Washington, D.C.: Publishing Corporation.

Jain, Ritu. 2003. 'Socio-Economic Impact through Self Help Groups', *Yojana*, 47 (7), pp. 11–12.

Jha, Abhas Kumar. 2000. 'Lending to the Poor: Designs for Credit', *Economic and Political Weekly*, XXXV (8-9), pp. 606–609.

Kabeer, N. 1999. 'The Conditions and Consequences of Choice: Reflections on the Measurement of Women's Empowerment', *UNRISD Discussion Paper 108*, Geneva: United Nations Research Institute for Social Development.

Klasen, S. 2002. *In Search of the Holy Grail: How to Achieve Pro-poor Growth?*, Munich: Department of Economics, University of Munich.

Krishna, A. 2003. 'Social Capital, Community Driven Development, and Empowerment: A Short Note on Concepts and Operations', *World Bank Working Paper 33077*, Washington, D.C.: World Bank.

Lalitha, N. 2007. 'Women Thrift and Credit Groups: Breaking the Barriers at the Gross Roots', *Peninsular Economist*, XII (2), pp. 188–195.

Malhotra, A., Schuler, S. and Boender, C. 2002. 'Measuring Women's Empowerment as a Variable in International Development', *World Bank Gender and Development Group Background Paper*, Washington, D.C.: World Bank.

Mayoux, L. 2000. 'Microfinance and the Empowerment of Women: A Review of the Key Issues', *Social Finance Unit Working Paper*, 23, Geneva: ILO.

Rajamohan, S. 2003. 'Activities of Self Help Groups in Virudhunagar District: A Study', *TNJC*, pp. 25–29.

Rao, Aruna, Feldstein, Hilary, Cloud, Kathleen and Staudt, Kathleen. 1991. *Gender Training and Development Planning: Learning from Experience*, Conference Report, Bergen: The Chr. Michelson Institute.

Rao, V.M. 2003. 'Women Self Help Groups, Profiles from Andhra Pradesh and Karnataka', *Kurukshetra*, 50 (6), pp. 26–32.

Swaminathan, Padmini. (ed.). 2012. *Women and Work*, New Delhi: Orient Blackswan.

Zaman, H. 2001. 'Assessing the Poverty and Vulnerability Impact of Micro-Credit in Bangladesh: A Case Study of BRAC', *World Development Report 2000/2001*, Washington, D.C.: World Bank.

CHAPTER 8

Youth for Sustainable Development

R.B.S. VERMA

Youth have always been a vital and vibrant human resource for bringing change and development. They, thus, have a right as well as obligation to actively participate in the task of national development and in shaping the destiny of nation. The need to involve this vast potential of human resource in the development process was duly recognized after Independence and it was felt that energies, aspirations and dynamism of youth should be channelized as far as possible towards constructive programmes. Our former Prime Minister, Indira Gandhi, expressing her concern for youth, used to view them as a distinct social section as compared to the others. All legacies for future can be safely passed on to them as the most reliable torch-bearer of the entire society.

Taking lead from this view and concern, an attempt is made here to construct a normative perspective and an index regarding the youth potential and performance in order to achieve sustainable development. A brief definitional explanation as to who is youth, what is sustainable development and what are the probable areas of youth involvement should clarify conceptual properties of this discussion.

The Concept of Youth

There are three prevalent views regarding youth with varying degree of ascending and descending relevances:

- The *first view* emphasizes biological factor and conceptualizes youth as a specific period or stage of life. As per this view, individual ceases to be youth as he/she crosses the age limit.
- The *second view* contemplates youth as quality of mind and mood which includes vigour, venture, freshness, enthusiasm, optimism and joyfulness.
- The *third view* considers both biological and psychological factors and visualizes youth as a stage in one's life when he/she happens to be most creative, active, innovative, receptive, challenging, agile and optimistic.

To conclude, it can be unequivocally maintained that youth is not a time of life but it is a state of mind. But for statistical feasibility and viable planning of programmes and formulating policy for this section of population, some age groups such as 14 to 21 years, 15 to 25 years and 18 to 35 years are prescribed by different state, national and international government and not by the Non-governmental Organizations. Thus, it is clear that in particular period of one's life span (probably 15–35 years) possibilities and prospects of becoming versatile, virtueful, vigorous, creative and active are comparatively more.

The Concept of Sustainable Development

Now let us examine the other key component of this discussion, namely, sustainable development. The World Commission on Environment and Development (The Brundtland Commission) was responsible for bringing the term 'sustainable development' into common parlance. This Commission has expressed the view that sustainable development is development that meets the needs of the present without compromising the ability of future generations to meet their own needs (World Commission on Environment and Development 1987: 8). Explaining the concept of sustainable development, Adiseshiah (1989: 32) has maintained that sustainable development is the development which meets the basic needs of all, particularly the poor majority for employment, food, energy, water and housing, and ensures growth of agriculture, manufacturing, power and services to meet these needs.

In that sense, sustainable development merges with economics and environment both in theory and decision-making practice. K.P. Geetha Krishnan (1990: 7) has explained this concept by maintaining that basically, when we talk of sustainable development, the easiest definition is that we, the present generation, have inherited a certain amount of ecology and environment surroundings in terms of land, water and air, when we should leave it at least in the same condition, if not in better condition, than what we inherited. This is the sum and substance of sustainable development, putting it into elementary terms.

The United Nations Division for Sustainable Development lists the following areas (as listed in alphabetical order) coming within the purview of sustainable development:

Table 8.1

The United Nations Division for Sustainable Development Identified Areas of Sustainable Development

Agriculture	Energy	International Cooperation for enabling environment	Sustainable Tourism
Atmosphere	Finance	Institutional Arrangements	Technology
Biodiversity	Forests	Land Management	Toxic Chemicals
Biotechnology	Fresh Water	Major Groups	Transport
Capacity-building	Health	Mountains	Waste (hazardous)
Climate Change	Human Settlements	National Sustainable Development Strategies	Waste (radioactive)
Consumption and Production Pattern	Indicators	Oceans and Seas	Waste (Solid)
Demographics	Industry	Poverty	Water
Desertification and Droughts	Information for Decision-Making and Participation	Sanitation	
Disaster Reduction and Management	Integrated Decision-Making	Science	
Education and Awareness	International Law	SIDS	

Srivastava (1996: 5) has summarized the following underlying principles and premises of sustainable development:

1. that, it is an alternative design for development, which by definition should be environmentally benign and eco-friendly;

2. that, the present generation should meet its need without compromising the ability of future generations to meet their needs, i.e. to ensure that the productive assets available to future generations are not unfairly diminished;
3. that, those who enjoy the fruits of economic development today must not make future generations worse off by excessively degrading the earth's exhaustive resources and polluting the earth ecology and environment;
4. that, there is symbolic relationship between consumerist human race and producer natural system;
5. that, environment and development are not mutually exclusive: healthy environment is essential to sustainable development and healthy economy;
6. that, economic development which erodes natural capital is often not successful;
7. that, environmental mistakes of the past need not be repeated as past patterns of environmental degradation are not inevitable;
8. that, development is not growth only, it should stand for broader goals of social transformation;
9. that, sustainable development in the long run has to do with ecology, resources and the people, along with their service agencies, institutions and other aspects of their social organizations;
10. that, sustainable development has two aspects: (i) internally sustainable development and, (ii) externally sustainable development. Without both, no real sustainable development would exist; and,
11. that, sustainable development is accountable to the poor, and hence, it should ensure that the poor have adequate access to development and secure livelihood.

Thus, it can be concluded that sustainable development is the development with justice both for men and environment of the present as well as of future generations. This kind of development takes place when individual organization and principles together move in an organized manner to achieve the said aim. One can relate these concerns with the Buddhist dicta of wisdom: (1) *Buddham Sharnam Gachhami* (inspiration from enlightened person); (2) *Sangham Sharnam Gachhami* (organized efforts) and, (3) *Dhamam Sharnam Gachhami* (principles and objectives should be clear).

Possible Dimensions of Involvement of Youth in Sustainable Development

There are several encouraging and positive outcomes of involvement of youth for sustainable development. It promotes equality of relationship between youth and planners and experts as well as encourages the bureaucrats for paving the way for creating favourable climate for sustainable development. It also helps in understanding core problems of this type of development. It helps in knowing people's values, attitudes, traditions, mores and expectations for an effective base for development. It offers the process of learning to all concerned, i.e. planners, administrators and youth. It provides awareness for development and helps in determining priorities in planning. It opens vistas for mobilizing and utilizing local resources and ultimately translates social policy and action for bringing about desirable change – both in youth as well as in society (Chaudhary 1998: 193–194).

The possible dimensions of involvement of youth in sustainable development may be detailed as under:

Community Education and Development

The purposes of community education have been the maintenance of the integrity and autonomy of the community and each individual, making them aware that they are the part of a greater world; making them feel that they are equal member of the larger society. In other words, it is about enabling them to build up the internal society of the community and also to integrate different communities and creating a new and vibrant community that will maintain its traditions and at the same time withstand the political, economic, social and moral pressures from outside.

The youth can further contribute to this goal by:

1. Determining community's needs, problems and resources.
2. Establishing contact with key functionaries and persons of the community.
3. Educating community about the present pressing needs and problems.
4. Motivating community members to pool their resources to solve these pressing needs and problems.
5. Encouraging community to tap and utilize resources outside the community, both governmental as well as non-governmental.

6. Making community members conscious about their circumstances and institutions/persons to be involved in meeting the challenges of the present circumstances.
7. Encouraging and motivating community for the construction and maintenance of community assets such as school building dispensary, panchayat ghar, roads/pavements, etc.
8. Educating community members in favour of immunization, health check-up, referrals, small family norms.
9. Encouraging for school enrollment, particularly girls enrollment;
10. Introducing ways and means for supplementing family income;
11. Organizing sanitation and civic drives.
12. Involving them in bringing out healthy recreation to the community.
13. Changing the attitudes and beliefs of our people to attribute everything concerning them including poverty to their destiny by convincing them that nothing can be achieved without action *(karma)* let alone betterment in their life and living conditions.
14. Exploring different types of extravagant habits of people such a smoking, betel chewing, tobacco eating, unnecessary pomp and show at the time of various ceremonies, illustrating evil effects and persuade people to give them up.
15. Exercising vigilance over the business community to ensure that good quality stuff becomes readily available to people at fixed prices, persuading businessmen to display their stock and price list and organizing mass protests and demonstrations against erring businessmen and pressurizing the government machinery to take suitable action against them without any hesitation.

Rural and Urban Development Programmes

Young persons drawn from rural as well as urban areas cannot only make valuable contribution in developmental programmes but many of them can also get good exposure to the needs and problems of the particular areas. In this dimension, our youth can:

1. Form youth clubs or profession based associations to take up the responsibility of helping poor sections.
2. Disseminate information of various developmental programmes of the government as well as of voluntary organizations such as: (i) regarding actual benefits available under them; (ii) their conditions of eligibility; and, (iii) procedural requirements, etc.

3. Render help and support to the members of weaker sections in actually getting the full benefits of these developmental programmes without any share of administrative machinery of the locally influential persons.
4. Distribute literature consisting of knowledge relating to growth of nurseries and plants and protection and maintenance of different varieties of trees.
5. Actively take part in: (i) Joint Forest Management (JFM) where the owner (the government) as well as the user (communities) manage the resource and share the costs as well as benefits thereof; (ii) in Community Forest Management (CFM) where the community takes the lead, manages the resource while the government is a passive supporter or an observer; (iii) in Participatory Forest Management (PFM) where the government takes the initiatives, manages the resource and the community participants in various forms, commonly as hired labour (Johnson 1995: 48–49).
6. Undertake initiative for soil conservation and development by constructing *bundhs* (small dams) in areas where flooding or water logging is caused.
7. Arrange testing of saline and waste land, advise its owners about methods and techniques of converting it into cultivable land and actually participate in the work of such conversion.
8. Take initiative from bringing waste land under cultivation as well as successful management and use of waste land.
9. Take initiative in cleaning the village ponds, etc. having overgrowth of water hyacinth, algae, etc.
10. Launch an educational campaign for the purpose of bringing about a change in the attitude of people towards nature, conservation of forests and preservation of wild life.

The above mentioned dimensions of sustainable development in which youth can be involved as per their talents, abilities, skills; training and aptitude are well delineated. But it is our bounden duty to motivate, educate, train, organize, guide and lead them in the gigantic task of bringing about sustainable development by innovation, advocacy an adoption.

Improvement in Education

In this field, the youth can:

1. Organize adult education for adult illiterates, particularly girls and women aged between 15–35 years.
2. Give assistance in running Balwadis for children of pre-school going age, especially of working women of weaker sections.
3. Play an important role in reducing the dropout rate by providing special coaching facilities to students who are weak in studies.
4. Make arrangements for rendering educational facilities to working children and as far as possible to motivate parents to withdraw their children from work and send them to school by explaining the significance of education for leading a happy and satisfying life.
5. Make arrangement for library and reading room facilities.

Population Education and Control

Here, the youth can:

1. Help in creating an awareness and understanding of the causes of population changes, impact of such changes on the quality of life of family/community and means by which population change can be influenced.
2. Organize special family welfare camps and assist the family welfare institutions in identifying the target couple for follow-up of population control measures.
3. Establish population education clubs for the purpose of creating favourable attitude towards the small family norm as well as render help in creating better appreciation of the relationship between the family size and available resources.

Legislative Enactments

In this context, the youth can:

1. Publicize various laws having a bearing on life and living of people as well as enactments made for the protection and conservation of environment.
2. Make the implementation machinery culturally aware of the persons with whom they are expected to deal and assist in proper implementation of various laws.
3. Impress upon and if necessary, even pressurize, the government machinery to sincerely implement the following laws directly helpful in correcting the exploitative conditions – such as: (i) Minimum Wages Act; (ii) Bonded Labour (system) Abolition Act; (iii) Reduction of exploitation and protection of Civil Rights Act;

(iv) Payment of Equal Remuneration Act, etc. They should provide necessary help and support in the enforcement of these laws.

4. Mobilize people's participation in the implementation of various laws by highlighting the social significance of their various provisions and need for people's effective participation in their implementation.

Health and Nutrition

While working in this area, the youth can:

1. Take part in mass and continuous immunization, health check-up and distribution of medicines.
2. Motivate people for undertaking services from health centres/sub-centres/*Anganwadi* centres.
3. Organize anti-drug addiction drives and prohibition awareness campaigns.
4. Mobilize community resources for undertaking various preventive and curative health measures and organize special health camps for people suffering from problems of ill health.
5. Educate people in various preventive health measures and make people aware of various health practices available in the area and help them in getting their maximum benefit.
6. Organize medico-social surveys, blood donation camps, eye relief camps, etc.
7. Identify cases of malnutrition, contact the agencies running nutrition programmes and motivate them to provide the needed nutrition to the undernourished.
8. Identify cases of various types of handicaps, report them to agencies concerned and established for providing services to them and assist the handicapped to get benefits timely.
9. Arouse consciousness among people towards health, sanitation, nutrition, etc. by organizing educational and extension services.
10. Popularize yoga, meditation, indigenous games and modern sports as well as nutritious dietary habits.
11. Contribute in the establishment of lifestyle education centres for the propagation of preventive measures against dangerous diseases like AIDS, etc.
12. Organize special campaign through special camps, rallies, *nukkad nataks* (street corner plays), wall writings, showing of

documentary films, composing and reciting of folk songs, pasting of posters, exhibitions, etc. regarding generation of awareness towards important health issues such as iodine deficiency, AIDS, child survival and safe motherhood, etc.

13. Take active part in the implementation of urban basic services programme in urban slums.

Eco-development

The 20th century has witnessed tremendous economic as well as scientific progress making man's life and living comfortable but showing indifference and even neglect towards ecological balance and environmental conservation resulting into dangerous ecological trends, disturbed rainfall cycles and rise in temperatures and sea levels. Air and water are increasingly getting polluted putting life on earth into dangerous situation. In this situation youth have special responsibility for the present as well as for future generations. Here, the youth can:

1. Launch a massive campaign for tree plantation, upbringing of the planted trees, etc.
2. Exercise vigilance over indiscriminate felling of trees and killing of animals and birds and for this vigilance committees or forest as well as animal protection committees can be established.
3. Arouse consciousness regarding the need for not indiscriminately exploiting and mastering natural resources, but for using them carefully and cautiously.
4. Acquaint people with scheme of social forestry and motivate them to benefit from it and do plantation on their land in a big way; act as a link between the Forest Department and public to make the required number of plants available to them on prescribed rates.

Thus, it can be seen from this normative exercise that the youth has multi-dimensional potential to break new grounds in achieving the objective of socially and economically sustainable development.

References

Adiseshiah, Malcolm S. 1989. 'Plan to Preserve Environment', *Yojna*, 33 (14–15), pp. 28–33.

Chaudhary, D. Paul. 1998. *Youth Participation and Development*, New Delhi: Atma Ram and Sons.

Geetha Krishnan, K.P. 1990. 'Sustainable Development in Operation', in Malcolm S. Adiseshiah (ed.), *Sustainable Development: Its Content, Scope, Price*, New Delhi: Lancer International.

Johnson, Stephen. 1995. 'Classified JFM Concepts', in S.D. Roy (ed.), *Enabling Environment for Joint Forest Management*, New Delhi: Inter-India Publications.

Srivastava, S.P. 1996. 'Sustainable Development: Issues and Considerations', in K. Gopal Iyer (ed.), *Sustainable Development: Ecological and Socio-cultural Dimensions*, New Delhi: Vikas Publishing House.

World Commission on Environment and Development (WCED). 1987. *Our Common Future*, London: Oxford University Press.

CHAPTER 9

Challenges of Climate Change and the Role of Youth

MITAL PETIWALE

Global Warming and Climate Change

Global warming and climate change are one of the most defining challenges of the 21st century. It has affected our world in such a way that for the first time, it has impacted each and every region or would be impacting each and every region to a lesser or greater degree. It has, for the first time, gathered the global community to find solutions in term of mitigation and adaptations to this potentially devastating global challenge. Each nation, be it developed, developing or underdeveloped, has only one goal and that is to save the planet earth. It is a challenge that is global in both its impact and its solutions but one that is not shared equally, as developing countries are likely to be among the most seriously affected by and the least able to address the consequences of climate change. Climate change affects each and every aspect of life. It acts as a major hurdle in development efforts with consequences ranging from immediate to long term. *The United Nations Framework Convention on Climate Change* (UNFCCC) defines climate change as 'a change of climate, which is attributed directly or indirectly to human activity that alters the composition of the global atmosphere and which is in addition to natural climate variability observed over comparable time periods'. Its impact-results are mentioned for the globe as well as the different continents in the International Panel on Climate Change (IPCC) reports. Some of the impacts are documented in the *IPCC Third Assessment Report: Climate Change 2001* which is as under:

- By the 2080s, substantial dieback of tropical forests and grasslands is predicted to occur, particularly in parts of South America and Africa.
- The availability of water in the rivers of Australia, India, Southern Africa, South America, Europe and the Middle East is expected to decrease.
- Cereal yields in Africa, the Middle East and India are likely to decline.
- A rise in sea level could inundate and erode coastal areas, increase flooding and salt-water intrusion; this will affect coastal agriculture, fisheries and aquaculture, freshwater resources, human settlements and tourism.
- The incidence of water-borne diseases, heat stress and vector-borne diseases such as malaria is expected to increase.
- All developing countries facing the problems of population and economic growth will be put under even greater stress as a result of these impacts.

Climate Change and Sustainable Development

Sustainable development is a development that meets the needs of the present without compromising the ability of future generations to meet their own needs. It contains within it two key concepts: the concept of 'needs', in particular the essential needs of the world's poor, to which overriding priority should be given; and the idea of limitations imposed by the state of technology and social organization on the environment's ability to meet present and the future needs (Brundtland Commission 1987). Sustainable development is based on socio-cultural development, political stability and decorum, economic growth and ecosystem protection, which all relate to disaster risk reduction. The long and short term consequences of climate change will directly impact development efforts and might slow down or hamper the achievement of internationally agreed development goals, including the Millennium Development Goals (MDGs). Major adjustments are required to promote more sustainable patterns of production and consumption at both the collective and individual levels.

Solid evidence exists that climate change will have a more serious impact than initially anticipated and that adaptation and mitigation will entail significantly higher costs if action is deferred than if the problem is addressed now. Addressing and adjusting to the challenge of climate change is certain to be a defining feature of the future of today's societies. It is, therefore, critical that this issue be addressed. For a country like India, a recently developed economy will have the challenge of balancing much needed economic development and right to pollute in term of carbon usage for its industrialization for its sustainable development. It is through its mitigation and adaptation measures that this can be achieved by increasing the societal resilience to climate change. The integration of disaster risk reduction, climate change and development is a must for sustainable development. The key words would be vulnerability reduction, adaptive capacity and resilience.

Climate Change and Social Work

Social work profession's contribution like other social sciences is vital in the field of global climate change. The recent research on the same indicates that it is the social – ecological system's resilience perspective which is enabling the commune of protectors to search for vistas of making communities, households and individuals more resilient. The profession has an important role to play in: helping people understand the issues; promoting sustainable energy production and consumption; mobilizing people to protect their futures through community social work; and proposing solutions to greenhouse gas emissions. Social workers can foster climate change endeavours that are equitable for all. The equity and justice based approaches of social work have much to contribute when dealing with inequalities in terms of policy decisions as well as distribution of risk. What people have learned about themselves, personal qualities, traits, and virtues that people possess, what people know about the world around them, the talents that people have, cultural and personal stories and lore, pride, and the community is not an exhaustive list of the various strengths that individual, family, group and community has. Social work professional has contributed to the environmental protection in the past through policy and advocacy all over the world. Similarly, the profession should start using the resilience approach in the field of climate change. Youth group is one such group which has immense potential to contribute in making communities more resilient.

Youth and Climate Change

There is no universal definition of youth as agreed upon but in sociological terms, youth is generally taken to denote a period of transition between the dependence of childhood and the relative independence of adulthood. Youth is defined in relation to the social roles, expectations and norms of contemporary society. Youth transitions have become more extended and more uncertain in recent years as a result of accelerating socio-economic change.

In today's world, one person in five is between the ages of 15 to 25, which is an accepted UN definition of the age that defines youth. About 85 per cent of these young people live in developing countries with 60 per cent in Asia. South Asian region is home to 22 per cent of the world's population. India is the second most populous country which holds 16.7 per cent of the total population of the world with 2.4 per cent of the world's total area. India with nearly 54 per cent of the population being below the age of 25 years is the youngest nation of the world.

Indians will be the largest working force and stakeholders in the development process which requires holistic vision on development, environment and leadership of the nation. Development and prosperity of any region is based on human environment relationship. The harmony with the environment makes a secure future and sustainable development of society. Rate of natural resource use, vulnerability to disasters and possibility of renewable resource use must be taken into account. Stress on our environment is much greater than the rest of our world. Population has direct impact on the environment.

Thus, the most energetic section of our society, the youth, will have to adapt to this situation. Children and young people are concerned, thoughtful citizens, capable of participating in and changing the society of which they are a part. They have an important role to play in addressing and affecting the issues of our world. In addition, children and young people have enthusiasm, imagination and abundant energy to undertake local actions, act as effective communicators in their communities and be involved in international arenas. Young people are not merely passive beneficiaries but effective agents of change. Dedicated, enthusiastic and creative, youth have been contributing to development by addressing society's most challenging issues.

Impact of Climate Change on Youth

Various segments of the society around the globe would face the wrath of climate change in various ways. It would encompass effects in terms of increased extreme events like drought, cyclones, hot temperature, cold temperatures, sea level rise, health, safety and security, livelihood, more stress on natural resources, scarcity of resources, etc. Young citizens would be more affected due to malnutrition impacting their health both physical and mental, the past incidences of natural hydrological disasters have shown that its always the women and children who have topped the loss of lives list, incidences of destitution also increases in case of children and adolescent girls, the young ones are easily trapped into crimes due to their tender age. In terms of lack of access to basic amenities of life like safe drinking water, health care facilities, educational facilities, institutional support, livelihood opportunities, the youth of any country would be most taxed. All these things may result in ecological marginalization, environmental discrimination, unequal access to resources, reduced economic scarcity, loss of livelihood, migration, etc. It would be an added burden for achieving the quality of life.

There is a vast difference between the consumption pattern of the rural youth and the urban youth at any given period of time, in any country be it a developed, developing or underdeveloped country. One point to be noted is that Europe and America are the ones who rank top on all the countries of the world in case of consumption of goods and services, energy, food, products, etc. as compared to the developing countries. The developmental model in terms of standard of living is more energy intensive. Five per cent of world population making the USA uses 50 per cent of resources.

Generally, the youth of today, especially in the urban and semi urban areas, are important consumers in terms of food, energy, services, etc. Thus, the majority of the youth who live in areas dependent on agriculture are bearing the brunt of youth living in urban and semi urban areas due to their loud lifestyles. Today's markets are more dominated by young consumers. As a result, this gives rise to regional imbalances, disparities and conflicts.

How does social work change this threat and turn it into an opportunity for the youth and increase their resilience and ultimately the resilience of the communities and the nation they belong to? For a young country like ours, what is the strategy to integrate climate change opportunities into sustainable development? Development is to be measured by questions of equality, justice, rights, security and peace. Society should evolve in a way so as to eliminate inhumanity in form of inequality, injustice, exploitation, violations of rights and degradation of life in general.

Youth and Climate Resilience

Today's youth is the citizen of today and tomorrow. Empowering youth will lead to transformation of any community, society or nation. If properly moulded, youth can become the champion of culture, custodian of a national pride and a trustee of the freedom of the country. Youth empowerment is the opportunity that each nation needs to mobilize and deploy. Empowerment is the ability to ask questions, make strategic choices and decisions that affect and influence one's life and environment. There are two stages of empowerment; first is the realization of freedom from fear and want and acquiring a sense of security and rights and another is acquiring a sense of confidence to make choices in one's own life and develop ability to go beyond one's self to make a positive difference in other's life; ability to initiate, inform, influence and inspire change and acquiring a sense of vision, mission and leadership. Youth should act as participants in social, religious and political processes rather than becoming consumers of services.

The case of involving young people in decision-making raises a number of related issues: it leads to better decision-making, strengthens commitment to and understanding of democracy; it protects young people's interests and it is a basic human right. Society benefits through the development of social responsibility and the fostering of social inclusion and, equally important, it also has personal benefits for the participants. Participation encourages the interpersonal and practical skills that give young people a sense of self-worth and self-confidence. The personal benefits help foster a sense of social cohesion and responsibility

Youth are our future to ensure sustainable lifestyles not based on oppression and exploitation, creating infrastructure to allow people to control their own lives and judiciously access resources. It can take shape as: (i) strong local self-governance enabling involvement in decision-making, (ii) policies, (iii) access to common resources, and (iv) constructive engagement of time. It is they who can find alternatives to harmful developmental paradigms.

It is imperative for the youth of today to join one or other struggle to make their presence felt and fill up the vacuum in political and administrative domain. They should be treated as partners and this partnership with youth in all social activities and that of governance should be properly encouraged. In fact, community activities should start in an active manner with the entry of the child into the golden age phase of 15–25 years. They must realize that they have already inherited the world while entering into the golden age. The youth needs to make transition from culture of violence to culture of peace. Such concerns as how to take care of refugees, old men, women, children and malnourished must occupy the imagination of the youth. The youth has to be self-vigilant that it does not get played up in the hands of terrorist outfits, rebels, violent greedy militia, pseudo-nationalist zealots and corrupt politicians. The social and environmental dangers that threaten us do not come from sources outside the human mind; they are reflections of it, mirroring the fears, greed and hostilities.

Youth have shown their engagement and concern about climate change in numerous initiatives all over the world. Young people and youth led organizations have been effectively participating in a wide range of adaptation and mitigation projects dealing with climate change. There are many examples of successful projects in which young people are being educated or educate each other on climate change issues. The *World Youth Report* (The United Nations 2010) highlights many of these positive initiatives.

Strategies of Youth Engagement for Climate Change Resilience

For making the societies resilient, the following strategies in form of Ten Commandments of climate change resilience can be helpful:

Promoting Education for Sustainable Development

The learning outcomes of climate change education and education for sustainable development should include acquisition of attitudes, knowledge, skills, and behaviour that promote scientific inquiry, ecological and social responsibility, community action and involvement, and global solidarity. The current interdisciplinary and cross cutting course curriculums being promoted is a step in this direction. Lifelong learning like in case of University Grants Commission should be given impetus. Workshops, seminars, project and outreach activities should be imminent part of the course curriculum right from the school days till lifelong learning programmes. Programmes like eco clubs, environment education, and community social services should be promoted in the earlier standards. Green campus can be made part of the education at the higher levels. Non formal education, hands-on training of the youth is an indispensable part of the strategy for sustainable education. Engaging youth in collaborative efforts also ensures non formal education. Education can be successfully used for increasing the resilience of individual, family, community and nation.

Promoting Access to Information of the Youth

Youth especially those where the access to information is very less, can be looped in for providing information through kiosks, information centres, clubs, workshops, awareness drives etc. In most remote areas, valid and authentic information is a lacuna. The age of cyber learning has also given rise to unauthentic and sometimes misleading information which needs to be filtered. Information regarding vulnerability, support groups, resources – natural, social, economic, technological and capital – agencies, policies, programmes, inclusion, etc. can invoke resilience or adaptive capacity.

Promoting Training and Capacity Building of Youth

Capacity-building involves raising awareness and also encompasses building analytical skills and enhancing decision-making abilities. These outcomes can be achieved through different approaches, including training, formal education, seminars and workshops and networking. In this information age, training and learning has acquired a new dimension.

Promoting Youth Engagement in Green Job

The work done in agriculture, industry, research and development, services, and administration that contributes to preserving or restoring the quality of the environment is known as green jobs. Career counselling should also encompass an introduction to green jobs. Green jobs represent a way for young people to contribute directly to the fight against climate change. They enable youth to move beyond adopting green behaviours in their private lives, making it possible for them to translate their convictions into action in the workplace. Awareness about environment and climate change has already started a wave of youngsters taking up green jobs.

Promoting Effective Communication

Effective communication is important because it is a tool that can be used to identify problems, encourage participation, invite innovation in problem solving, and promote adaptation and mitigation. Climate change is a complex issue that presents its own challenges for effective communication. Uncertainties on the response of the climate system, the environmental and socio-economic impacts, greenhouse gas emission reduction targets, and the reliability of climate model output further clouds the decision-making to respond.

Promoting Youth Participation

The participation of youth in environmental protection and climate change can be sought at all levels and locations ranging from grass-roots activism and participation in conservation projects to policy-making bodies and NGOs. The role and participation of youth can be institutionalized in policy-making through advisory bodies such as youth councils. Many national governments have ministries or departments with youth affairs as part of their portfolio.

Promoting Behaviour Change in Youth

For sustainable lifestyles and sustainable development, the youth need to modify their own behaviour for adaptive capacity. They need to understand their own consumption patterns, assess their own values as well as understand the values of others. Debates and exchange of ideas with peers, employers and decision makers can enable them to choose sustainable lifestyles.

Promoting Advocacy

Advocacy is a powerful tool for checking and shaping the political will and policies related to climate change. Issues of inclusion, equity and justice need to be interwoven in the policy matters. Moreover, while agreeing to international treaties and carbon emission cut off rates, the underdeveloped and developing countries too will need strong advocacy for balancing their acts of development and energy consumption.

Promoting Volunteerism

The spirit of youth can match the spirit of volunteerism. In developing and underdeveloped countries, the need for volunteerism is much more than in the developed countries. The developed countries can afford to create new jobs for the issues of climate change but for economically struggling countries which are mostly the underdeveloped countries, it is very difficult to create jobs especially to deal with climate change. Moreover, volunteering also provides a sense of fulfilment to the youngsters that they are contributing meaningfully to the cause of nation. Many countries have such examples of mobilizing youths as volunteers.

Promoting Leadership

For developing leadership of future torch bearers, the youth must be given chance to exhibit and develop their leadership qualities. A leadership with vision and mission is an essential component of a resilient community. Political vision will make politicians more accountable for mitigation and adaptation issues related to climate change. It will enable the politician to make plans based on long term vision and mission. Similarly, the youth of today will be good leaders of tomorrow by learning while acting as pressure groups. Engaging in the political and administrative services will also sharpen their own skills to become good capable leaders.

Summing Up

Thus, social work profession has much to offer in making the communities more resilient to climate change. The strength perspective when used with the most promising segment of our society, the youth, promises ray of hope in otherwise pessimistic world of climate change. It will enable to exploit the opportunity that climate change offers by allowing to choose between informed choices for sustainable living, sustainable development and a sustainable world. The powers of youth are tremendous which can change the planet and hand it over as a better home to their children then what we are passing on to our children.

References

Brundtland Commission. 1987. *Report of the World Commission on Environment and Development*, Published by United Nations. Also published as *Our Common Future*, London: Oxford University Press.

Domilline, Leena. 2011. 'Climate Change: Social Workers' Roles and Contributions to Policy Debates and Interventions', *International Journal of Social Welfare*, 20 (4), pp. 430–438.

Fahmi, Eldin. 2006. *Young Citizens: Young People's Involvement in Politics and Decision Making*, London: Ashgate Publishers.

Satapathy, Sachidananda. 2007. *Youth Vision 2020 towards Building an India of Our Choice*, New Delhi: Serial Publications.

Taking IT Global. 2007. *Climate Change: Youth Guide to Action*, Ontario, Canada.

The United Nations. 2010. *World Youth Report: Youth and Climate Change*, New York.

CHAPTER 10

National Service Scheme in Higher Education: Some Critical Observations

H.S. SURESH

Nation, Youth and the NSS

Nurturing and tapping the talents and energies of young men and women for the advancement of the individual and the society has always been considered as crucial for the overall growth of a nation. Youth in every country is the supreme symbol of reserved and potential strength. It is, therefore, very necessary for any society to recognize the potential of youth and make special efforts to develop them to the optimum level so as to ensure that they become the contributing members of the society (Navale 1996). This is not so easy and simple as it sounds. Often the idea of this nature passes through a long historical journey and takes several *avtaars* before it settles into a full-fledged national level intervention. This major and ambitious intervention was launched in 1969 on the birth centenary year of Gandhi who originally saw the potential in youth. His all new ideas of constructive and reformist initiatives depended on youth of the times. Then, after many decades, in Independent India came another attempt on these lines. Sekhar has noted as follows:

> The Government of India from 1948 onwards worked on the idea and entrusted to a number of committees and experts the task of designing an appropriate programme or a package of activities for the students. Among them, K.G. Saiyidain's report entitled 'National Service for Youth' (1961), which was based on the experiences of different countries, is a comprehensive one. The report insisted on

> making the scheme voluntary, and the Education Commission (1964–66) called for the association of students at all stages of education with some kind of social service. Both these propositions constitute the ideological base of the NSS (2002: 99).

The idea of NSS has traversed a long course. Let us take a close look into it in order to make correct assessment of its genesis potential, achievements and the challenges. Advising the students and the teachers to form the active and intimate contact with the community in whose midst their institution is located, Mahatma Gandhi suggested that instead of doing pure academic research about economic and social issues, problems and disability, the students should do 'something positive so that the life of the villagers might be raised to a higher material and moral level' (NSS 1997: 1).

Dr Radhakrishnan, the eminent scholar, educationist, philosopher and statesman, was appointed the Chairman of the University Grants Commission. Under his leadership, the UGC recommended the setting up of national service in the colleges and universities on voluntary basis. He had two aims in mind. One was to develop mutually beneficial contacts between the students and the teachers on the one hand and establishing a symbiotic relationship between the university or a college and the community on the other hand. It is interesting to note that a great deal of churning and exchange of ideas took place on this issue. There was a consensus on assigning some role to youth in nation-building through social service but it was not becoming clear in terms of its logistics. The same idea of engaging the youth was placed before the Central Advisory Board of Education (CABE) at its meeting held in January 1950. The CABE recommended that '... the students should devote sometime to manual work on voluntary basis and the teachers should also associate with them in such work' (NSS 1997).

After a brief interval and hibernation, the idea was again revived and activated when the new nation decided to adopt a planned approach to socio-economic development by following the socialist path of rapid economic growth. In 1952, the Government of India decided to adopt centralized planning and prepared the draft of the First Five Year Plan. The need for social and labour service for students for a period of one year was re-stressed. As a result of this modest beginning, 'labour and social service camps, campus-work projects, village apprenticeship scheme, etc. were put into operation by various educational institutions.' Then after a lull of about five–six years, in 1958, 'the then Prime Minister Pandit Jawaharlal Nehru in his letter to the Chief Ministers mooted the idea of having social service as a prerequisite for graduation. He further directed the Ministry of Education to formulate a suitable scheme for introduction of national service into the academic institutions' (NSS 1997: 1). Nehru's enthusiasm and the commitment to nation-building is amply reflected in this effort of his. Usually nation-building is equated with such productive sectors as agriculture, industry, international trade and commerce, business, finance, banking, infrastructure and so on. In this sense, it is encouraging to see that software like sectors such as education and social service were being thought as equally important sectors to be deployed and engaged in nation-building processes right from the beginning.

Blurring the lines between the Centre and the states, once again in true federal spirit and partnership, the two joined hands in advancing this mission of youth engagement. Therefore, in 1959, the Education Ministers' Conference was convened to discuss the draft outline of the scheme. This Conference was unanimous on having such a scheme for national service and it made useful recommendations. All these initiatives and efforts towards evolving such a programme received a great deal of encouragement and that in turn, brought out certain voids in the existing system of college and university. It was felt that the imparting of only classroom education was not helping the youth enough. Some innovative supplementation on the lines of proposed national service scheme was felt desirable. But the Conference was too big a body/assembly to work out the detailed steps in that direction.

Hence, it suggested an appointment of a small group or a committee to explore the scope of such a nationwide programme. It began its exercise by proposing a pilot project on experimental basis. As a result of these deliberations, a Committee was appointed under the Chairmanship of C.D. Deshmukh on 28 August 1959 to make concrete suggestions for structuring national service programme. After about a small gap of about five–six years, once again interest in this issue got enlivened. The Kothari Commission on Education worked during 1964–1966 and made pioneering recommendation that the '... students at all stages of education should be associated with some form of social service' (NSS 1997: 2).

The *NSS Manual* (1987, 1997) contains the complete narrative on the history, philosophy, basic concepts and components, objectives and administrative structure at university level, composition of NSS volunteers as well as the profile of the activities to be undertaken.

Youth constitute one-third of India's population. Recognizing the role and responsibility of educated youth in upholding norms and the freedom of the country, the Government of India, introduced the National Service Scheme (NSS) in our educational system for the proper development and deployment of student-youth resources for constructive purposes.

NSS attempts to make education relevant to the needs of the society by raising the level of social consciousness among the students. Education through community service is the goal of NSS and the development of student's personality is the ultimate gain. The colleges implementing NSS reach out to the community through their staff and student volunteers, basically with a view to learning by exposure, experience and community interaction. The scheme envisages taking the students beyond the confines of the classroom and curriculum to make learning meaningful. It is believed, while the classroom activities cater to the intellectual pursuits of a student, community based activity and the consequent social interface will develop in them the competence required to perform as useful members of the community.

The NSS intended to engage the students and the teachers in social service. The most important feature of the NSS is that it has left the students and the teachers free to make their own plans of social service which suit the needs of the community around them and their colleges and universities. As is known, the village India (also known as Bharat, the other India) is neglected and is away from the mainstream of growth, development, progress and enlightenment. The dictates of global political and social economy is such that somehow it ends up as a loser in comparison to the cities. Villages are late receivers of benefits of national and regional development. This gap needs to be bridged. The focal point of NSS is to make its contribution in this regard.

Historical Development of Education in India

However, in order to understand and appreciate the vision and mission behind this semi-educational endeavour called NSS, it is necessary to take a quick look at the historical development of education in India. First, let us have a peep into deep history of Indian traditions of higher education which had a strong component of community dimension to it. Then we shall have a brief glimpse into the modern system.

> A system of education is a unique legacy; a human society inherits from its ancestors. All great cultures of the world have had their grooving in their philosophical traditions and philosophical bases are built over their educational foundations. Communities that do not have a strong base of educational system appear to have failed in building any distinct social ethos. (Mishra 1998: 5)

Traditional System of Education in India

The Indian society has always considered education with paramount importance and has given it an eminent place. Nalanda, Takshshila and Tamralipti were considered to be the ancient universal centres of learning. The philosophical teachings found in the scriptures of Hinduism, Buddhism and Jainism and the wisdom portrayed in the great epics of *Ramayana, Mahabharata* and the *Upanishad*s are regarded as great contributions to universal culture and civilization.

Sanskrit literature abounds with *shlokas* (verses of eternal value), maxims and adages on education that give us an insight into the functions and social expectations of education in those days. Some of the lofty ideals and values nourished and cherished by our ancestors are passed down from generation to generation in the written as well as oral traditions over the centuries.

Our ancestors visualized education as a liberating force. Their definition of education was *Sa Vidya ya Vimukta*ye (education is that which liberates). Their concept of education transcended the national boundaries when they proclaimed *ano bhadrah kritavo yantu vishwatah* (let noble thoughts come to us from every part of the world) because they considered the world itself as one family (*udara charitanam tu vasudhaiva kutumbakam*). And again it is because they knew very well that 'truth is one but scholars interpret it variantly (*yekams sat vipra bhahudha vadanti*) as the scholars are equipoised (*panditaha samadarshinah*)'.

They placed knowledge and action on equal footing as they believed that 'a scholar is one who is functional (*yah kriyavan sa panditaha*)'. Similarly, the concept of teaching is beautifully coined in two words '*shishyadicchet parajayam*' which means that a (true) preceptor desires to be excelled by his own pupil. Then how does the learning take place? Here is another verse:

Acharyat Padamadatte
Padam Shishyah Swame

Padam Sahbrahmacharibhah
Padam Kalakramenacha

A student gets one-fourth of his learning from his teacher, one-fourth from his peers, one-fourth is learnt out of his own intellect and rest is taught by time.

Modern Education System and NSS

The idea of including the community concerns in the process of gaining knowledge by university students through NSS was stated in the objectives of the programme. The need for education is given great importance by one and all, which is reflecting in: (i) the number of universities which are continuously set up in the country; (ii) the education commissions periodically set up to look into the problems; and, (iii) the various education delivery mechanisms that are created at both national and state levels. It has also made education an inclusive value for all sections of population.

The objective of education as visualized by the leaders was to serve a dual purpose at one go. It gave a formal education in the class-rooms through various undergraduate and post-graduate courses in multiple disciplines. This so acquired learning from colleges and universities was to be the basis for social use by supplementing the social, economic and cultural growth in the community and the country.

Incorporating NSS programme first for university and college students and gradually for 10+2 school level students was precisely to bring about the use of the opportunity of dual benefit of obtaining formal education and extending it to the community along with many social service programmes. This called for extension work wherein the learning from the institutions was to be taken at the door steps of the people in the community. In doing so, one requires to choose and adopt a suitable method and skill in making it effective and beneficial. This extension services were considered to be the third dimension of higher learning along with teaching and research. The NSS, thus, can and will prove to be an important link between higher education and community.

Evaluating NSS: Achievements

The government sponsored programme of the NSS has sustained itself for now over four decades. Millions of students from10+2 school level, colleges and universities have associated with this programme and will hopefully continue associating and benefitting from this effort of the NSS. No such programme as the NSS can survive and sustain itself in the midst of changing social conditions, social priorities and social relevance in the era of LPG. Various internal and external push and pull factors of the programme either cause hindrance or provide promotion to the implementation. The urban youth has greater awareness and opportunities for self-development (unlike the rural and under-privileged youth) and, hence, they are able to benefit to a greater degree.

Education itself is perceived as an investment in HRD and the NSS is being one of the inputs. This concept is shared by many Programme Officers as NSS is essentially an experimental learning programme. An experimental approach to learning is neatly summarized in a Chinese proverb: *'What I hear I forget. What I see I remember. What I do I know'.*

A book may yield information but a look yields inquisitiveness. Teaching the techniques of leadership is not a classroom exercise. The students have to be given the responsibility to lead in order to discover what leadership is all about. Talking about community service is not enough. Student must become involved in community action to appreciate what community service really means.

Development of the student's personality is the ultimate objective of NSS. Intellect is one aspect of a student's personality that is subjected to tests and examinations in our university system, but the physiological and social traits of the personality mostly remain unattended, un assessed. Apart, from intellect, it is the ideals, values, beliefs, attitudes, interests, imaginations, emotions, feelings, experiences, skills and situations that contribute in the making of one's personality. NSS programmes and policies are also directed towards meeting these needs.

It is also observed while education transforms one into a 'man power' by enhancing his ability, capacity, skill and knowledge, it becomes a 'human resource' when this man power is fitted against opportunities. The NSS activities recognize the truth that the knowledge gained in the classroom becomes a 'resource' only when it is applied to solving problems for critical thinking and to create ideas. National Service Scheme is a noble experiment in academic expansion. It inculcates the spirit of voluntary work amongst the students and teachers through sustained community interaction. It constantly endeavours to identify the needs of the individuals and the community and to bridge the gap in precept and practice.

What really motivates a student to join NSS is the opportunity for fellowship and intellectual stimulation it provides and openings it offers to discover himself in the group (identity) and the altruistic nature of the youth. It is possible that a smaller percentage of the student force are motivated by pragmatic considerations such as increasing job opportunities by possession of a National Service Scheme certificate and a few incentive marks that might stand them in good stead towards employment opportunities.

A few skills or a set of skills are no doubt essential to secure a job. The campus recruitment agencies as well as other employers look for something beyond this. Analytical power, creativity, skills of observation, articulation of problems ideas and concepts are needed more than ever. These are some of the traits of personality a volunteer would like to learn and acquire from his National Service Scheme experience. It is in the interest of NSS to ensure that our volunteers leave colleges with some marketable skills. They should also leave with a sense of obligation to serve the society. They are also required to be taught how to withstand the brief spells of unemployment, should it happen in a market guided economy and new hire and fire norms.

If the NSS Programme Officers can help their volunteers through well designed programme content, develop their faculties in the actualization of their needs and aspirations, the future does belong to NSS. The indomitable spirit of youth and their uncompromising stand on ideals and values they cherish, the limitless energy they possess and the promises they hold for the future-all are exalted through the two words in one of our *vedic* hymns – *NAMO YUVABHYAH* – (salutation to youth) which alone is sufficient to understand the importance of youth.

Some Challenges

The NSS, being a government programme faces perennial resource crunch. This limits its reach to the students and teachers (Hans 1995). It is observed that in such initiatives, incentives play a positive role in generating favourable response from the targeted groups. In such situations of paucity of funds, it requires extra effort in convincing and motivating them. Often it is noticed that if successful in convincing and motivating them, then sustaining their interest and continuing their involvement as well as participation become a major challenge.

The programme, on the whole, is run on excessively bureaucratic norms and procedural mindset. This takes away lots of creative energy into preparing and maintaining records and following procedures. Over-enthusiasm for accountability increases lot of paper work and account-keeping. This, in turn, divides the attention and time of the teacher from field activities and participating students. The camp experiences have shown that supervision cannot be lowered. It results in laxity and volunteers often suspend the work or compromise on quality. The programme objectives remain either unfulfilled or partially fulfilled. A poor quality of unsupervized work may defeat the object of creating the durable community assets in whatever form intended – say, digging a new or deepening the existing water pond, repairing a rural road, building makeshift or semi-*pucca* toilets and drainage/sewage lines, re-designing the existing school compound for various local games/sports, etc.

The interest and priorities among youths are changing. This has an impact on their profile, aspirations, values and goals. The advent of modern e and p media, offering variety of programmes and tempting output, have had corrupted the youth. They are prevented from recognizing the role, value and the need for sports and community/social service. The magnifying and glorifying world of TV has become all pervasive. There is also positive impact of TV. Some youth have started using TVs and computers as a medium for awareness, information and creativity. This prevents them from associating with programmes like the NSS. They view their association with NSS from the perspective of job opportunity. It is sad that the NSS loses out to their urgency of acquiring technical or skilled training.

Normally, a youth shapes his world view from his contact and engagement with the community. He learns and understands about life from what he sees around. This limits his imagination. Youth needs to have an acceptable role model for adaptation as a leader, someone who is inspiring and can be followed (Sinha 1997).

The NSS programme needs to be reviewed time and again in light of the changing social and economic scenario rather than preferring to continue with the existing inherited format. Modification in its policy, focus and activities can be suitably made to evoke interest of the teacher, students and the community for mutual give and take benefits. Manageability and creativity can be the prime concern in its continuity at all levels of implementation. It must be recognized by one and all that the youth and NSS are interwoven and integrated.

They mutually reinforce each other in the service of the community and the nation.

References

Government of India. 1964–66. *Education Commission Report (1964–66)*, New Delhi: Ministry of Education.

Hans, Gurmeet. 1995. 'Student Volunteers for Social Service', *Indian Journal of Social Work*, LVI (1), pp. 39–52.

Mishra, S. 1998. *Dr B.R. Ambedkar*, Aurangabad: Marathawada University.

Navale, Anil S. 1996. 'Youth and Development' (Unpublished Mimeograph), Baroda: Centre for Operational Research and Training (CORT).

NSS. 1987, 1997. *National Service Scheme Manual*, New Delhi: Department of Sports and Youth Affairs, Ministry of Human Resources Development, Government of India.

Sekhar, Kottu. 2002. 'Three Decades of the National Service Scheme: The Social Work Component and Development Issues', *International Social Work*, 45 (1), January, pp. 99–114.

Sinha, Durganand. 1997. 'Ambiguities of Role-Models and Values among Indian Youth', *Indian Journal of Social Work*, 38 (3), pp. 241–247.

CHAPTER 11

Corporate Social Responsibility: Some Important Dimensions

SURENDRA SINGH

Business enterprises are the basic cells of modern economic life and their phenomenal success in converting earth's resources into economic wealth is quite remarkable. They have transformed the life and landscape in the social and physical world. Basically they are the institutional members of society. If individual members have an obligation to improve the level and standard of society, then corporate houses have also responsibility to enrich the society as per its requirements. Like individuals, corporations are also citizens and citizens have civic duties and responsibilities. The corporate performance does affect economy and creates social problems. An equal amount of social responsibility is needed to match their social power. If each institution performs its social role in an orderly relationship with other institutions, we can solve the problem of society in the easiest possible manner. Thus, the measurement and reporting of social performance of profit oriented corporate houses and firms forms the core of corporate social responsibility (CSR).

The term corporate social responsibility reflects the impact of a corporation's activities on society. This embodies the performance of its economic function and other actions taken to contribute to the quality of life. These activities may extend beyond meeting the letter of the law, the pressures of competition or the requirements of contracts. The National Association of Accounts (1977: 2) has identified four major areas of social performance: (i) Community Development, (ii) Human Resource, (iii) Physical Resources and Environmental Contribution, and, (iv) Product or Service

Contributions. The responsibility of business itself indicates the desire to ensure the optimum use of resources, development and expansion, operation and management, promotion of research environment management, etc. since corporate have to draw on the community in which they operate for all resources; they also have obligations to their multiple stakeholders. Stakeholders are defined as those who get affected by corporate policies and practices. Today, it is acknowledged that business has not just financial accountability but also has the social and environmental responsibility – popularly known as the triple bottom line of good governance. Earlier, business was expected to serve that purpose of its stockholders as a creator of financial wealth. But now business is assigned to fulfil the expectations of different stakeholders like consumers, employees, shareholders, society, community, environment and government.

Approaches towards CSR

There are three approaches to the concept of corporate social responsibility and they constitute the basis for assessing corporate social performance:

1. The first approach originates in classical economic theory as expressed in the hypothesis that the firm has one and only one objective, which is to maximize profit. By extension, the objective of a company should be to maximize shareholders' wealth. It is asserted that in striving to attain this objective within the constraint of the existing legal and ethical framework, business corporations are acting in the best interests of society at large. This classical interpretation of the concept of corporate social responsibility has been advocated as there is one and only one social responsibility of business – to use its resources and engage in activities designed to increase its profit, as long as it stays within the rules of the game, which is to say, participation in open and free competition, without deception or fraud. Few trends could so thoroughly undermine the very foundations of our free society as the acceptance by corporate officials of a social responsible firm other than to make as much money for their shareholders as possible (Friedman 1962: 133).
2. The second approach, developed in the 1970s, recognized the significance of social objectives in relation to the maximization of profit. In this view, corporate managers should make decisions which maintain an equitable balance between the

claims of shareholders, employees, customers, suppliers and the general public. The corporation represents, therefore, a coalition of interests, and the proper consideration of the various interests of this coalition is the only way to ensure that the corporation will attain its long term profit maximization objective (Johnson 1979: 33).

3. The third view regards profit as a means to an end and not as an end in itself. In this view, 'the promoters/executives of a company have the problem of reconciling the demands of employees for more wages and improved benefit plans, customers for lower prices and greater values, shareholders for higher dividend and greater capital appreciation-all within a framework that will be constructive and acceptable to society. Accordingly, organizational decisions should be concerned with the selection of socially responsible alternatives. Instead of seeking to maximise profit generally, the end result should be a satisfactory level of profit which is compatible with the attainment of a range of social goals (Schrader 1987: 6).

The classical economist Adam Smith who wrote the bible of capitalism *Wealth of the Nations*, more importantly also wrote a *Theory of Modern Sentiments,* in which he emphasized that sympathy and a proper regard for others was the basis of any civilized society. Mahatma Gandhi believed in the trusteeship model, whereby the wealth you create has to be ploughed back for the benefit of society. In fact, today the debate is not about whether corporate need to take on social responsibility, because that is taken as given, and the only dilemma is how this responsibility is to be discharged and how it is to be measured, audited and continuously improved upon. Most often, the success of companies was measured by their turnover, size, market capitalization, profit after tax or shareholder value created. The real purpose of industrial corporations is to improve the quality of life in society.

Scope of CSR

Ernst and Ernst (1978: 14) have identified six areas in which corporate social responsibility is expected to be expressed:

1. Environment
2. Energy
3. Fair business practices
4. Human resources

5. Community involvement
6. Product

Let us now take a bit detailed view of each of the above.

Environment

This area involves the environmental aspects of production, covering pollution control in the conduct of business operations, prevention or repair of damage to the environment resulting from processing of natural resources and the conservation of natural resources.

Corporate social objectives are to be found in the abatement of the negative external social effects of industrial production, and in adopting more efficient technologies to minimize the use of irreplaceable resources and the reduction of waste.

Energy

This area covers conservation of energy in the conduct of business operations and increasing the energy efficiency of the company's products.

Fair Business Practices

This area concerns the relationship of the company to special interest groups. In particular it deals with: (i) Employment of minorities; (ii) Advancement of minorities; (iii) Employment of women; (iv) Advancement of women; (v) Employment of other special interest groups; (vi) Support for minority business; and (vii) Socially responsible practices abroad.

Human Resources

This area concerns the impact of organizational activities on the people who constitute the human resources of the organization. These activities include:

- Recruiting practices
- Training programmes
- Experience building-job rotation
- Job enrichment
- Wage and salary levels
- Fringe benefit plans
- Congruence of employee and organizational goals
- Mutual trust and confidence

- Job security, stability of workforce, layoff and recall practices
- Transfer and promotion policies
- Occupational health

Community Involvement

This area involves community activities, health-related activities, education and the arts and other community activity disclosures.

Products

This area concerns the qualitative aspects of the products, for example their utility, life-durability, safety and serviceability, as well as their effect on pollution. Moreover, it includes customer satisfaction, truthfulness in advertising, completeness and clarity of labelling and packaging. Many of these considerations are important already from a marketing point of view. It is clear, however, that the social responsibility aspect of the product contribution extends beyond what is advantageous from a marketing angle.

Objectives of CSR

Following three objectives are important in the context of social responsibility:

1. To identify and measure the periodic net social contribution of an individual firm, which includes not only the social costs and benefits internalized to the firm, but also those arising from externalities affecting different social segments.
2. To help in determining an individual firm's strategy and practices, which directly affect the relative resource and power status of individuals, communities, social segments and generations are consistent with widely shared social priorities, on the one hand and individuals' legitimate aspirations on the other.
3. To make available in an optimal manner to all social constituents relevant information on a firm's goals, policies, programmes, performance and contribution to social goals (Ramnathan 1996: 8).

There has been a long-standing debate over scope of the corporate social responsibility but it is a fact that its scope is affected by the change available in the business environment. Social responsibility of business is a continuous process as the business is a regular and on-going activity and it is composed of two-way traffic. The businesses as well as the different sections of the society have mutual interests.

It is an accepted tenet of the present day scenario that change is the only unchanging constant. Managing change has been acknowledged as one of the most important and challenging tasks faced by the corporate today. The crucial issue that needs to be addressed in this context is the *modus operandi* of changing the current model of the corporate management to ensure the continuous well-being of the society. To protect the interests of the shareholders and employees, it can be said that the primary business of a business is to stay in business. The institutions of business exist only because they perform invaluable services for society. Society gives business its charter to exist and the charter can be amended at any time if it fails to run according to societal requirements.

The fundamental idea embedded in CSR is that business corporations can no longer act as isolated economic entities in detachment from the broader issues of society. Although there is a clear difference between CSR stemming from a desire to do well (the normative case) and CSR that reflects an enlightened self-interest (the business case) – in many cases a firm's reasons for embracing CSR reflect a mixture of both these motivations. Therefore, if a running business has to retain its existing social role, it must respond to society's needs. Corporate houses must win over the confidence of workers and avoid class conflicts in their own interest. If the corporate wants to establish a good public image, it will have to show convincingly and tangibly that it supports social goals.

Conceptual Framework of Corporate Citizenship

The growing domination of global economic forces is pushing the business to acquire greater responsibility for social well-being. As a result, a new concept is emerging in the new millennium: 'Corporate Citizenship' resembling the corporate social responsibility. A company's reputation in terms of corporate citizenship can be a key asset in attracting and retaining customers, opening up new markets, and attracting and retaining a loyal and productive workforce. A corporate which fails to undertake this social responsibility faces the prospects of shrinking consumer base and consequently profits. Some of the world's most successful companies, including Shell, Nike, Union carbide and Exxon, operating entirely within the law have experienced devastating public relations and disasters due to negative public perceptions of their social responsibility. These perceptions have hurt the reputation and credibility of these companies, and correspondingly that of the shareholders' perception of its value.

CSR encourages increased understanding and active participation of corporate in equitable social development as an integral part of good business practice. It focuses in finding ways for corporate houses to behave in a manner that maximizes their society's wealth and consequently stake holder's value. Corporate social responsibility is defined as the continuing commitment by business to behave ethically and contribute to economic development while improving the quality of life of the workforce and their families as well as of the local community and society at large. Corporate social responsibility is considered a must for any company in the public gaze (Schrader 1987: 6).

CSR is not a concept Indian corporate houses are unfamiliar with, though their activities may not always have carried the CSR tag. For instance, as long back as the 1920s, Tata Steel was engaged in philanthropic activities like maternity benefits, payment of provident fund, working hours, etc. More companies have begun thinking on similar lines. With MNCs focusing on CSR, many Indian corporate houses now keep aside sums ranging from 0–15 per cent of their profits after tax for CRS. Understanding corporate social responsibility is a fledging area of serious economic activity.

Corporate responsibility norms seem to rise as wealth increases. Growing demand for more responsible corporate behaviour creates business opportunities. Firms that meet the demand at an early stage stand to win; laggards are put at risk. A company that puts the interests of its stakeholders first through good corporate governance finds its stock more attractive to investors.

The manner in which the business community is contributing to the developmental issues is also undergoing a change. The old style paternalistic philanthropy of 'doing for the community' – building schools and hospitals in the name of the company founder – is giving way to the idea of 'working with the community'. These ideas include: sharing marketing, technical and managerial skills; using communities as channel members to distribute the company's products; setting up ancillary units managed by communities and supplying products and using employees as volunteers, trainers and mentors.

In simple terms, being socially responsible makes good business sense and firms could be rewarded by increased patronage.

Corporates are expected to continuously improve their social, environmental, health and safety, sustainable development, human rights, ethics, gender equity, customer relations, etc. The World Business Council for Sustainable Development in its publication *Making Good Business Sense* clearly stated how companies' behaviour affects many people, including the flora and fauna, and not just the shareholders. A company should be a responsible member of the society in which it operates. That means contributing to sustainable development by working to improve the quality of life of employees, their families, the local community and stakeholders up and down the supply chain. It can mean a day-care facility for working mothers, a new clinics, health insurance, playgrounds; it can also mean biodegradable packaging, cleaner fuel for buses and trucks, community tree plantation drives, reduced water and energy consumption (Dewhurst 1989: 18).

Regulatory Base of CSR

In practice, following regulatory base as provided by the Accounting Standards Committee of the Institute of Chartered Accounts in England and Wales (1975: 13) is being used to comply with the corporate social responsibility:

1. Legislation which outlaws undesirable social activities. Many examples exist of public concern with undesirable features of business activity, and of legislation to suppress such activities. For example legislation relating to child labour in India has made employment of child less than 14 years as illegal.
2. Licensing systems may be employed to limit the extent of activities which are useful to society, but present a potential social problem. The licensing of trucks, for example, has been made the subject of certificates or road-worthiness, and attention is now being paid to the control of exhaust emission. Thus, licensing may be qualitative as well as quantitative.
3. It has been argued that taxation is convenient manner of internalizing external social costs of activities having negative effects on society. The objective is to impose taxes on the firm equal in magnitude to the damage sustained by society from the firm's activities.

The obvious purpose of these taxes would be to encourage firms to abate the effects of such activities or alternatively to finance public programmes for controlling these effects. According to some advocates of the taxation approach which deal with social costs, business firms would be free to choose between abating the social nuisance and avoiding tax, or continuing as before and paying the tax. According to other advocates of this approach, there should be a tariff of taxes to encourage firms to locate an area where their methods of production would do least harm to the environment. The Environment Protection Control Act, 1988, has made necessary provisions with regard to pollution control process.

These theoretical problems are implicitly recognized in the debate about corporate social accountability. That is why corporate social performance is to be assessed under these contexts.

Corporate Social Communication Process

Social Performance Reports are the latest trend in corporate communication indicating the level of compliance of social responsibility. The growing popularity of corporate social reporting and organizations' desire to hear their stakeholders' view on corporate social performance suggests two possibilities. First, that the stakeholders are interested in corporate behaviour, and business attitudes are changing from a predominantly managerial emphasis to collaborative one. Second, that there is an infrastructure of management information systems underpinning the whole process of reporting and providing the information behind organizational decision-making. Social accounting systems identify and measure social performance. If an organization then chooses to disclose this information in the interests of transparency and openness, its stakeholders must be confident that the information is true (Ditzler 1983: 62).

Reliable information systems reduce the risk that reporting of inaccurate information could damage the firm's reputation. Many organizations collect information that is pertinent to stakeholder groups, but no one chooses to disclose it. Most companies routinely collect information on employees; meeting customer requirements; working with suppliers; occupational health and safety; and environmental issues. Thus, corporate attitudes towards stakeholders are changing, rather than holding the stakeholders at arm's length, many organizations are now seeking to engage with them. It is a definite change from the hostile encounters that gave rise to early forms of social auditing and reporting. Corporate social reporting is increasingly popular for communicating data about social performance of corporate to multiple constituents. The wave of corporate communication is underpinned by existing management information system. But while popular management accounting tools are being used for social responsibility decision-making, they require skillful adaptation if they are to demonstrate transparency and accountability. They have to perceive the value of business as holistic and not as additive.

The organizations take advantage of their good social reputation in their marketing campaigns. Social image of organizations is extremely important for several stakeholder groups. The groups they identified are similar in all forms of organizations: communities, customers, employees, environment, shareholders and suppliers. But the priority given to different stakeholder groups varies. The organizations are planning to develop links between the externally reported measure and their internal reporting. But, despite lacking in such a system, the firms are concerned about their social performance. The issues such as recruitment and induction process, coupled with the social values, meant that employee group control and self-control influenced social performance. Each organization has its explicit values. The findings of Spicer (1978: 138) suggest that following measures are required to ensure effective compliance of social responsibility:

1. Establish an implementation team that includes a management accountant and managers. This should be led by a manager. Consult managers about the social information and performance measures they need.
2. Develop links between the organization's mission statement/objectives and its internally reported social measures.
3. Develop internal social performance measures for each of organization's stakeholder groups.
4. Check that the internally reported social performance measures include both input and output measures.
5. Set up a system for the internal monitoring and management of social performance.
6. Develop explicit links between managers' evaluation and their contribution to the organization's social performance.

The social values and culture of an organization are critical factors affecting its social performance – often through informal group control and self-control. External social reporting is important, but so is management information on social performance. Ultimately, it is the strategic and operating decisions of managers and other employees that determine the social performance of an organization.

Issues with regard to Corporate Social Responsibility

There are different stakeholders who are seriously interested in better corporate performance compliance and social responsibility:

> Consumers are demanding more than available products from their favourite brands. Employees are choosing to work for the companies with strong values. Shareholders are more inclined to invest in businesses with outstanding corporate reputations. Quite simply, being socially responsible is not only the right thing to do; it can distinguish a company from its industry peers.
>
> Employees are our greatest assets is the favourite corporate cliché. And yet in their profit and loss accounts, employees are put down as costs and not as assets. With the advent of information technology and service industry, corporates have suddenly realized that employees today represent the most valuable 'intellectual property' which is their most precious asset. Not every employee is seen as an asset but good employees are certainly sought after and need a nurturing and challenging work environment.

Earlier, corporates dumped their industrial production wastes with impunity in the environment. With the growing awareness and concern about environmental degradation, depletion of natural resources like water and fossil fuels and the phenomenon of global warming; there is moral and legal pressure on corporates to realize that the earth needs to be preserved and looked after so that our children and future generations are not adversely affected. The adverse implications of undesirable corporate performance are:

1. Rising health costs due to growing air and water pollution.
2. Depletion of natural resources like deforestation, endangering sustainable development.
3. Loss of revenue due to reduced international tourism.

The lack of concern for the environment and the society can be very detrimental and can actually shake the foundations of a business that has been built over decades. This is best illustrated by the examples of Union Carbide in India and Asea Brown Boveri which has been fighting a long protracted asbestos liability suit in the US.

In the field of energy, co-generation, tri-generation, using bio-mass for power, solar energy, wind and hydro power are all present day means of generating power either efficiently or through natural resources without the burden of pollution. The government can and should play a vital role in promoting clean fuels by offering subsidies, carbon credits, tax benefits and the like. This is an area where governments and corporates can work together for maximizing opportunities and improving social performance (Pearce et al. 1989: 84).

Should corporate houses manufacture anything that can sell and would generate profits or do corporates have a responsibility to ascertain whether they fulfil a genuine need in keeping with the value system of the community? For instance, should a company manufacture and sell alcohol, cigarettes and guns? One view could be that as long as the law of the land permits it a corporate could produce anything that can be sold. For example, they cannot produce heroin or cocaine, even if there is a huge demand, because it is illegal. This is a very touchy and debatable issue, but it is important that enlightened corporate houses, with a high sense of social consciousness, would question what they are producing from an ethical point of view and its impact on society.

The corporate houses are not islands unto themselves, but exist in the community. In the long run, in their own enlightened self-interest, they need to invest in the community because it is from there they get their talent pool, their customers and the shareholders. The more educated and prosperous the community, so more the business will eventually benefit.

Corporate Social Responsibility in Indian Scenario

There are several instances of exemplary demonstration of social responsibility by Indian corporate. Mention can be made of Late Sri Jamshedji Tata, who with his vision to create an Indian iron and steel industry, transformed an unknown, backward village named Sakchi, later renamed as Jamshedpur, into a model of town planning and community care. The Houses of Tatas, Godrej, Birlas are known for their commitment to developing social infrastructure. Recently B. Muthuraman, Managing Director, Tata Steel Ltd. (*Business Line* 2004: 4) opined that Tata Steel in future will not deal with companies which do not conform to a certain minimum standard of corporate social responsibility. He said: 'We will not either buy from or sell to companies that do not measure up to Tata Steel's social responsibility standards.' He further opined that we have been striving towards the global bench mark for corporate social responsibility. The purpose of the company was to improve the quality of life in the society.

The National Dairy Development Board (NDDB) has transformed huge areas in Indian villages by empowering producers and creating a marketing outlet for their produce. Operation Flood, popularly known as White Revolution, is a result of this initiative. Infosys Technologies currently commits up to 1.5 per cent of its profit after tax annually for social and community causes, which include education, women's projects, health care, community development, and preservation of art and culture. Wipro, through the Azim Premji Foundation, has dedicated itself to the cause of universalization of elementary education in India and currently runs 1,900 schools in various parts of the country.

These are all laudable efforts. But given the extent of the poverty in India, the low levels of literacy especially among women and the abject health care facilities available to the weaker sections of the society, a lot more needs to be done – especially by the corporate sector which has the financial and organizational muscle. In partnership with the government and the NGOs, it can make a significant and measureable contribution in improving the lot of the less fortunate men, women and children of our country.

Corporate Social Responsibility in India: Problems in Measurement and Reporting

Assessing corporate social performance is at its infancy stage in India. There are various reasons and problems for its slow growth. The possible reasons for the inadequate disclosure of corporate social performance may be:

1. There are no standard guidelines available for the preparation of social performance statement though various models have been given but none is complete in itself.
2. The Indian Companies Act, 1956, does not require a very detailed disclosure of corporate social performance in annual reports. So, the companies do not take botheration to prepare social accounting statements. Many consider it as hectic work and wastage of time. Though, with an amendment made in the Companies Act in 1988, the disclosure of energy conservation, foreign exchange earnings and pollution control measures, etc. have been made mandatory.

3. Preparation and audit of corporate social performance statements are also a problem. Since the variables to be identified, measured and reported in social accounts are the interdisciplinary, so these statements cannot be prepared and audited by the accountants alone. It is suggested that a committee consisting of an accountant, social scientist, a legal expert and psychologist can perform this job. But it is often difficult to get a proper match of such persons belonging to different fields.
4. The companies do not define their social goals in specific terms. Until goals are defined and identified, the statements cannot be prepared accurately. Some companies are also unable to differentiate between social goals and financial goals.
5. There is always some element of subjectivity in quantifying the benefits and costs of social programmes (Porwal 1988: 27). Porwal further argues that, 'Social accounts do not remain authentic, and imaginary calculations of social benefits and costs cannot give accurate results. Results drawn from such calculations may be void and useless.'
6. The corporation is basically an economic institution. It is not a charitable agency or a community service institution. Outlays for general social responsibility activities will distort the allocation of scarce funds available to a firm and will turn the firm into a vast wasteland in the long run. Social problems can be successfully solved only by those institutions best fitted to deal with them.
7. Managers of the enterprise are not trained to pursue social goals. They do not have an appropriate apparatus to destroy the public 'bads' and concentrate on public 'goods'. They are not competent to orchestrate the non-economic objectives successfully and decide the issue of turning corporate 'bad guys' into corporate 'good guys' applying their value judgments. If these pious intentions are to be turned down by the society, they may find themselves suddenly in a no-win position. Since there is considerable disagreement among the public as to what should be done, corporate managers will be criticized no matter what is attempted.
8. Corporations are not magicians. Society cannot expect the corporations to perform miracles. They cannot offer goods at fair prices, satisfy ever-hungry working groups, fatten the coffers of shareholders, keep the inflation monster under check, pay

exorbitant taxes and also bless the numerous unrelated social projects in a selfless manner. 'Business corporations are not bottomless cornucopias able to solve all society's ills.' Attempts to soft-pedal profit maximization policies would prove to be disastrous for the firm in the long run. Profit implies socially preferred behaviour. It means placement of funds to the best advantage; loss means impoverishment of society. Profit is dynamic element and motivating force behind economic development and all round progress. Further, social responsibility is a fair weather concept; enterprises cannot dream of philanthropy unless profits are sufficient.

9. A competitive business cannot be genuinely selfless. Enterprise cannot commit funds irrationally just to satisfy public expectations in areas where there are no direct or indirect benefits. If an enterprise spends lavishly on social action programmes and its competitors do not emulate the example, it will significantly increase the loss of socially responsible enterprise as the price difference and, hence, loss will result. A competitive enterprise, therefore, has no discretion to indulge in this type of extravagance.

In spite of above constraints, a significant number of corporates recognize CSR as the means to enhance their long-term stakeholder value. The genuine reasons for implementing such CSR are:

1. It is the most important driver for good corporate citizenship and CSR initiatives are directly linked with improved brand reputation.
2. It provides an opportunity to improve relationships with local communities.
3. It creates brand equity factor about the company, which is increasingly instrumental in retention of talented professionals.
4. It develops customer preference for companies with a social conscience.
5. It sensitizes the needs of society to expect more from the business corporation.

Most companies do not have a systematic approach to CSR implementation and they do not commit resources for it in a planned manner. The factor hindering adoption of CSR on a wider scale is lack of comprehension and capacity to implement it. Industry associates have also a critical role to play in shaping of experiences and rewarding best practices. CSR should be included as a subject in business schools to ensure that the managers of the future are imparted with the requisite skills and sensitivities.

New circumstances need new responses. The crises faced by humanity can be solved only by the application of concerted corporate action. The advent of the multinational enterprise, and the globalized markets have together formulated the direction and dimension of the modern corporation to its acme and zenith, where it can pose and present a formidable challenge to the power and influence of even a nation-state.

We cannot do without business corporations. It is imperative, that we exercise adequate and collective control over the way business corporations conduct their affairs so that they support, and not sabotage, the ecological environment and the balance of nature. When corporations realize that they are instruments of social purpose that they are established within society in order to accomplish some useful and social objectives, then they have a moral and ethical right for a continual existence, a license to use natural resources, and the concomitant responsibility to produce socially beneficial products and services.

Many corporations have inherited commercially-oriented and profit-centred culture and values that they tend to display a lackadaisical disposition and disregard to the social and environmental fallout from their business activities. Ecological and community issues often take a backseat in the discourse of their business management theory. These issues are vital and pivotal for the survival of life in this planet and it is also crucial and central in terms of social justice. We need a new business economics, which redefines corporate responsibility to include natural resources as well as human resources – both inside and outside the organization – within its ambit of accountability.

Building sustainable organizations requires a radical change of mind-set from the mainstream business thought and practice. Large-scale shift in strategy necessarily involves treading on the toes of the organizational culture. The culture of the company is usually described as 'the way we do business around here.' It comprises the values, norms, symbols, myths, behaviour, and conduct which obtain in an organization – the collective genius and consensus of the population at work. The surge of human energy, consequent to this metamorphosis, is the matrix from which a new culture will arise like the phoenix; and then, it will get further rejuvenated and invigorated to become *per se* a powerful change agent. It is this persistent and consistent process of transformation, which will support and renew the community, the economy, and the planet. It is this process which will impart a holistic purpose and mission to a business enterprise; and not to make it a mere tool and technique for accumulation of material wealth and mundane prosperity.

At a time when business in emerging economies are often fighting with their backs to the wall on globalization, WTO, IPR and a host of other challenges, corporate social responsibility must not be seen as another noose around its neck, rather it should empower them to deal better with their community. However, industrial corporations must have an overarching goal of doing good to the society of which making profits is only a part. This ensures long term success whereas companies with the only goal of making profits do not succeed in the long term.

References

Accounting Standards Committee. 1975. *The Corporate Report*, England and Wales: Institute of Chartered Accounts.

Dewhurst, J. 1989. 'The Green Resource Audit', *The Accountant*, February.

Ditzler, Patricia. 1983. 'Corporate Social Performance', *Management Accountant*, February.

Ernst and Ernst. 1978. *Social Responsibility Disclosure Survey*, Cleveland, Ohio: Ernst and Ernst.

Friedman, M. 1962. *Capitalism and Freedom*, Chicago: University of Chicago Press.

Johnson, H.C. 1979. *Disclosure of Corporate Social Performance*, New York: Praeger.

Muthuraman, B. 2004. 'Social Responsibility Vital for Tata Steel Dealings', *The Hindu Business Line*. 03 July, p. 4.

Pearce, D.W.A. et al. 1989. *Blueprint for a Green Economy*, London: Earthscan.

Porwal, L.S. 1988. *Accounting Theory*, New Delhi: Tata McGraw Hill.

Ramnathan, K.V. 1996. 'Towards a Theory of Corporate Social Accounting', *The Accounting Review*, July, pp. 516–528.

Schrader, D.E. 1987. 'The Corporation and Profits', *Journal of Business Ethics*, 6 (8), pp. 589–601.

Spicer, Barry H. 1978. 'Investors' Corporate Social Performance and Information Disclosure', *The Accounting Review*, January.

The National Association of Accounts. 1977. *The National Association of Accounts Committee Report, Part III.*

CHAPTER 12

Social Development through Corporate Social Responsibility: A Case Study of Karnataka

Y.S. SIDDEGOWDA AND JAGADISH B.

The concept of corporate social responsibility of large industrial groups has occupied a prominent place in the wider national discourse on economic issues since the pre-Independence era in India. Mahatma Gandhi described large businesses as 'trusts' of the people or as 'wealth of the people held in trust' and thus emphasized on the larger social purpose that industrial wealth should serve in Independent India (Sudip and Kumar 2005).

Today, in the age of globalization, corporations and business enterprises are no longer confined to the traditional boundaries of the nation-state. In the last 20 years, multi-national corporations (MNCs) have played a key role in defining markets and influencing the behaviour of a large number of consumers. The ongoing revolution in communication technology and the effectiveness of knowledge-based economies has created a new model of business and corporate governance (ASOCIO 2004). A growing awareness about the need for ecological sustainability and the New Economy framework, with an unprecedented stress on communication and image merchandising, have paved the way for a new generation of business leaders concerned about the responses of the community and the sustainability of the environment. It is in this context that we need to understand the new trends in corporate social responsibility (CSR).

ASOCIO (2004) has stated in its policy paper that '...the major drivers for CSR among companies are: enlightened self-interest, social investment, transparency and trust and increased public expectations of business. It further states that in recent years companies have realized that a strong CSR programme is essential for achieving good business practices and effective leadership and have concluded that their impact on the economic, social and environmental front directly affects their relationship with the stakeholders'.

What is CSR?

Corporate social responsibility can be described as the continuous commitment by corporations towards the economic and social development of communities in which they operate. CSR comprises efforts towards sustenance of depleting environmental resources, emergence of effective workplace practices and narrowing the gulf between the rich and the poor (Sandhya 2006).

CSR is nothing but what an organization does to positively influence the society in which it exists. It could take the form of community relationship, volunteer assistance programmes, health care initiatives, special education/training programmes and scholarships, preservation of cultural heritage and beautification of cities. Basically, the philosophy is to give back to the society, what it (business) has taken from it, in the pursuit of wealth creation. Corporate social responsibility is operating a business in a manner which meets or excels the ethical, legal, commercial and public expectations that a society has from business.

The term CSR is often used interchangeably with such other terms as Corporate Citizenship and is also linked to the concept of Triple Bottom Line Reporting (TBL), which is used as a framework for measuring an organization's performance against economic, social and environmental parameters.

CSR: How Does it Help?

First, there exists a well-defined and generally agreed notion of the wider public interest for companies to follow; second, this notion of the public interest can be identified with the pursuit of social and environmental objectives – the triple bottom line; third, the 'soft regulation' of corporate social responsibility serves as a way of inducing corporations to promote the public interest; and, finally, this body of soft regulation of companies should be developed further.

Drivers of CSR

As shown in Figure 12.1 the private sector business has widespread social, environmental and political effects on society. Support and pressure for corporate responsibility comes from shareholders, managers and employees, consumers, business partners, communities and governments. Socially responsible practices have a direct and positive impact on a company's productivity.

Figure 12.1

Drivers of CSR

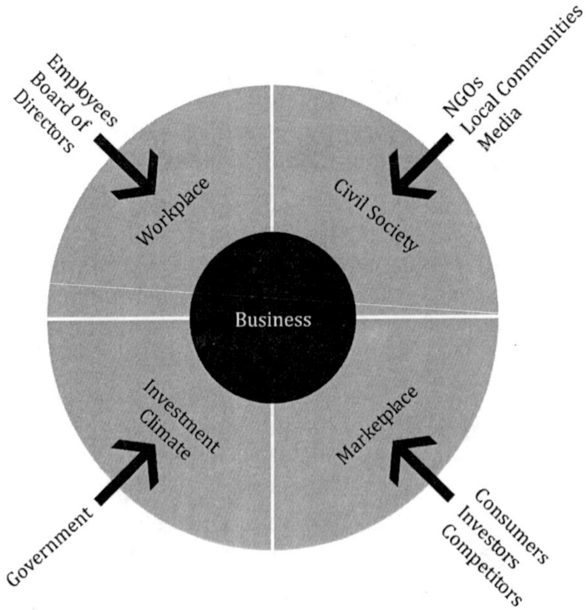

Public Sector Enterprises, CSR and Liberalization

India began her industrial journey with a large public sector with several huge corporations and companies operating in various sectors like petroleum, heavy industries, aviation, mining, steel, equipment manufacturing and shipping. The Indian public sector has had a long tradition of corporate social responsibility and the initiatives of corporations like the Oil and Natural Gas Commission (ONGC), Steel Authority of India Ltd (SAIL) and Gas Authority of India Limited (GAIL) have been critical in the development of several backward regions of the country. Indian Airlines and Bharat Heavy Electronics have been widely acclaimed for their disaster management efforts (Brown 2001).

Families of CSR

The Indian corporate houses and firms constitute a veritable industrial sector. Indian industrial scene really offers a spectacular profile of economic might of the nation. Classifying them into various categories and groupings is a tough and complex task. However, an attempt is made here as follows to gather some sense about their pre-CSR social commitments:

1. For long-established industrial dynasties, such as the Bajaj, the Birlas and the Tatas, concepts of nation-building and trusteeship have been alive in their operations decades before CSR became a popular cause.
2. Alongside these are the leading Indian companies with strong international shareholdings, such as Hero Honda, HUL (Hindustan Unilever Ltd), ITC, and Maruti Udyog, where local dynamics fuse with the business standards of the parent or partner.
3. Another tradition emerges from the public sector enterprises, such as BHEL (Bharat Heavy Electricals Ltd), HDFC (Housing Development Finance Corporation), NTPC (National Thermal Power Corporation), and ONGC (Oil and Natural Gas Corporation), where social obligations remain an integral part of their business despite the advancing of privatization.
4. And then there is the new generation of enterprises that has surged on the back of knowledge-based globalization, such as Dr Reddy's, Infosys, Ranbaxy, and Wipro, where less emphasis is on minimizing negative impacts and more on maximizing the positive spill-over effects of corporate development.

CSR: Growing Importance

The concept of CSR is neither the brainchild of a single person nor a single organization. There has always been an ethical perspective to the business strategies practiced all over. There are several moral and normative edicts which the organizations have been following for several decades. One such ethical perspective is the desire to offer help, being conscious of the fragility of the environment we are living in.

In many countries, national and local governments have taken a 'hands off' approach to regulating business due to the following reasons:

1. In response to liberalization and globalization of trade and commerce, the role of state is shrinking.
2. Shrinking of resources: Most of the governments at the national and local levels are experiencing shortage of funds and a shrinking resource base.

The four major factors, which are catapulting the CSR issue in the forefront, encouraging and demanding the corporate to expand their efforts in these areas are:

1. Large size of the modern day's corporations.
2. A growing number of companies recognizing the business benefits of CSR interventions.
3. Increasing pressures from customers, suppliers, employees, communities, investors and other activist organizations representing stakeholders.

Andrew Carnegie, writing in the year 1989, believed that rich had the moral obligation to give away their fortunes and that personal wealth beyond the family's needs should be regarded as trust fund for the benefit of the society. 'The Trusteeship Concept' advocated by M.K. Gandhi is very similar. Carnegie also believed that the money should be given during the benefactor's lifetime to ensure that it achieved the maximum good. Carnegie had identified seven best uses to which a millionaire can devote the surplus of which he must regard himself as only the trustee.

Tom Cannon has stated that business creates wealth, produces goods and services, creates employment and generates income. Society provides a means of exchange, legal mechanisms, banking systems, trained manpower and social infrastructure like roads, schools, hospitals, etc. In addition to the above, with the advent of the joint stock company (as a form of organization) the society has granted two very special rights to business. The first is potential immortality and the second is limited liability. Thus, business does have social responsibility (Cannon 1994). This is summarized rather well in Table 12.1:

Table 12.1

Profile of Society-Business Interface

Society Provides	*Business Provides*
Means of exchange	Products and services
Trained manpower	Direct and indirect employment
Legal and banking systems	Income generation in terms of wages, dividends, taxes, interest, etc.
Social infrastructure like roads, schools, hospitals, etc.	

Thus, according to Cannon, in return for these special privileges being granted to business, it does have a responsibility to fulfil certain moral and material obligations and expectations of the society at large.

Key Initiatives and Frameworks

Today, a large and increasing number of companies are reporting to their social, environmental and ethical performance, both as a communication to their stakeholders and as a management tool. Though standardization in reporting is yet to be achieved, a number of multilateral organizations voluntary agencies and international standard organizations have launched reporting initiatives, important among these being the following:

The UN Global Compact

It has 10 universal principles in the areas of human rights, labour, environment and anti-corruption.

Global Reporting Initiative (GRI)

It provides a framework for sustainability reporting. The Global Reporting Initiative (GRI) is multi-stakeholder initiative, formed to develop globally applicable guidelines that can be used voluntarily by reporting organizations.

Ethical Trading Initiative Base Code

The global standards on employment and working conditions (linked to the ILO conventions) are available today. The UN Declaration of Human Rights and Rights of the Child have also emerged as major protective mechanisms under global watch. It is a partnership between the companies, trade unions and the NGOs.

Organisation for Economic Cooperation and Development (OECD) Guidelines

It contains recommendations addressed by governments to MNCs operating in or from adhering countries.

Tata Index for Sustainable Human Development

A comprehensive set of indices, processes and frameworks followed by all Tata group companies.

Accountability 1,000 (AA 1,000)

AA 1,000 developed by the Institute of Social and Ethical Accountability is a 'process standard' setting out principles and a method for social reporting that focus on the process rather than the content of the social report.

Social Accountability (SA 8,000)

Social Accountability International launched SA 8,000 which is a standard addressing labour and workplace conditions. It is modelled on International Standards Organization (ISO) 9,000. It builds on ISO auditing techniques: specifying corrective and preventive actions, encouraging continuous improvement, focusing on management systems and documentation proving these systems' effectiveness.

Coalition of Environmentally Responsible Economies (CERES)

The CERES Report is a standardized format for corporate environmental reporting developed through collaboration by companies, institutional investors and environmental organizations.

In the Indian context, very little systematic documentation of CSR initiatives is available so far. One such study was done by Business Community Foundation for TERI (Ritu 2004). Some of the findings of the study are as follows:

1. Serious and committed approach to CSR is widening its reach, but there is vast ground yet to be covered.
2. Collaboration work between companies and NGOs is increasing.
3. Corporates are realizing that 'good for people is good for business too.'
4. Most interventions made so far are philanthropic in nature, rather than strategic.

According to the results of a Global Survey conducted in 2002 by Ernst and Young[1], 94 per cent of companies believe that the development of a CSR strategy can deliver real business benefits; however, only 11 per cent have made significant progress in implementing the strategy in their respective organizations.

There is an increasing recognition of the triple bottom line: *People, Planet and Profit.* The triple bottom line stresses the following:

1. The stakeholders in a business are not just the company's shareholders.
2. Sustainable development and economic sustainability are to be rigorously pursued.
3. Corporate profits to be analysed in conjunction with social prosperity.

In the traditional paradigm, most corporate bodies viewed CSR as the extension of a financial input for a humanitarian cause. However, the contemporary context is more complex: 'A company that undertakes activities aimed at communities (be they philanthropic, social investment or commercial initiatives) but does not comply with business basics cannot be termed socially responsible' (Srivastava and Venkateswaran 2000). These words have widened the scope of our understanding of CSR. Business basics may be re-termed as 'business ethics'.

Impact of CSR

It must be stated that CSR is an extensive and multi-dimensional phenomenon. Its impact, therefore, is bound to be varied, multi-dimensional and differentiated.

From Philanthropy to Stakeholder Participation: Emerging Trends

The conceptualization of corporate social responsibility until the 1990s was purely in terms of philanthropy or charity. Welfare programmes or initiatives were introduced not as a duty or a responsibility but as a form of charity that was supposed to indicate the virtues of the company or the organization. However, the post-liberalization phase has seen a fundamental shift from this philanthropy-based model of corporate social responsibility to stakeholder – participation based model. A definitive element of continuity in the said CSR effort by the industry is added. It is no more a onetime doling out for photo clicks and be done with. The best example of this new responsible model is reflected in the way Wipro and Infosys Technologies respond to CSR obligations. They show genuine social concerns of the corporate giants. Internationally viewed, we find Bill and Melinda Gate Foundation as one such example.

Revolution at the Grass-roots Levels

The focus has been on initiatives that are people-centric with active community participation at all levels. Further, the corporations themselves have moved away from the charitable initiatives like giving financial grants or sponsorships to providing products and services in a manner that would make a real difference in the target communities.

The most important perceptible change has been the introduction of a host of innovative programmes and schemes in several areas like education, health care, rural development, environment protection, protection of artistic and cultural heritage and disaster management that are customized to meet the specific needs of the target group. Corporations devote not only financial resources but expertise, manpower, products and services for the successful implementation of schemes. Some of the examples are as follows:

- ITC, which positions its *e-choupals* as an 'instrument for converting village populations into vibrant economic organizations', already serves 3.5 million farmers in 36,000 villages. The plan is to have a network of 20,000 *e-choupals* and 700 *choupal saagars* across 1,00,000 villages within the next decade. The *choupal saagars*, a progression from *e-choupals,* serve as hubs for warehousing and as hypermarkets for a variety of goods. The total outlay is around ₹ 5,000 crore.
- Lupin India Limited has started a project for providing sustainable development in 154 villages across Rajasthan. The scheme consists of a holistic action plan for agricultural income generation scheme, land cultivation and fruit plantation programmes, fodder preservation schemes, sericulture, water-recycling programmes, establishment of medical and educational centres, adult literacy programmes and credit schemes.
- ICICI Bank is banking with the unbanked. It hopes to provide 'touch points' within 10 km of every rural customer and is making plans to increase its rural portfolio to 25 per cent of total advances by 2010 (up from 12% today).
- A grand alliance, involving Tatas, Birlas, Ruias and Jindals, for example, is taking shape in Jharkhand, a state battling huge developmental odds. It is looking to bring health care to the 32,620 villages of the state.

- Usha Martin, Lupin, the Tatas, Confederation of Indian Industries (CII), United Nations Development Programme (UNDP) and the Ministry of Non-Conventional Energy Sources in a partnership is harnessing renewable energy to meet the entire energy needs of clusters of villages in Rajasthan and Jharkhand.
- In addition to conducting HIV-detection, prevention and control drives, Reliance at Mora in Surat, has also put 110 people on Anti-Retroviral Therapy.
- Cipla, another Indian pharma major, has found a novel approach to fulfil its CSR obligations by offering to sell a cocktail of three anti-HIV drugs, Stavudine, Lamivudine and Nevirapine, to the Nobel Prize-winning voluntary agency, Medicine Sans Frontiers, (MSF) at a rate of $350, and at $600 per patient per year to other NGOs over the world. This offer has led to a significant decrease in the prices of these drugs worldwide. This, in turn, has increased the accessibility of these drugs, especially in the developing countries.
- Ranbaxy operates seven mobile health care vans and two urban welfare centres that reach over a lakh people in various parts of northern and central India.
- Tata Consultancy Services (TCS) has set up a fully-equipped computer training laboratory for children from the Society for the Welfare of the Physically Handicapped and Research Centre in Pune for imparting basic computer knowledge.
- NIIT has launched a highly popular 'hole-in-the-wall' scheme where it places a computer on a public wall in urban and rural areas so that neighbourhood children can learn computer basics using the play-way method.
- Bharat Electronics Limited built cyclone proof houses for the victims of the super cyclone with the help of the victims themselves so that the houses are built according to their needs.
- Ion Exchange has founded a profitable venture for environmental protection through water treatment, forestation and organic farming.
- Sudha Murthy of the Infosys Foundation, the social initiative arm of the IT major Infosys, explains the great efforts that corporations are making to ensure that the projects they are involved with are actually genuine and serve a purpose. Murthy further explains: 'We get a lot of projects, so we do a round of elimination .... make a shortlist after a lot of verification, so as to decide

which are the good ones. Then we supervise the implementation part by visiting the area. But we have to work very hard, during all holidays, weekends and 18 hours every day.'

- Several organizations like Gas Authority of India Limited (GAIL) have introduced benchmarking exercises for their CSR activities and industry bodies like Confederation of Indian Industries and FICCI have introduced cross-sectoral programmes, for the first time, in CSR related areas.

Private businesses are at the heart of economic success. Private investment, and the increases in productivity it generates, actually drives sustainable growth (Bouton and Sumlinski 2000).

Figure 12.2

Process of Poverty Reduction by Private Sector Industries

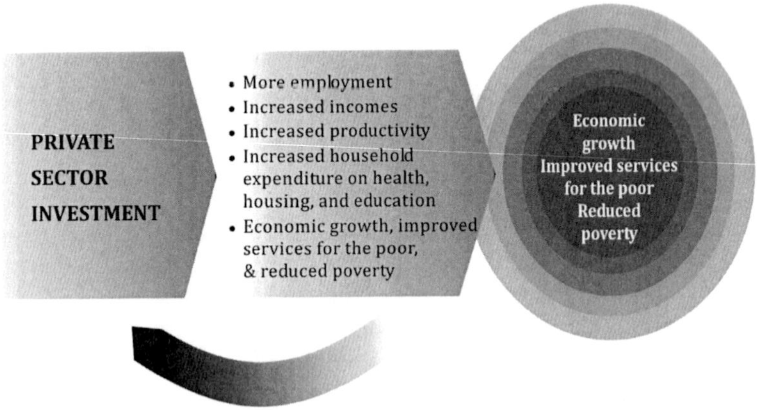

A study of 84 countries from 1960–2000 found that increased productivity accounted for 41 per cent of economic growth (Bosworth and Collins 2003). Corporate social responsibility focuses on what an organization does that affects the society in which it exists.

The idea of corporate social responsibility is positive and broadly focused, amounting to a transformation of the objectives of the company and so of the market system. It is not enough, in this view, for companies to pursue profits within the constraints of law and the principles of honest dealing. Companies are seen as having a leading role as agents of social, environmental and economic progress. Business should enthusiastically embrace and adopt the notion of 'corporate citizenship' (Henderson 2001: 35).

As shown in Figure 12.2, Businesses can help to reduce poverty:

- by investing, producing, and paying wages and taxes, they can contribute to growth;
- by respecting labour standards and encouraging local sourcing, they can contribute to pro-poor growth; and
- by creating jobs, providing skills, training and producing products that meet the needs of the poor, their operations can have a direct impact on the poor.

The main findings of the study *Corporate Social Responsibility Initiatives of NSE Nifty Companies: Content, Implementation Strategies and Impact* are as follows:

1. Approximately 57 per cent of the responding companies, have a formally adopted 'ethics code' while only one-third of the companies have an 'Ethics Officer' or 'Ethics Counselor'.
2. Large proportion of the responding companies are active in the areas of Education/Training (80%), Health care (66%), Environment (60%), Welfare of underprivileged sections (57%) and Rural development (23%).
3. As far as the areas of CSR activities are concerned, a surprising result is obtained. None of the responding companies have said that they are doing anything in the areas of religious and/or spiritual developments.
4. Less than 50 per cent of the companies have done anything during natural or other calamities.
5. In the context of decision-making process, more than one-third of the companies have institutionalized the process through specially constituted committees or Board of Trustees.
6. Four distinct implementation strategies have been identified and companies seem to have adopted more than one strategy. Most frequently adopted strategy has been making monetary contributions. The second most popular one is collaborating with other government, semi-government and voluntary organizations. Very few companies have an in-house department for CSR activities; even fewer seem to involve their employees in the effort.

Social Development through CSR in Karnataka

Presently, corporate houses in Karnataka are focusing on areas like education, health care, rural development and environment.

CSR Initiatives by Infosys Foundation

Infosys Foundation is a public charitable trust founded in 1996. Following are the areas in which it is working:

Health Care

- Conducting rehabilitation camps at tribal areas, drought hit areas, etc.
- Construction of hospitals.
- Upgrading hospitals with significant equipment like ultrasound scanners, ambulance, significant drugs in certain cases, etc.

Social Rehabilitation and Rural Upliftment

- Construction of orphanages.
- Construction of common halls at orphanages, old age homes, etc.
- Rehabilitation of *devadasis* (temple dancers) in Karnataka.
- Rehabilitation of mentally retarded through other local organizations.
- Rehabilitation of children on railway platforms, streets and slums.
- Assisting the promotion of social awareness among the tribal or other backward communities where evil and superstitious practices are followed.
- Donation of passenger vans to certain rehabilitation centres.

Learning and Education

- Setting up libraries for every rural Kannada medium school by donating a set of about 200 books worth about ₹ 2,000 under our educational project called *Shalegondu Granthalaya.*
- Donating corpus fund to good but economically weak schools.
- Donating for the construction of additional classrooms or re-construction of old classrooms/school building.
- Donation of other equipment to schools like computers, furniture, etc.
- Construction of science laboratories.
- Assisting the promising students of economically weaker sections by means of scholarships or contributing to pay their annual fees.

Art

- Promotion of deprived art or culture by organizing stage-shows.
- Donating for such organization which promotes creative artistic talent.

CSR Initiatives by Wipro

Azim Premji Foundation was established in 2001 with a vision to contribute to education that facilitates a just, humane and equitable society. The approach has been to focus on systemic change and improvement in quality of education in the government schools. The Foundation is focusing on the following key areas while working with the government:

Teacher Education

Teacher education programmes have sought to build capacity in the existing education functionaries in terms of their perspectives, subject matter knowledge, competencies and motivation levels. Since inception, it has worked with over 50,000 government school teachers across eight states.

Education Leadership and Management

The Foundation has developed about 3,500 education functionaries in the state of Karnataka, including principals of schools in a unique effort involving training of master development facilitators for extended periods of time through classroom training and field projects.

Examination Reforms

Foundation has worked in about eight districts in five states and changed the way examinations are conducted for students up to 5th standard and the state of Karnataka has introduced external competency based evaluation.

Technology in Education

There is a consistent international trend to explore and utilize computer aided learning to augment the teaching-learning processes in the classroom. The Foundation initiated the Computer Aided Learning programme in the year 2002 to harness the potential of computer technology for education. The objectives of the programme were to make learning enjoyable and assessment fun, for all students.

To this end, the Foundation created syllabus-based bi/trilingual multimedia content. It is probably the largest developer of Digital Learning Resources that address curricular issues of children from classes 3 to 8 in 18 languages (including four tribal languages). About 2.5 million children in 20,000 schools have used these resources across 16 states.

CSR Initiatives by MphasiS

MphasiS works with the voluntary sector in implementing projects in the communities. It involves employees, clients, and other stake-holders, and encourage them to actively contribute their skills, time and expertise to such initiatives.

Assimilation of Persons with Disabilities into the Workforce

It has recruited over 320 persons with disabilities in various capacities across its verticals. In order to evolve and deal with a long-term strategy of employment opportunities, the Company has partnered with Enable India, a pan-Indian NGO that works towards placement of persons with disabilities in the corporate sector.

Inclusiveness of Persons with Disabilities into Mainstream Society – Nannagu Shale (A School for Me Too)

To address the employment needs of persons with disabilities, MphasiS, in partnership with Fourth Wave Foundation (FWF), has developed an intervention programme by creating a model that impacts all segments of society, and helping them take responsibility in making this work. FWF has envisaged two different implementation models for two geographical areas, one for rural Karnataka and the other for urban and rural Bangalore. They plan to replicate these models across India enabling inclusion of children with disabilities into the society, ensuring their right to education.

Aalamba Programme

Aalamba programme is an employability and entrepreneurship programme aimed at youth who are school dropouts and fall into a policy black hole. MphasiS aims to empower over 300 youth with employment and skills training, and support with employment exchange services. It also aims to support 30 bright young people in developing their own enterprises, as part of the business and employment co-operative, within one year of training. It has helped setting up a catering unit initiated by the Self-Help Group of women, called Sangam Foods, and a Potter's Shop (a sales outlet of pottery products) at Pottery town in Bangalore, India.

Swachcha Grama, Badami Taluk, Bagalkot District, Karnataka

MphasiS extended its support to the Badami Taluk in Bagalkot district in the aftermath of the severe floods that hit North Karnataka. MphasiS ensured that more than 1,600 households from 22 villages were provided dry rations, blankets, buckets, etc. in partnership with headstreams. MphasiS is also promoting *Swacha Grama* (clean village) concept by building 50 toilets for two villages in Badami Taluk.

Nurture Merit

This is a programme to nurture the merit of students from disadvantaged families to enable them to realize their potential. MphasiS provides assistance in the form of college fees, examination fees, tutorials, and coaching for meritorious and needy students. They also provide text and career related books, computer facilities, career guidance, training and also facilitate students' holistic and personality development to excel in professional and personal life through various training programmes.

Namma Halli

Namma Halli is a CSR initiative of Confederation of Indian Industries (CII), Karnataka. Under this initiative, CII-Karnataka had invited its members to adopt villages in rural Karnataka. MphasiS has adopted four villages in Doora Panchayat – Doora, Talur, Muradagalli, and Dodda Katuru – located 130 km from Mysore in Karnataka. The goals behind this initiative include sustainable economic development, improved health, and over all human development with increased and improved access to education, adult literacy, clean village and environment. MphasiS is committed to support this initiative for an initial period of three years.

Specific Participatory Interventions taken up by the Corporate Sector are:

Education and Training

1. Construction of school building (TVS).
2. Merit scholarships to employees and others (TVS).
3. Adult literacy classes (TVS).
4. Vocational training to women and youth (MphasiS).

5. Enhancing teachers' performance (Infosys, Wipro).

Health care

1. Medical camps (Jubilant).
2. Mobile medical services (Jubilant).
3. Pulse polio programme (TVS).
4. Construction and/or revamping of municipal hospitals (TVS, MphasiS).
5. Cancer and AIDS awareness, prevention and treatment.
6. Health awareness in schools (Wipro, MphasiS).
7. Infant health (TVS).

Environment

1. Recycling of pollutants and wastes (Toyota).
2. Tree plantation (Toyota).
3. Natural resource management (Toyota).
4. Rain water harvesting programme (Ashok Leyland).
5. Awareness programmes in schools/colleges (Toyota).

Rural Development

1. Agricultural guidance (TVS, Jubilant).
2. Provision of drinking water (Toyota, TVS).
3. Agricultural extension (TVS).
4. Rural roads and other infrastructure (TVS).
5. Promotion of rural income generation schemes (TVS, Jubilant, Nestle).
6. Solar lighting to villages (Applied Materials).

The Way Forward

There is a need to develop a more coherent and ethically-driven discourse on corporate social responsibility. CSR is still sometimes seen as 'green wash' to clean the sins of pollution, or 'white wash' to provide a facelift to the company's public image. It is often seen as old wine in a new bottle – just another trendy name for good old philanthropic initiatives by companies. There is a need to move beyond such transitory illusions about corporate social responsibility.

The focus of international development is the Millennium Development Goals (MDGs) which represents a shared commitment to work to eliminate world poverty. If the incomes of the poor are increased and their access to health and education services is improved, then the MDGs will be achieved. It is a startlingly simple equation: in most developing countries, increasing the income of poor households leads to better educated and healthier poor people (Pritchett and Summers 2002).

There is a need for Indian corporate houses to graduate from thinking in terms of just charity, to the concept of responsibility. There is also an urgent need to integrate CSR with business strategy, i.e. to link company's core business and strengths on the one hand with resources available with the organization internally and needs of the external environment, on the other (Stoner et al. 2001).

Suggestions

- Companies should ensure better understanding of CSR within the corporation at all levels. This can be achieved by creating task-specific working groups on CSR issues and encouraging adherence to the CSR policy by means of rewards.
- Companies should stress that CSR leads to reputation enhancement of the corporation.
- Corporations should create CSR structures to involve the community, labour and other relevant stakeholders in decision-making and compliance mechanisms.
- Transparency in the value chain has to be improved since this will lead to a better identification of bottlenecks through the chain.
- Mother companies should allocate budget to daughter companies so they can address CSR issues.
- The business case of CSR should be clear. Therefore, profitability statements or a business plan should be formulated together with the CSR policy.
- The 'roots' of CSR in the company should be assessed by looking at the structure and processes in place which enable the enforcement of CSR principles.
- Companies should share examples of efforts, e.g. joint partnerships, that removed bottlenecks to CSR.
- A toolkit should be developed for self-assessment of companies on CSR performance.
- The mother company should be made accountable as it enjoys the (financial) advantages of global branding. Mother companies should connect the use of the brand name to compliance with its CSR policy.

- Companies should install a CSR cell within their company in order to facilitate stakeholder engagement. Without an internal structure, it is not possible to involve the community.
- To give more priority to environmental issues, greening costs should be part of the project costs.
- Civil society should be more involved with monitoring of CSR and networking
- NGOs need to build capacity to engage with the private sector.
- Research should focus on the business case of CSR elements and categories.
- Universities and other institutes should work together to put CSR on the agenda, especially of business schools, research institutes, etc.
- Sector specific round tables on CSR should be promoted.
- The Frame of Reference of CSR should also contain development goals, a focus on decent employment generation and stable vendor relationships with suppliers.
- Much more work is needed to educate Indian consumers on the needs for and the benefits and costs of CSR.
- NGOs should develop sector specific CSR best practices after a meaningful dialogue with the industry.
- NGOs should lobby with media corporations to regularly publish and do ranking on not only financial but also on CSR benchmarks.

CSR activities are known to achieve best results when these activities have natural links with the company's business. Proactive intervention by selecting areas like health, education, poverty alleviation, rural development and concentrating on them will go a long way.

Note

1. The fifth issue of its quarterly newsletter on *Corporate Responsibility* informs about Ernst and Young's (2002) most important and interesting corporate responsibility projects in four areas: Workplace, Marketplace, Environment and Community.

References

Asian-Oceanian Computing Industry Organization (ASOCIO). 2004. 'Corporate Social Responsibility', Policy Paper, June.

Bosworth, Barry and Collins, Susan M. 2003. Quoted in the World Bank's *World Development Report 2005*, Overview (www.worldbank.org/wdr/).

Bouton, Lawrence and Sumlinski, Mariusz A. 2000. 'Trends in Private Investment in Developing Countries: Statistics for 1970–1995', *Discussion Paper 21*, Washington, D.C.: International Finance Corporation.

Brown, K. 2001. 'Corporate Social Responsibility: Perceptions of Indian Business', in M. Mehra (ed.), *Entrepreneurship: People, Planet and Profit*, Calcutta: Centre for Social Markets. Retrieved from www.csmworld.org/public/pdf/socialrespons.pdf (Accessed 10 February 2011).

Cannon, Tom. 1994. *Corporate Responsibility – A Textbook of Business Ethics, Governance, Environment: Roles and Responsibilities*, London: Pitman Publishing.

Henderson, David. 2001. *Misguided Virtue: False Notions of Corporate Social Responsibility*, Wellington: New Zealand Business Roundtable.

Pritchett, L. and Summers, Larry. 2002. *The Elusive Quest for Growth*, Cambridge, MA: MIT Press.

Ritu, K. 2004. *The State of CSR in India 2004: Acknowledging, Progress and Prioritizing Action*, New Delhi: The Energy and Resources Institute (TERI).

Sandhya, U. 2006. 'Corporate Social Responsibility', *The Hindu*, 9 August.

Srivastava, Harish and Venkateswaran, Shankar. 2000. *The Business of Social Responsibility*, Bangalore: Books for Change.

Stoner, F.A.J., Freeman, E.R. and Gilbert, R.D. 2001. *Management*, New Delhi: Prentice-Hall of India Private Limited.

Sudip, M. and Kumar, V. 2005. *Emerging Trends in Corporate Social Responsibility: Perspective and Experiences from Post-Liberalized India*, Hyderabad: National Academy of Legal Studies and Research, University of Law.

CHAPTER 13

Empowering the Indigenous Groups through Peoples' Institutions: A Case of Social Transformation of Tribes in Andhra Pradesh

KOTESWARA RAJU PENMETSA

The Thematic Argument

This article portrays an approach aimed at empowering the indigenous groups through building peoples' institutions by ushering community driven development initiatives with a focus on social transformation (Roy Burman 1979; Heredia 1995; Pandey 1997; Naidu 2009). A process driven programme called *Maa Thota* is being supported by NABARD with financial support from Tribal Development Fund and being facilitated by local NGOs to bring harmony between tribal ecology and their development in a holistic manner. The focus is on rejuvenating and putting to its best use of the local natural resources and building stable livelihoods around the immediate ecosystem. The facilitating NGO's role is to transfer their managerial and organizational skills to the indigenous groups by creating peoples' institutions robust enough to manage the institutions created by the facilitation of the NGO, alternatively termed as Project Implementing Agency (PIA).

The Tribal Context

The tribes constitute a small but important element in India's population. These descendants of some of the earliest inhabitants of this sub-continent have contributed to the variety and richness of cultural forms in the country (Adhikary 2009; Munshi 2012). Over the centuries, they have preserved that richness which evolved into a distinctive style of life. In terms of the quality of life and cultural ethos most of the tribes stand out in sharp contrast to the general village populations of the land.

However, the tribes suffered a lot at the hands of the alien rulers as well as, in some cases, at the hands of local ruling compatriots (Bharikoke and Devi 2006). They bear the scars of oppression, exploitation, isolation and neglect, resulting in their relegation to a position of penury and often serfdom. Efforts were made by the Indians and Europeans at alleviating their problems through various approaches such as 'isolation', 'assimilation' and 'religious conversion' or 'proselytization'. But these efforts often met with partial success as they failed to understand the real needs and problems of the tribes and did not offer lasting solutions to their plight and predicament.

With the dawn of Independence, a modest beginning has been made to help mitigate the suffering of the tribes. From the First Five Year Plan onwards the policy towards tribal welfare and development has been undergoing changes – from the stage of Special Multi-purpose Tribal Development Block to that of the present concept of Sub-Plan strategy with integrated approach (also known as Integrated Tribal Development Project). In all, efforts of the plans have been made to eliminate exploitation, inequalities and ensure equitable distribution of the fruits of development. This has been much more marked from the Fifth Five Year Plan onwards. In spite of the ever increasing emphasis on growth with social justice, the social benefits have not been distributed equally and inequalities, both regional and local, continue to exist.

The richness of the wide variety of cultural life is the most invaluable heritage of the great Indian tradition. Life is nowhere more spontaneous and vivid in its fullness than in the small traditions of its tribal communities. More than 200 such communities are spread over the country from the Himalayas to the Indian Ocean and from Arabian Sea to the eastern frontiers adjoining Burma (now known as Myanmar). There are groups as large as a few millions and as small as a few hundred. Each of these groups, no matter what their number, is a proud community, participating in the national life, yet retaining its own identity.

Problems of Tribal Sustainability

The major casualty in any tribal belt is environment. Environmental imbalances and ecological degradation are rampant due to a host of reasons. This had devastating impact on the livelihoods of the indigenous groups who are totally dependent on their immediate ecosystem, triggering further environmental concerns. In order to address this menacing problem, NABARD (National Bank for Agriculture and Rural Development) has come up with a unique process driven programme called *Maa Thota* where the focus is on preserving the immediate ecosystem and regenerating the ecology through soil-moister conservation, rainwater harvesting and developing sustainable livelihoods through the development of orchards. Around this core programme there is the satellite programme of women development, educational advancement, health promotion and creation of wealth through capitalization of their forest produce as well as farm produce through value addition and market penetration. The indigenous tribes are supposed to acquire the organizational and managerial skills over a period of time, say seven years, in association with the facilitating NGO.

The Approach

Having realized the context the following vision and mission is evolved by DNR College to achieve the goals set by NABARD. The name of the project meant for the promotion of sustainable participatory livelihood programmes (*Wadi* model) in the tribal areas of West Godavari district; Andhra Pradesh with the service provision of DNR College was *Maa Thota*.

Vision

Facilitating the promotion of sustainable participatory livelihood programmes through farming and associated non-farm activities, aiming at the empowerment of the tribes, culminating in the improvement of the quality of the land and the people living on the land, through resource mobilization, management and conservation.

Mission

- To sensitize the tribal community regarding the importance, need, and advantages of pro-active management of natural resources in terms of mobilization, management and conservation.

- To mobilize the sensitized beneficiary tribal families to form into support groups.
- To build the capacities of the beneficiary tribal families in pro-active management of natural resources, crop production and harvesting techniques.
- To provide continuous technical, social, economic and market support to the beneficiary tribal families.
- To avert the tribal exodus in the wake of the desperation due to the failure of making use of their own natural resources in their vicinity.
- To initiate or collaborate with processing units and launching own or co-branded products produced by beneficiary tribal families for enlarged market generation, penetration and market capitalization with the value addition to plough back more wealth to the beneficiary tribal families.
- To institute systems of internal control, process documentation and certification of high standards with diligent practices of social audit by the constituent stakeholders.
- Above all to sustain the local initiative, by the time of the conclusion of the project, in a well-defined institutional framework, robust enough to enable and empower the tribes to take charge of their lives with full and adequate enjoyment of social security as a result of the human and social capital generated out of the efforts of the project *Maa Thota.*

Activities

- Situational analysis of livelihoods of beneficiary tribal families in the project area.
- Sensitizing the beneficiary tribal families in the need and advantages of pro-active natural resource management.
- Needs assessment of the beneficiary tribal families – livelihoods, financial and non-financial such as health, education and social security.
- Addressing the needs of the beneficiary tribal families.
- Initiating farming with an eco-friendly perspective and providing continuous technical, social, economic and market support to the beneficiary tribal families.
- Taking up exposure visits of beneficiary tribal families and arranging meets to share best practices to step-up the motivated efforts of the principal stakeholders.

- Collaborating with academic, research and market organizations in the field of cashew and other suitable and remunerative orchards, medicinal plantations, etc. with multiple cropping patterns for immediate, short-term and long-term incomes and also to enhance biodiversity, for effective crop management, harvesting technologies, post-harvest mechanisms, processing, value addition, market generation and penetration and capitalization.
- Instituting prudent and diligent system of internal control, following ethical values in process documentation and adopting systems of social audit by the stakeholders.
- Working in synergy with governmental, non-governmental and corporate organizations to tone up the thrust in attaining the stated objectives and overall human and social development issues.
- Endeavouring to create human and social capital so that the target community takes care of its own future affairs as a benefit accrued from the mechanism of sustainability of the project. A gradual withdrawal strategy too is of equal concern.

Project Structure

The project structure should be amenable for transforming the institutional approach into a community driven initiative. While most projects have a pyramidal structure of organizational management, as an institution that is committed to the evolution and progression of community based democratic institutions, DNR College has planned to work in unison with people in a manner of evolving organic integration of the different segments of the stakeholders. In synergy with the institutional framework being followed and advocated by NABARD, there will be three integral and internal arms for the project as shown in Figure 13.1.

The Management Advisory and Support Team

The management advisory and support team will comprise members from the PIA and the beneficiary community to usher the community driven approach. From the PIA, the president, secretary, treasurer, one nominated member of governing body of the DNR College Association along with the Project Director *Maa Thota* will be the members. From the beneficiary tribal community, the president, secretary, treasurer and one nominated member of the *Samutu*, the Federation

Figure 13.1

Three Integral and Internal Arms for the Maa Thota Project

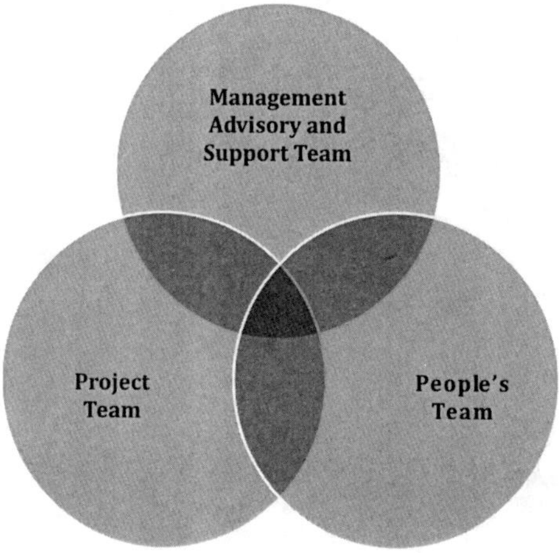

of Village Organizations being covered under the project will be totalling altogether to nine members.

The Project Team

As shown in Figure 13.2, the project team will be constituted by the project director, as the team leader, endeavouring to accomplish the project goals. He is to be supported by the deputy directors in functional areas and the participation of the heads of *Samutu* and *Gram Siris*-the Village Organizations, support groups and beneficiary families will further buttress the efforts to achieve the project goals.

The Peoples' Team

The peoples' team will comprise the constellation of the *Samutu* at the core and the *Gram Siris* in a radial manner as profiled in Figure 13.3. By the close of the project period, this peoples' team is expected to rise to the level of the PIA. This team will be facilitated to acquire the competencies and convictions of the PIA over the project period.

Community coordinators in association with the *Vikaspreraks*, being nucleus in the facilitation of the Support Groups, play the roles of a facilitator, enabler, and emancipator leading to the empowerment of tribal communities in areas of social, economic, health, educational and cultural spheres, culminating in the enhancement of quality of life of people with mechanisms for full and adequate enjoyment of social

Figure 13.2

Composition of the Project Team

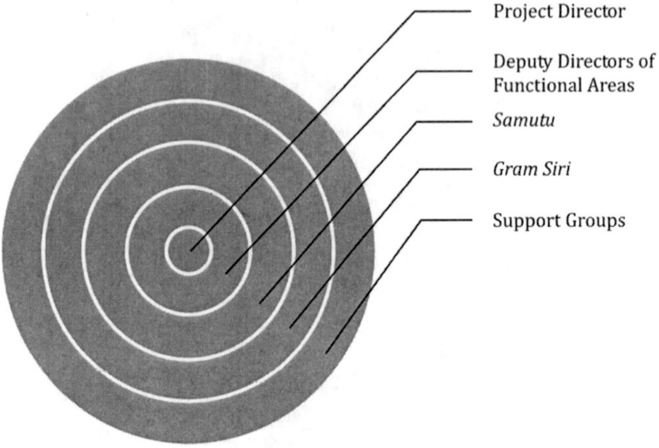

security by the beneficiary families, albeit through pro-active natural resource management.

Sustainability Mechanism and Withdrawal Policy

As an institution committed to the values of justice and empowerment through democratic processes, the focus would be on the creation of

Figure 13.3

The Constellation of People's Team

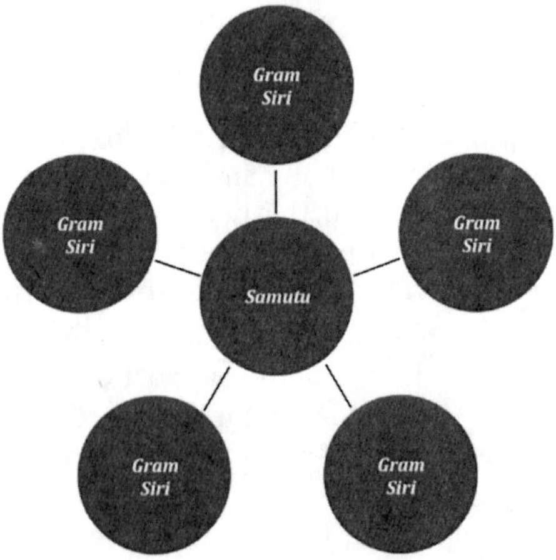

human and social capital whereby the primary stakeholders take charge of their lives. By ushering a community driven development approach through the facilitation of formation of human and social capital, a systematic withdrawal policy begins by the start of the third penultimate year and progresses in the ratio of 60 per cent, 80 per cent and 100 per cent, respectively, so that the transition of managerial responsibilities and transformation of the competencies of the principal stakeholders is not abrupt and inadequate.

Organogram

Executive Director

Deputy Directors

- Natural Resource Management
- Crop and Harvest Management
- Finance and Market Management
- Livelihoods and Institution Building

Cluster Coordinators

Community Coordinators

Focal Areas

- *Samutu Maa Thota* – building peoples' institutions.
- *Maa Thota* – the *wadi* component.
- *Gram Siri* – the community livelihoods and resource centre.
- *Sowbhagya* – the comprehensive approach to total tribal well-being.
- *Samvardhani* – Building capacities.
- *Samvidha* – Collectivization.
- Trinity – the synergic convergence between GOs, NGOs and corporate houses.

Samutu Maa Thota is the nucleus to transform the initial institutional approach of the *wadi* being facilitated by the Project Implementing Agency into a community driven approach to ensure sustainability of the project initiative. It does not lead to merely growing *wadis,* but generating wealth through value addition and market capitalization through people's institutions such as the village and *mandal samakhyas* (federations of village and *mandal* level productive enterprises-the *Gram Siri* and the *Vana Siri*). The new found practice wisdom of managing the project, is facilitated by the Project Implementing Agency, the DNR College. The age-old world view of the tribes, which has been very much founded on the tenets of sustainability, has to be channelized for advancing the tribal value of perpetual conservation as against the non-tribal characteristic of total and immediate exploitation of the resource potential of the region.

The *Maa Thota* – the *wadi* component takes care of developing and nurturing orchids as part of promoting sustainable livelihoods founded on the principles of resource mobilization, utilization and conservation.

Gram Siri strategizes on how the village level organization would function as a productive enterprise in terms of enhancing the livelihoods of the people while being discharging the functions of a community resource centre. Value addition of products and produce like tamarind, honey, *adda* leaves and cashew and their marketing through co-branding and branding operations and wealth maximization through collectivization is the principal goal of the *Gram Siri.*

Sowbhagya – the comprehensive approach to total tribal well-being explains how a holistic approach towards the development of human capital through harnessing and dovetailing the resources and services in the areas of health, education, livelihoods, housing and social security can enhance the access and availability of the same to the tribal people. Through awareness generation, sensitization, linkages and referral services and subscription, the access to and availability of these vital social services that fosters the human capital would be made available to the tribal people of the project for their integrated development.

Samvardhani dwells on the mechanism of building the capacities of the primary and secondary stakeholders of the project, with an enlarged emphasis on the women folk in view of their potential contribution to productive and collective efforts for individual and community development.

Samvidha paves the way for community sensitization for collectivization, social mobilization and participation for partnering with the project initiatives, since community's voluntary participation is essential both for individual and collective advancement.

Trinity – the Synergic Convergence conceptualizes how best a functional relationship can be established between the different key stakeholders working for the tribal development. The different sectoral and target oriented programmes of the government such as Comprehensive Land Development, the project mode activities of District Water Management Agency and the Horticultural mission along with ITDA programmes are potential areas for convergence. The service potential and the knowledge management activities of the non-governmental organizations are to be roped in. Market opportunities and services under corporate social responsibility of the corporate sector are other opportunities of collaboration. The incremental services from service organizations would be used for resource optimization for enhancing quality of life of the people of the project area. Regular advocacy-cum-partnership meets are the processes of this convergence.

The Peoples' Institution

The following are the principal goals of the PIA: (i) to promote and sustain social capital through the facilitation of human capital, (ii) thereby to improve the quality of life of people, focusing on the marginalized and vulnerable, through fundamental missionary approaches of human facilitation, social mobilization and community action, (iii) to ensure with rights-based perspective, social justice and equity aimed to address social exclusion, that is guided by the core values of conviction for human dignity and worth, democratic self-governance and compassion, (iv) to excel in service delivery, and (v) to realize the goal of ensuring the people universal access to social services.

The PIA strives to create an enabling environment for the persons working for and with the project, such as: (i) the primary and secondary stakeholders together creating community awareness, in a multidimensional manner, (ii) sensitization of the general public on the need for a positive response towards making use of the support systems, and (iii) community mobilization with a synergic convergence between GOs, NGOs and corporate organizations, to improve the universal access to services of welfare and development so that people realize their individual and social needs.

Through the facilitation of an active participation of all the stakeholders together, the PIA would endeavour to improve the functioning in terms of community programme vision through the promotion of social capital whereby the rights of the people are best protected through community action and advocacy issues. It would be further toned up with the interface of leadership programme, vision for better articulation in terms of influencing and mobilizing people out of the credibility and legacy established, in conjunction with scientific programme vision. This will be accomplished by developing the mechanisms for absorbing the strides of scientific development aiming to promote the human and social well-being.

The *Samutu* – Federation of the Peoples' Organizations

The tribal communities are known as the little republics. Their social life is built on the principles of democratic processes. All adult members in the community enjoy the right of self-determination. They are actively involved in all the decisions concerning their lives. This very democratic fabric helps in transforming the institutional approach into a community driven approach by fostering the support groups and their federations. The *Gram Siri* is the village level federation with an executive committee and general body. While all the beneficiary tribes are the general body members of *Gram Siri* (the VDC), the executive committee is elected by the general body, which should be constituted by positions like President, Secretary, Treasurer and six other members from the different groups of the village. The *Gram Siri* is a village level productive enterprise to take care of the livelihood issues and value addition and marketing of their products and produce. Apart from this they should function as community resource centre to discharge a variety of roles and responsibilities to cater to the needs of the community people.

All such *Gram Siris* would elect an apex body at the project level, by forming into a federation, which was traditionally known as *Samutu* in the local dialect. It should take care of project level productive enterprises called *Vana* Siri. While these organizations are the custodians of the project funds right from the beginning and monitor its progress, from the fourth year onwards they assume the executive powers in a phased manner. From such stage they gradually replace the project staff in a phased manner and even start receiving remuneration from the project funds and are, thus, attuned to operate the processes of the project. The details of the transition are indicated in Appendix 13.I and the budget costs are furnished in Appendix 13.II.

During the project period surplus generation and wealth creation is to be facilitated through the *Gram Siris* and *Vana Siris* to create a corpus for the project which can sustain the budgets, particularly the costs of the institutional structures of the people, for the continuity of the *Maa Thota* initiatives.

The project being facilitated by DNR College is in the third year of its partnering and hopes to be successful in attaining the declared mission of empowering the indigenous groups through their own institutions.

Appendix 13.I

Year-on-Year Remuneration for Institutional Structures and Community Driven Structures (in Rupees per month)

S. No.		*Designation in the Project*	*1stYr (₹)*	*2ndYr (₹)*	*3rdYr (₹)*	*4thYr (₹)*	*5thYr (₹)*	*6thYr (₹)*	*7thYr (₹)*
1.	(a)	Project Director	6,000	6,000	6,000	6,000	6,000	6,000	6,000
	(b)	President	—	—	—	1,000	1,500	2,000	2,500
2.	(a)	Project Coordinator and Dy Director	9,000	9,500	10,000	10,500	11,000	11,500	12,000
	(b)	Institution Bldg/Secretary	—	—	—	1,000	1,500	2,000	2,500
3.	(a)	Dy. Director Livelihoods	6,000	6,500	7,000	7,500	8,000	8,500	9,000
	(b)	Treasurer	—	—	—	1,000	1,500	2,000	2,500
4.	(a)	Dy Dire-Natural Resource Management	6,000	6,500	7,000	7,500	—	—	—
	(b)	BhooSamrakshak	—	—	—	1,000	1,000	1,000	1,000
5.	(a)	Deputy Director-Plant Protection and Harvest Management	6,000	6,500	7,000	7,500	8,000	8,500	9,000
	(b)	VanaSamrakshak	—	—	—	1,000	1,000	1,000	1,000
6.	(a)	Deputy Director-Social Audit and Monitoring	3,000	3,500	4,000	4,500	5,000	5,500	6,000
	(b)	Paryavekshak	—	—	—	1,000	1,000	1,000	1,000
7.	(a)	Community Coordinators	2,000	2,000	2,000	2,500	2,500	2,500	2,500
	(b)	Vikasa Prerak	—	—	—	1,000	1,000	1,000	1,000
8.	(a)	Accountant	3,000	3,000	3,000	3,000	3,000	4,000	3,000
	(b)	Karanam	—	—	—	1,000	1,000	1,000	1,000

Notes: All entries prefixed with '(a)' are indicating the remuneration of institutional structures and likewise all entries prefixed by '(b)' are for community driven structures.

Appendix 13.II

Financial Commitment towards Institutionalization of Community Driven Approaches

Designation in Project	*1st Year*	*2nd Year*	*3rd Year*	*4th Year*	*5th Year*	*6th Year*	*7th Year*
President	—	—	—	1,000	1,500	2,000	2,500
Secretary	—	—	—	1,000	1,500	2,000	2,500
Treasurer	—	—	—	1,000	1,500	2,000	2,500
Bhusamrakshak	—	—	—	1,000	1,000	1,000	1,000
Vanasamrakshak	—	—	—	1,000	1,000	1,000	1,000
Paryavekshak	—	—	—	1,000	1,000	1,000	1,000
Vikasaprerak-(0,0,0,5,5,10,10)	—	—	—	5,000	5,000	10,000	10,000
Karanam	—	—	—	1,000	1,000	1,000	1,000
Monthly Financial Commitment	—	—	—	12,000	13,500	20,000	21,500
Yearly Financial Commitment*	—	—	—	1,44,000	1,62,000	2,40,000	2,58,000

Note: All figures are in ₹

* The grand total is 8,04,000

References

Adhikary, Ashim Kumar. 2009. *The Tribal Situation in India: Structure, Change and Continuity*, New Delhi: Abhijeet Publications.

Bharikoke, Neera and Devi, Uma. 2006. *Tribal Rights in India*, New Delhi: Serial Publications.

Heredia, R.C. 1995. 'Tribal Education Development: Need for a Liberative Pedagogy for Social Transformation', *Economic and Political Weekly*, 30 (16), pp. 891–897.

Munshi, Indra. (ed.). 2012. *The Adivasi Question*, New Delhi: Orient Blackswan.

Naidu, P.R. 2009. *Tribal Development in India: Curtain Raiser*, New Delhi: Adhyan Publications.

Pandey, A.K. 1997. *Tribal Society in India*, New Delhi: Manak Publications.

Roy Burman, B.K. 1979. 'Challenges and Responses in Tribal India', in M.S.A. Rao (ed.), *Social Movements in India*, New Delhi: Manohar.

CHAPTER 14

Communitization of School Education for Development: Analysing Role of Village Education Committees in Punjab

D.P. SINGH AND RITU MOR

The Background

Community participation in education in India is not a new concept. Community has always been thought of as an integral part of the educational set-up. The initial years of post-Independence India were marked by the centralization of education. The efficiency of the local decentralized bodies was suspected and criticized so far as the question of their ability to use the power was concerned (Wankhede and Sengupta 2005). A notion prevailed that everything belonged to the government and not to the community. This idea could not sustain for long as centralization failed to affect a change in the quality of school education (Noronha 2003).

The First Education Commission clearly spelt out the need of decentralization of school education and involvement of local bodies in the processes related to school improvement in 1966. According to the Commission, the immediate goal was to associate communities with the schools in their locality (GOI 1986). Community participation as a primary strategy for ensuring decentralization in school education got another major boost with the adoption of National Policy on Education, 1986 (GOI 1986). The Policy laid primary emphasis on decentralized planning and management of elementary education in the country (GOI 1997). The Policy visualized direct community involvement in the form of Village Education Committees (VECs) for management and improvement in school education at the village level. The Programme of Action (POA) 1992 further strengthened the Village Education Committees by providing that the state government will lay down general guidelines regarding the constitution of village education committees and established norms of accountability in respect of the heads of these institutions.

The 73rd and 74th Constitutional Amendment Acts, 1993 provided for decentralization of the activities and facilitated the transfer of power and participation of the local self-government institutions or the Panchayati Raj Institutions (Govinda and Diwan 2007). *Sarva Shiksha Abhiyan* (SSA) assigned greatest importance to systematic mobilization of the community and creation of an effective system of decentralized decision-making. The Right to Education Act, 2009, also recognizes the role of local governance in school education by necessitating the formation of a School Management Committee (SMCs) in each school (GOI 2010). Thus, we see that community participation, as a novel and unique approach of development and school governance, has always been emphasized in all the education related policy documents in India in order to build a synergic relationship between the community and the government with a view to create a sense of ownership, better resource management and overall development at the grass-roots level (GOI 2005; Govinda and Diwan 2007).

Communitization of School Education in Punjab

The state of Punjab has been accorded a fair amount of importance to education in the major policy initiatives. Over the years promotion of education has been one of the top priority areas for the state government. A vast network of schools and institutions of education have been set up. A number of schemes and incentives have been launched to motivate the parents so that the children go to school. The Census figures reveal that there was a substantial increase in the literacy rates in Punjab since 1971. The data shows that the literacy rate of Punjab in the year 1971 was 34.12 per cent which increased to 43.37 per cent in 1981 and 58.5 per cent in 1991. The rate of literacy of 69.95 per cent in the year 2001 shows an increase of more than 11 points from the previous figures (GOP 2004).

Similarly, there has been a substantial increase in the number of primary and upper primary schools. Since 1966, when the state of Haryana was carved out of Punjab, the primary schools have witnessed an increase of 52 per cent up to the year 2000. Likewise, the upper primary schools increased by 34 per cent. At primary level, the percentage increase in the number of teachers has been 49 per cent during the 1966–2000 period. During the period 1991–2001, the percentage increase in the number of literates has gone up by 49.55 points (GOP 2004).

As regards the school infrastructure, Punjab is considered to be one of the best in school infrastructure in the country. In fact, as per the Educational Development Index (EDI) 2011, prepared by National University of Educational Planning and Administration (NUEPA), Punjab is at the top in infrastructural parameters in the country followed by Pondicherry and Andaman and Nicobar Islands. The EDI reflects remarkable gains made by Punjab on parameters of school accessibility, infrastructure and teaching facility outcomes. According to District Information System for Education (DISE) 2009–10, more than 98 per cent habitations in the state are covered by a primary school within one km. There were just 2.9 per cent single classrooms schools and only 3.39 per cent single teacher schools in the year 2009–10. The average number of classrooms was 3.6 and in 99.45 per cent schools, drinking water facility was available in the premises while 99.02 per cent schools had girls' toilets. The average number of teachers per school was 3.2 while the student-classroom ratio was at 25 and the student-teacher ratio was 27 (GOP 2010).

Thus, it is evident that the state has achieved a considerable success in the field of school education in terms of teachers and infrastructure. Being fully aware of the social commitments, the Government of Punjab continues to ensure that all communities get access to and the advantage of educational facilities. Giving unqualified priority to school education, the Punjab state government has introduced various innovative approaches like mobilizing community support and introducing decentralized planning to help achieve the goal of universalization of elementary education.

The Village Education Committees (VECs) known as Village Education Development Committees (VEDCs) are in place since 2002. The *Sarva Shiksha Abhiyan* (SSA) which hinges around decentralized planning and community participation is being religiously implemented by the Government of Punjab since 2002 (GOP 2002). The SSA has empowered the local community by their involvement in all aspects of plan formulation. Community based planning process is being carried out by delegating powers to Panchayati Raj Institutions

(PRI) and constituting the Village Education Development Committees (VEDCs). The equity issues related to girls and children from socially disadvantaged groups and with special needs are being properly attended under the programme.

The programme has helped bridge the social gaps and to a great extent ensured that no child aged 6–14 years remains out-of-school in the state. Since the implementation of the programme, there has been a visible impact on the school infrastructure as well as quality of school education (GOI 2000). Considerable progress has been on access related in terms of getting out of school children into the school and ensuring that they stay there. The quality dimensions of school education are also being addressed by ensuring that the teachers are present and quality teaching learning takes place. Broad strategies under the SSA are institutional reforms in order to improve the efficiency of delivery systems and to reach out to the educationally deprived children across all communities (GOI 2002). Incentives such as stipends and scholarships, free books and uniforms and mid-day meals, etc. have been initiated in all government schools in order to improve the attendance and to boost overall literacy.

The Study

The above background provides that the link between community participation and equitable quality education is very crucial. This link necessarily forms the basis of social development at grass-roots level (Govinda and Varghese 1991). Keeping this in view, the present paper is based on the findings of a research study on the contribution of Village Education Development Committees in improving school education thereby ensuring development of the community. The specific objectives of the study is to explore the contribution of Village Education Development Committees in the promotion of elementary education in terms of increase in enrollment, improvement in school result and reduction in school dropout rate, contribution of members in individual capacity, conduct of meetings and activities undertaken with reference to improving infrastructure, fund-raising and incentives to students.

Methodology

The present study attempts to evaluate the functioning of the Village Education Development Committees (VEDCs) in the two of the least literacy districts namely Mansa and Muktsar of the state of

Punjab. The process of formation, composition and functions of these committees have been studied primarily from the secondary sources largely consisting of the documents, reports, circulars and guidelines of the state as well as the central government (GQP n.d.-a, n.d.-b, n.d.-c).

For the sample, a total of 52 villages as per required indices, have been selected from both the two educationally backward districts of Punjab. Accordingly 26 villages from Mansa and 26 villages from Muktsar were selected from the sample. The selection of a village eventually led to the selection of a school and the respective Village Education Development Committee (VEDC). Ultimately, 52 rural primary schools and 52 VEDCs were studied for the present investigation. A total of 411 members of the VEDCs constituted the sample for the present study. The members of the VEDCs comprised head teachers, Panchayat members, members of the PTA, ex-servicemen, retired teacher and philanthropist/NRIs.

Village Education Development Committees in Punjab

Village Education Committees (VECs), known as Village Education Development Committees (VEDCs) or in Punjabi addressed as *Pendu Sikhiya Vikas* Committees (*Pasvak*), were formally announced in October 2002 in Punjab. After the announcement, VEDCs actually started functioning after the panchayat elections held in June 2003. Formation of these bodies has legitimately ensured people's participation in the school related activities at the village level by involving the teachers, parents, women representatives and social activists. The VEDCs act as local management committees for each school which actively participates in the development activities of a school and implements them. The VEDCs are expected to be helpful in improving the standard of school education in the village through community involvement. VEDCs are viewed as a medium to accelerate the pace of development of primary education in the state. The VEDCs provide representation to both the elected local bodies like PRIs and the common people. A VEDC consists of eight members. Two members are from the village panchayat, two members are from the PTA, one member each has to be an ex-military personnel, a philanthropist/NRI and a retired teacher of the Government of Punjab. The head teacher of the school concerned is the secretary of the VEDC (GQP 2002).

Working of Village Education Committees: Structural-Functional Aspects

The guidelines amended as per Memo No. E-media/2010/VEDC/ 30340–379, Dated: Chandigarh, 19 March 2010 states that the chairman of VEDC will be elected by majority from amongst the VEDC members other than the ex-officio members. The Panchayat shall pass a resolution for nominating the PRI members and send it to the head teacher. The tenure of Panchayat members as the members of VEDC shall be co-terminus with the tenure of the Panchayat. With the formation of new Panchayat, new nominations shall be done. The nominations of the PTA members will be done by the school PTA by passing a resolution. Only those PTA members shall be the members of the VEDC whose children study in that particular school. PTA members shall remain the members of the VEDC till the time they are members of the PTA.

The headmaster shall nominate the ex-serviceman, philanthropist, retired teacher and the senior-most teacher. For ex-serviceman, the highest rank and length of service shall be given preference. As philanthropist such person from amongst the villagers shall be nominated who has donated the maximum amount to the school. The senior-most teacher from among the school-staff excluding the headmaster shall be the member of the VEDC. The senior-most teacher is authorized to act as the secretary of VEDC in the absence the head teacher. The formation of VEDC shall be sent to DEO (EE) by the head teacher for approval. The DEO (EE) shall approve the formation and send it back to the head teacher.

The tenure of VEDC shall be three years from the date of approval by the DEO (EE). By passing a resolution, the VEDC can change any unfit member but such a change can be made only with the approval of the DEO (EE). In case any member of the committee remains absent in three consecutive meetings, his membership shall be cancelled and a new member shall be nominated in his place. In any case, the position of any VEDC member shall not remain vacant for more than three months. The monthly meeting of VEDC is compulsory. If need arises, more than one meeting can also be held. This meeting will be held in the school as per pre-decided date and time. The notice of the meeting shall be issued by the member secretary. The quorum of the VEDC meeting shall essentially be 1/3 of its total members. The VEDC meeting or any other work of the committee shall not remain interrupted due to the absence of a member. The VEDC is fully authorized to take any appropriate decision in the interest of the school. The VEDC shall pass resolution for all its decisions or the works to be undertaken in future. Every resolution shall have the signatures of each participating member. It is the responsibility of the member secretary to record the minutes of the meetings and to enter the passed resolutions in the school register.

The VEDC shall open a separate account for the grants received from SSA (GOP n.d.-a). This account shall be jointly operated by the member secretary and the chairman. The VEDC chairman or any other member of the VEDC shall not, in any case, ask to bring any school record outside the school premises. The VEDC meeting shall be held within the school only. For signing any school record and cheque, the VEDC chairman shall himself come to the school. If such a thing is not done or observed, the member secretary shall report the matter to the district head quarter. On the basis of this report, the DEO shall issue a show cause notice to the concerned chairman or member and in case of an unjustified explanation; they can be removed from their position. It is the sole responsibility of the member secretary to maintain the accounts and get all SSA work and activities completed as per the guidelines. The VEDC will hold at least one meeting between 2nd and 7th day every month. The records of the resolutions passed in these meetings will essentially be duly maintained (GOP 2002).

The Findings of the Study

The Contribution of VEDCs in Increasing Enrollment

It was found that before the formation of VEDCs in the high literacy villages, the gross enrollment increased by 0.51 per cent during the year 2000–01 and 2001–02 and by 2.10 per cent during the second year (2001–02 to 2002–03). After the formation of VEDCs, the gross enrollment increased by 2.25 per cent during 2003–04 and 2004–05 while by 11.46 per cent during 2004–05 and 2005–06. This shows that the rate of increase in the gross enrollment in the high literacy villages was higher after the formation of the VEDCs in comparison to the period of two years when VEDCs were not in place. Thus, it can be said that the Village Education Development Committees contributed positively towards the rate of increase in the gross enrollment in the high literacy regions.

Across gender, the VEDCs had a positive contribution towards increasing girls' gross enrollment as well as boys' gross enrollment in the high literacy regions. In the low literacy regions, before the formation of VEDCs, there was a decrease of 5.03 per cent during the year 2000–01 and 2001–02 whereas in the following year (from 2001–02 to 2002–03), the enrollment increased by 3.54 per cent. After the formation of the VEDCs, the gross enrollment dropped by 2.72 per cent during the first year (2003–04 to 2004–05) and by 3.13 per cent in the following year (2004–05 to 2005–06). Thus, from the findings it is concluded that the formation of VEDCs did not make any significant contribution with regard to the increase in enrollment of students in the low literacy villages. Across the gender similar pattern was followed. Hence, it is concluded that VEDCs did not have any role across gender of students.

Improving School Results

In high literacy villages, before the formation of VEDCs, the number of failures declined by 42.33 per cent during the year 2000–01 and 2001–02, while the number of failures increased by 62.02 per cent during the year 2001–02 and 2002–03. After formation of the VEDCs, the number of failures increased by 24.27 per cent in year 2003–04 and 2004–05, while it decreased by 11.7 per cent during 2004–05 and 2005–06. Thus, from the findings, it is suggested that the VEDCs did not play any role in improving the school results in the high literacy villages. In the low literacy regions, before the formation of VEDCs, the number of failures increased by 1.29 per cent during 2000–01 and 2001–02 and by 5.73 per cent during 2001–02 and 2002–03. After the VEDCs were formed, there was a drop of 56.7 per cent in the number of failures during 2003–04 and 2004–05 and further a drop of 22.89 per cent was witnessed during 2004–05 and 2005–06. Thus, it is suggested that since the school results have improved after the formation of VEDCs in the low literacy regions, the VEDCs have played a positive role towards reducing the number of failures, thus improving the school results.

Reducing Dropout

In high literacy villages, before formation of VEDCs, the dropout rate has decreased by 16.67 per cent during 2000–01 and 2001–02 and by 34.28 per cent during 2001–02 and 2002–03. After the formation of the VEDCs, the dropout increased by 19.67 per cent during 2003–04 and 2004–05 and there was a decrease of 65.21 per cent during 2004–05 and 2005–06. This means that the VEDCs did not play any positive role in reduction of dropout rate in the high literacy villages.

In the low literacy villages, before the formation of the VEDCs, the dropout rate has witnessed an increase of 57.14 per cent from 2000–01 to 2001–02 whereas the dropout rate decreased by 32.72 per cent during 2001–02 and 2002–03. After the VEDCs were formed, the dropout rate increased by 105.17 per cent during 2003–04 and 2004–05 and it got reduced by 35.25 per cent during 2004–05 and 2005–06. From the findings, it is suggested that the VEDCs did not play any significant role in reducing the school dropout rate in the sampled schools situated in the low literacy villages.

Contribution of VEDCs Members in their Individual Capacity

The findings revealed that only about one-fifth (20%) members discussed the problems of the school with the appropriate officials or the parents while a little more than one-fifth (22.4%) members had paid one or two visits to the school with an aim of monitoring the school environment. As regards the member-teacher interaction on issues relating to school improvement, only 35.8 per cent members gave an affirmative reply. About 44 per cent members had collected money for organizing sports activities in the school and contributed towards arranging funds/donations for the school. In general, the findings suggested that the contribution of individual members of the VEDCs with regard to school improvement has not been very encouraging except for the head teachers. Thus, the study underlines the need for initiating some programme for morale boosting of the VEDCs members so that they develop a feeling of belongingness towards their school and contribute significantly in their individual capacity.

Conduct of Meetings

The present study finds that the meetings of the VEDCs are not held in accordance with the guidelines laid down by the *Sarva Shiksha Abhiyan* Authority of Punjab and most of the norms regarding conduct of meetings of these bodies are not followed in letter and spirit. The meetings of the VEDCs are not at all a monthly feature. In fact, no formal meetings of the VEDCs are held. The meetings of the VEDCs are held on papers only. Whenever a grant is received, the head teacher/secretary after recording the minutes of the meeting on his own, sends the register to the residences of the VEDCs members for signatures. This way the paper formality is completed. The VEDC members do not come to the school for meetings in spite of requests from the secretary. It is the primary reason why the VEDC meetings are to be held in circulation. A huge majority (89.5%) of the VEDC members themselves agreed that they don't give any importance to the VEDC meetings as they viewed the meetings of VEDCs just as a formality. As per them, the VEDCs meetings don't serve any purpose; attending or not attending them does not make any difference. The study finds that there is a general lack of interest among the teachers as well as the VEDC members towards VEDCs. Therefore, it is suggested that there is a need to reorient the VEDC members in such a way that they begin to value the importance of VEDC meetings.

Issues Discussed in the Meetings

There are two major issues that always find a place in the minutes of the VEDC meetings. The first relate to making provisions for infrastructural facilities like construction of rooms, repair of buildings, purchase of furniture and other such civil or maintenance jobs while the second is regarding the utilization of grants. The major focus of VEDCs remains on the issues relating to financial matters. An omission in the matters involving money (such as not discussing them in the VEDCs meetings) entails serious disciplinary action. Therefore, the secretary/head teacher is particularly careful in completing all the paper work in this regard. To escape any reprimand or punishment from the higher authorities, such issues are always recorded in the minutes of the VEDCs meetings. The issues like quality of teaching-learning material, classroom processes and learning achievements, etc. are not considered of much worth for the meetings as avoidance of these issues don't entail any serious punishment.

Activities Undertaken to Improve Infrastructure

Majority (81.1%) of the VEDC members informed that the main activities undertaken by the VEDCs were about repairing and constructing the classrooms followed by repairing and constructing the toilets and ramps (70.4%). Nearly one-third (28.19%) respondents told that the VEDC repaired/constructed boundary wall of the school whereas a little more than one-tenth (11.1%) of these respondents informed that the Committee purchased furniture for teachers and students. The VEDCs do not give any importance to fund-raising activities. About 87.3 per cent VEDC members replied in the negative when asked if the VEDC had undertaken any fund-raising activity in their community. About 12.7 per cent members informed that the VEDC they represented had collected donations for organizing some sports events.

Activities as Incentives to Students

The VEDCs participate only in those activities which are sponsored either by the state or by the central government. As regards the incentives to students, 82.5 per cent VEDC members informed that the VEDCs organized exposure visits for the school children whereas 79.6 per cent respondents told that free text books/notebooks schemes were being monitored by these committees. As per 77.6 per cent respondents, the VEDCS were involved in giving cash prizes to the first three toppers of each class in every school. Other activities where the VEDCs participated related to vocational courses for girls like the course on computer literacy, embroidery and soft skills. There was no scheme/incentive known to have been launched by the VEDCs themselves, i.e. by generating their own funds.

Miscellaneous Activities

As regards the activities of general nature, a huge majority of respondents (85.4%) were of the view that the VEDCs did not undertake any activity other than those mandated under government norms. Only about 14.6 per cent respondents told that the VEDCs they represented had undertaken one or the other activities for increasing enrollment and school results and reducing the dropout rate. These activities were about putting up of bill boards at various places within the village displaying the details of civil works and utilization of grants, making announcements from the *gurdwaras* from time to time regarding various school related issues, organizing cultural programmes and sports, holding door-to-door meetings, organizing lectures and speaking to local activists/community leaders about the problems at the school.

Conclusions

Overall, the contribution of VEDCs towards school related activities other than those mandated under SSA norms is very poor. There is a general lack of initiative and motivation among the VEDCs members. The VEDCs, by and large, remain a male bastion and the personal merit of a woman remains overshadowed by the patriarchal stereotypes and culture factors adverse to gender equality. Age still remains an important criterion in determining the leadership positions in rural areas particularly in the school related activities. The VEDCs in Punjab continue to be dominated by the not so young people. In the absence of specific reservation provisions, the people of dominant castes tend to monopolize the leadership positions in villages with reference to community participation in the school related activities.

Nevertheless, in spite of the not so good scenario, the involvement of community through Village Education Committees in Punjab has given a good start in operationalizing the participatory decentralized model of development in all kinds of activities of the school governance. The process of community participation has created a space of its own with regards to school improvement and thus accelerating the process of social development at the grass-roots levels.

References

Government of India. 1986. *Programme of Action: National Policy on Education*, New Delhi: Ministry of Human Resource Development, Department of Education.

____. 1997. *DPEP Guidelines*, New Delhi: Ministry of Education, NCERT.

____. 2000. *Sarva Shiksha Abhiyan - A Programme for Universal Elementary Education: Framework for Implementation*, New Delhi: Ministry of Human Resource Development, Department of Elementary Education and Literacy.

____. 2002. *Janshala: Towards Empowered Community Schools*, New Delhi: Ministry of Human Resource Management (Online available at http://www.education.nic.in/Janshala/contents/pdf).

____. 2005. *National Curriculum Framework 2005*, New Delhi: National Council of Educational Research and Training, December.

____. 2010. *Compilation of 50 Years of Indian Education: 1947–1997* (Online available at http://www.education.nic.in/cd50years/home.htm.).

Government of Punjab. 2002. *Norms for Village Education Development Committees*, Chandigarh: *Sarva Shiksha Abhiyan* Authority.

____. 2004. *Punjab Human Development Report*, Chandigarh.

____. 2010. *District Information System for Education, 2009–10*, Chandigarh.

____. n.d.-a. *Guidelines for Maintaining Accounts under Village Education Development Committees*, Chandigarh: *Sarva Shiksha Abhiyan* Authority.

____. n.d.-b. *How the Construction Works are to be Done under Village Education Development Committees*, Chandigarh: *Sarva Shiksha Abhiyan* Authority.

____. n.d.-c. *Guidelines for Rural/Urban Education Development Committees*, Chandigarh: *Sarva Shiksha Abhiyan* Authority.

Govinda, R. and Diwan, Rashmi. (eds). 2007. *Community Participation and Empowerment in Primary Education*, New Delhi: Sage Publications.

Govinda, R. and Varghese, N.V. 1991. *The Quality of Basic Education Services in India: A Case Study of Primary Schooling in Madhya Pradesh*, New Delhi: National Institute of Educational Planning and Administration.

Govinda, R. 2007. 'Dynamics of Decentralized Management in Primary Education: Policy and Practice in Rajasthan and Madhya Pradesh', in R. Govinda and Rashmi Diwan (eds), *Community Participation and Empowerment in Primary Education*, New Delhi: Sage Publications.

Noronha, Anjali. 2003. 'The Community in Charge: Shades of Experience from Madhya Pradesh', in R. Govinda and Rashmi Diwan (eds), *Community Participation and Empowerment in Primary Education*, New Delhi: Sage Publications.

Wankhede, G.G. and Sengupta, Anirban. 2005. 'Village Education Committees in West Bengal, India: Planned Vision and Beyond', *International Journal of Educational Development*, 25, pp. 569–579.

CHAPTER 15

Risk Behaviour of PLHA and Social Development in India

SANGEETA SHARMA DHAOR

Understanding Social Development

Social development is an all-encompassing term. It necessarily requires balancing of all kinds of its sub-categories such as economic, political or social. The world over concerned academic scholars in most social science disciplines have been relentlessly trying to make comprehensive sense of the term by offering a wide range of its definitional meaning and explanation. Since the main objective of this chapter concerns more with its empirical status in a particular case site rather than semantic and theoretical arguments over this term, I have limited its scope in favour of the former rather than the latter. Being a social work professional, researcher and academician, I have taken recourse to Gore's following explanation of the term 'social development' as a starting point for this discussion and clarity:

> The concept of social development is inclusive of economic development but differs from it in the sense that it emphasizes the development of the totality of society in its economic, political, social and cultural aspects. In this sense, social development planning is not concerned with planning exclusively for social services, any more than it is with exclusive planning of economic growth (2003: 20).

Indian experience in terms of development has been more of chasing the path of development treaded by the western or developed countries rather than carving an indigenous niche for itself. We began with a goal of large scale rapid industrialization. But in the process we forgot to check the effects of the same in terms of rapid migration, reducing agrarian economy, increasing service sector with an emerging middle class and an ever expanding poor class owing to uncontrolled inflation and reduced job opportunities partly as a result of population explosion. Lately, globalization has accelerated the race for material possessions. The boom in information and technology sector and concomitant emergence of business processing outsourcing service industries in all major urban centres of various sizes have put a new income in the hands of young educated strata of the society. As a result, an impressive growth rates could be achieved on account of the gross domestic product touching about 8 per cent on an average basis during 2004–2012. But behind this impressive GDP figures, what we are watching is polarity of incomes. It was inadvertently forgotten that within 'shining India' and in the midst of '*Bharat Uday*', we have a poor India where poverty line has been defined as income of ₹ 32 per day.

The internationally renowned scholar James Midgley, has most succinctly argued that:

> 'The phenomenon of persistent poverty in the midst of economic affluence is one of the most problematic issues in development today. In many parts of the world economic development has not been accompanied by an attendant degree of social progress. The phenomenon has often been referred to as distorted development' (1995: 3–4).

In this kind of chequered scenario, distributive justice must be sought with an aim to provide opportunities to every one. Warning bells to this effect have been periodically sounded by eminent social work scholars. Gore (2003) is one such scholar who has emphatically argued that the intervention of the state was expected to ensure that the social justice aspects of development were not lost sight of in the pursuit of goal of economic growth. It is found that losing the sight of social development has resulted in a slow progress of our other related human development goals. India is ranked at number 134 out of 187 countries in the human development ranking by the United Nations.

AIDS as Challenge to Social Development

Health is one of the most important components of human development and healthy people being one of the most important contributors to social and economic development. The most important resource a country could have, is its healthy people;

especially its youth. Young persons are the forerunners of social change and social development. They are the most productive force of the nation. How this young force conducts itself determines the direction a nation is heading to. A nation full of energetic, educated (as well as semi-educated) and well-guided youth is an asset; and is usually way ahead from the one burdened with the liability of illiterate, weak, disoriented and diseased youth. There are numerous studies on wastage of youth due to it being badly enslaved and entangled in the addictions of tobacco, liquor, sex or drugs. Such *lumpen* (i.e. unemployed and unemployable) youth easily becomes fodder for political and criminal exploitation by the vested interests in the political parties of all hues as well as in society. Among all the diseases striking the humans with varying degrees of morbidity and mortality like cancer or Ebola virus, AIDS stands out as a unique challenge to humanity as a whole. AIDS is a multi-dimensional affliction. Its infectious spread is a major challenge to physical sciences and also as much as to social sciences. Let us begin with the profile of its prevalence in India.

Table 15.1

HIV Prevalence in Women and Men in India by Age

Age	*Total (%)*	*Women (%)*	*Men (%)*
15–19	0.04	0.07	0.01
20–24	0.18	1.17	0.19
25–29	0.35	0.28	0.43
30–34	0.54	0.45	0.64
35–39	0.37	0.23	0.53
40–44	0.30	0.19	0.41
45–49	0.33	0.17	0.48
50–54	NA	NA	0.34

Source: National Family Health Survey Data, 2005–06.

India is home to 2.5 million of HIV positive persons. It is reported that the total number of *People Living with HIV/AIDS* (PLHA) in India is estimated at 23.9 lakhs (19.3–30.4 lakhs) in 2009. Children less than 15 years account for 3.5 per cent of all HIV infections. Whereas 83 per cent infected persons are in the age group of 15–49 years. Of all HIV infections, 39 per cent (9.3 lakhs) are among the women (Government of

India 2012). HIV/AIDS is affecting people belonging to reproductive age group of 15 to 45 years. Within it, the most are falling in the age group category of 15–35 years which covers and represents the youth.

AIDS stands for acquired immunodeficiency syndrome. 'Acquired' as per Oxford Dictionary and Thesaurus stands for, 'to buy, come by, to earn, to get, to obtain, to procure, to purchase.' This clearly means that this infection is not 'caught' like other airborne infections but is acquired. This implies that the person has a control over the means of getting infected. The first stage of getting infected involves the introduction of virus into the blood stream. HIV, as it has come to be known, is an untreatable viral infection acquired through all or any one or more of the following four modes:

1. Unprotected sex with an infected partner.
2. Sharing infected needle and syringes.
3. Transfusion of infected blood or blood products.
4. From infected pregnant mother to her unborn child.

These four risk factors are described to everyone during pre- and post-test counselling of persons with possible HIV infections. Two categories of infected persons come for these sessions – one which comprises those who either volunteer on their own as a result of increased risk perception or are referred to by their consulting doctors for HIV test when they visited them due to some associated illness under investigation.

The basic objective of these counselling sessions is to prepare a person mentally for any adverse results of these tests. In case the person is diagnosed positive, counselling is done to him/her for safe behaviour for the protection of the loved ones. Such a person is also guided for timely treatment. But this process is not easy. It is full of obstacles caused by PLHA's complex behaviour patterns which are risky for others in contact with the PLHA. A workable pragmatic strategy is suggested as follows:

> Counselling of HIV patients was based on social cognitive theory that describes the individual as a complex being, molded by personal factors, environment and learned behaviour. This emphasizes a technique called self efficacy, whereby one can come to self regulate anti-social behaviour through an understanding of one's environment and by developing certain expectations about the outcome of a certain behaviour. Social worker can use these insights in order to counsel people suffering from anti-social behaviour (this quote is cited from: www.ehow.com/about_5438150_modern_social_work_theory).

BCC as Interventionist Strategy: An Empirical Inquiry

This counselling strategy is popularly known as behaviour change communication (BCC) and it is presumed that an informed person, by virtue of his knowledge would behave in a more responsible manner and keep him/her as well as the loved ones protected from the infection. These efforts are made with the purpose of increasing risk perception among the PLHA individuals so that their behaviour is positively monitored and checked in order to prevent HIV infection. Di Climente's convictions and suggestions in this regard are of particular relevance and interest. He says that, 'Social Cognitive theory has proven particularly useful as a foundation for developing HIV risk reduction intervention, especially for adolescents and multi-culture populations. Cornerstone of this model includes the provision of timely and accurate information, developing and mastering social competency skills through observational learning techniques' (DiClimente 1997: 193–194).

These behavioural theories and interventionist practices for monitoring and preventing certain risky behaviour of the PLHA generated an extremely useful perspective on the issue. It helped during the research work in making an assessment of the behaviour of persons living with HIV/AIDS and gave the researcher an idea as to what extent our 'behaviour change interventions' and strategies are effective.

Profile of the Respondents

In the empirical research, 105 HIV positive persons were contacted and in-depth interviews were conducted along to obtain insights into the quantitative profile of the problem. Apart from it, in order to overcome the deficit of qualitative insights into the issue, some focused group discussions on major issues were conducted. In this research exercise, more than half the respondents (53.3%) were from the age group of 30–60 years whereas 47.7 per cent respondents were from the age group of 18–30 years.

Operationally, for the purpose of this research investigation, only two groups were formed. For a better understanding of this behavioural phenomenon, a further break-up of the category was made to know the exact range in which most of the PLHA got classified.

Table 15.2

Distribution of the Respondents by Age

Age Group	*Frequency*	*Per cent*	*Cumulative Per cent*
18–24	09	8.5	8.5
25–29	29	27.6	36.1
30–34	28	26.6	62.7
35–39	18	17.1	79.8
40–44	07	6.6	86.4
45–49	10	9.5	95.9
50–54	03	2.5	98.4
55–60	01	0.9	99.3
Total	105	100	100

As can be seen in Table 15.2, most of the PLHA in the sample fell in the age group of 25–39 years. A big number of 75 respondents out of 105 belonged to this age group.

Table 15.3

Distribution of the Respondents by Education Level

Education Level	*Frequency*	*Per cent*	*Valid Per cent*	*Cumulative Per cent*
Illiterate	34	32.4	32.4	32.4
Upto Middle School	47	44.8	44.8	77.1
Middle School Above	24	22.9	22.9	100.0
Total	105	100	100	

The literacy level of the respondents, as presented in Table 15.3, was found to be low with 32.4 per cent respondents being illiterate and 44.8 per cent respondents were reported as educated only upto middle school. Only 22.9 per cent were educated beyond middle school.

In this sample size, more than half, i. e., 57 per cent respondents were male, 38 per cent were females and 5 per cent were transgender. Figure 15.1 shows graphic break up of respondents by sex. In this study, the awareness of HIV transmission among the respondents was explored along with their sexual preferences and actual behaviour to see if they still are in risk behaviour after being diagnosed with HIV.

Figure 15.1

Distribution of Respondents by Sex

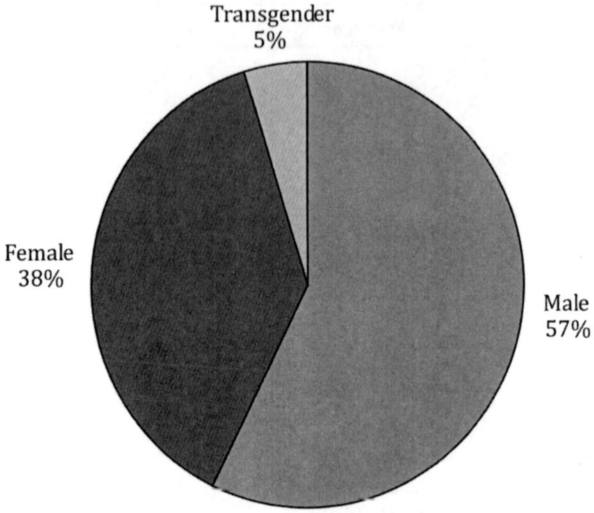

Table 15.4

Distribution of Respondents' Awareness about Modes of HIV Transmission

Causes of HIV Transmission	*Frequency*	*Per cent*	*Valid Per cent*	*Cumulative Per cent*
None	09	8.6	8.6	8.6
1 mode	05	4.8	4.8	13.3
2 modes	09	8.6	8.6	21.9
3 modes	29	27.6	27.6	49.5
4 modes	53	50.0	50.0	100.0
Total	105	100.0	100.0	

As per Table 15.4, 53 (50%) respondents were aware about all the four modes of transmission of HIV. If we look closely, we find that 13.3 per cent persons knew only one or no mode of transmission. We found that due to rigorous interventions on awareness generation of masses for HIV transmission, only 27.6 per cent knowing only three, and 50 per cent of the respondents knew of all the four modes of transmission. This was disheartening, as rigorous interventions on information, education and communication (IEC) was done with this group.

Figure 15.2

Distribution of Respondents by their Native States

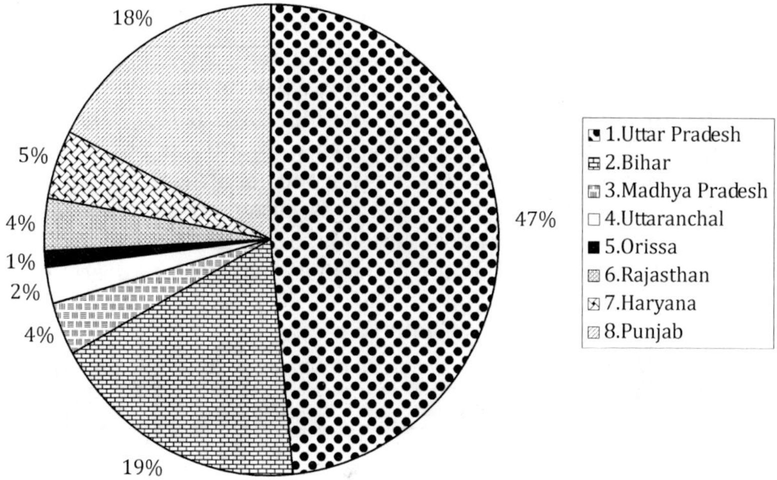

The respondents' profile in Figure 15.2 suggests that most of them had migrated from neighbouring states, though some had come from far off states like Orissa. Nearly half of them, i.e. 47 per cent, had come from Uttar Pradesh, 19 per cent were from Bihar, 4 per cent were from Madhya Pradesh, 2 per cent were from Uttaranchal, 1 per cent has migrated from Orissa, 4 per cent were from Rajasthan, 5 per cent were from Haryana and 18 per cent were from Punjab.

As shown in Table 15.5, it was found that in all, 84 (80%) respondents got attracted to the persons of opposite sex, as compared to 14(13.3%) persons who were feeling attracted to same sex and 07(6.7%) respondents getting attracted to both the sexes.

Table 15.5

Sexual Attraction to Persons of Different Sex by Age of the Respondents

Attraction to	*Age 18 –30 n=49*	*Age 30–60 N=56*	*Total N=105*
Opposite sex	40(81.6)	44(78.6)	84(80)
Same sex	06(12.2)	08(14.3)	14(13.3)
Both	03(6.1)	04(7.1)	07(6.7)
Total	49(100)	56(100)	105(100)

Notes: Chi-square cannot be computed as in some cells the expected frequency is less than 5. Figures in parentheses are percentages.

Out of the two age groups, the younger age group had a higher per cent of persons 40 (81.6%) getting attracted to opposite sex and only 44 (78.6%) respondents of the older age group got attracted to persons of opposite sex.

In the younger age group, six respondents (12.2%) reported getting attracted to persons of same sex, whereas eight (14.3%) got attracted to same sex persons from the older age group. Only three (6.1%) persons of the younger age group were attracted to both the sexes whereas four (7.1%) of older age group got attracted to persons of both sexes. Interesting conclusion is drawn from these data. Attraction to person of same sex was found to be slightly higher in older age group. Similarly bisexuals are found more in the older age group.

Table 15.6

Success in Making Relations with Person of Choice by Age of Respondents

Success	*Age 18–30 n=49*	*30–60 N=56*	*Total N=105*
Yes	35(71.4)	34(60.7)	69(65.7)
No	14(28.6)	22(39.3)	36(34.3)
Total	49(100)	56(100)	105(100)

Note: Figures in parentheses are percentages.

It has been found that persons belonging to younger age group in the sample were more successful in forming sexual relations with persons of their choice as 35 (71.4%) were successful in forming relations with persons of their choice as compared to only 34 (60.7%) persons belonging to older age group. This analysis shows that younger people are sexually more active.

Table 15.7

Attraction to the Persons of Opposite, Same or Both Sexes by the Income of the Respondents

Attraction to	*No Income n=30*	*₹ 500–4,000 n=47*	*₹ 4,000/and Above n=28*	*Total*
Opposite sex	27(90)	41(87.2)	16(57.1)	84(80)
Same sex	02(6.7)	05(10.6)	07(25)	14(13.3)
Both sexes	01(3.3)	01(2.1)	05(17.9)	07(6.7)
Total	30(100)	47(100)	28(100)	105(100)

Notes: Chi-square cannot be computed as in some cells the expected frequency is less than 5. Figures in parentheses are percentages.

Table 15.7 indicates that with the increase in income level, more persons are getting attracted to persons of same sex. Only two respondents (6.7%) belonging to no income category feel attracted to person of same sex. A meagre total of five (10.6%) respondents belonging to ₹ 500–4,000 income category feel this way and six (25%) respondents belonging to ₹ 4,000 above income category feel attracted to same sex persons.

This may imply that as a person becomes financially better, he is able to explore his/her sexuality and express it as against those with no income. When the person is dependent on family especially when s/he is not earning he may behave in normatively and socially acceptable ways. With increase in earning capacity and, thereby, in the income, a person becomes more empowered and expressive of sexuality.

Table 15.8

Attraction to the Persons of Opposite, Same or Both Sexes by the Marital Status of the Respondents (3.1 by 1.6)

Attraction to	*Married n=63*	*Unmarried n=19*	*Widow/ Deserted n=23*	*Total*
Opposite sex	53(84.1)	10(52.6)	21(91.3)	84(80)
Same sex	07(11.1)	06(31.6%)	01(4.3)	14(13.3)
Both sexes	03(4.8)	03(15.8)	01(4.3)	07(6.7)
Total	63(100)	19(100)	23(105)	105(100)

Notes: Chi-square is 11.55071, hence not significant. Figures in parentheses are percentages.

In our overall assessment, based on data presented in Table 15.8 the attraction to opposite sex was found to be the highest among 80 per cent respondents. In the category of married respondents, 84.1 per cent felt attracted to the person of opposite sex, 11.1 per cent feel attracted to the same sex and 4.8 per cent felt attracted to both the sexes. This is far more accentuated in case of unmarried respondents where only 52.6 per cent feel attracted to opposite sex, 31.6 per cent feel attracted to same sex and 15.8 per cent felt attracted to persons of both the sexes. We fail to reject the null hypothesis that attraction to persons is not associated with marital status of the respondents.

This shows that due to social pressure people with different sexual orientation are marrying (to person of opposite sex) but still feel attracted to person of the same sex or both the sexes. According to generally observed trends, this particular category tends to become a highly vulnerable group, as they may indulge in homosexual activity; in protected or unprotected sex, and thus pose a great risk to all the prospective partners including their wives/spouses.

Table 15.9

Success in Forming Relation with Persons of Choice by Marital Status of the Respondents

Successful	*Married n=63*	*Unmarried n=19*	*Widow/Deserted n=23*	*Total*
Yes	49(77.8)	12(63.2)	08(34.8)	69(65.7)
No	14(22.2)	07(36.8)	15(65.2)	36(34.3)
Total	63(100)	19(100)	23(100)	105(100)

Notes: Chi Square is 13.89137, hence significant at .01 levels. Figures in parentheses are percentages.

This small and modest empirical investigation (Table 15.9) has yielded a very interesting finding. It has revealed that a majority of 49 (77.8%) respondents in the 'married persons' category were able to form relation with persons of their choice. This is followed by unmarried at 12 (63.2%) and drastically low for widow or deserted category at eight (34.8%).

We can safely conclude from this analysis that in all 22.2 per cent of the married persons are not able to form relation with the person of their choice; 36.8 per cent of the unmarried category and 65.2 per cent of the 'ever married now single' category are not able to form relation with person of their choice. It must be noted that his information was received in response to an open question where no time frame was given.

Conclusion: We conclude that marital status determines the success in making relation with person of one's choice.

Table 15.10

Distribution of Respondents by their Participation in Commercial Sex Activity

Participation in Commercial Sex Activity	*Frequency*	*Per cent*	*Valid Per cent*	*Cumulative Per cent*
Yes	39	37.1	37.1	37.1
No	66	62.9	62.9	100.0
Total	105	100	100	

The role of commercially available sex in spreading the AIDS is intensely debated issue in this genre of research. Our study reports new findings and generates fresh insights into the behaviour of this phenomenon. The evidence reported in Table 15.10 shows that only 37.1 per cent of the respondents participate in commercial sex activity. A big segment of 63 per cent respondents did not take to commercial route to sex.

Table 15.11

Commercial Sex Activity by Marital Status of the Respondents (3.5 by 1.6)

Commercial Sex Activity	*Married n=63*	*Unmarried n=19*	*Ever Married Now Single n=23*	*Total n=105*
Yes	19(30.2)	14(73.4)	06(26.1)	39(37.1)
No	44(69.8)	05(26.3)	17(73.9)	66(62.9)
Total	63(100)	19(100)	23(100)	105(100)

Notes: Chi Square is 13.38699, significant at .01 levels. Figures in parentheses are percentages.

However, when this category was further broken into married and unmarried segments, we observed that commercial sex activity was found to be highest in unmarried respondents at 73.4 per cent. This was found much low in married at 30.2 per cent and even lesser at 26.1 per cent amongst 'ever married now single' group.

We reject the null hypothesis that commercial sex activity is not affected by marital status of the respondents. Hence, we conclude that 'commercial sex work activity' is affected by marital status and that the unmarried persons participate more in commercial sex activity. This is an important finding reported by this research exercise.

Findings on Status of Protective Usage

Usage of protective devices or aids like condoms is considered to be a safe practice in abating the spread of HIV/AIDS the world over. Suitable awareness campaigns are initiated and rigorously put in effect by keeping in mind the cultural and social context of a particular ethnic, caste or race, community, country or the continent. In this regard, it may be safe to assume that the awareness strategies and initiatives which work for Asia or Africa may not work for Europe or Australia and vice versa.

Table 15.12

Consistency of Condom Usage by the Marital Status of the Respondents

Consistent Condom Use	*Married n=63*	*Unmarried n=19*	*Widow/Deserted n=23*	*Total*
Yes	29(54.7)	02(11.8)	04(28.6)	35(41.7)
No	24(45.3)	15(88.2)	10(71.4)	49(58.3)
Total	53(100)	17(100)	14(100)	84(100)

Notes: Chi square is 10.95528, significant at .01 levels. Figures in parentheses are percentages.

In our research study (Table 15.12), condom usage among the respondents was found to be low. In all, only 35 (41.7%) respondents used condoms when engaged in sexual activity. As against this, 49 (58.37%) respondents did not use condoms. Amongst those using condoms, the highest 29 (54.77%) were the 'married respondents'. This was followed by 'ever married now single' category with four (28.67%) respondents using condoms. From the unmarried group only two (11.87%) respondents reported using condoms during sexual activity which is very low, especially for HIV positive persons as this is one of the four routes of its widespread transmission. A total of 10 (71.47%) 'ever married now single' category respondents, 15 (88.27%) unmarried and 24 (45.37%) married persons reported not using condoms. We conclude that condom usage is affected by marital status of the respondents. For a greater methodological clarity, it must be stated that this question was applicable and asked to only those 84 respondents who reported having sexual activity on the basis of last week's recall.

Table 15.13

Condom Usage by the Age of the Respondents

Condom Usage	*18–30 n=41*	*30–60 Yrs n=43*	*Total n=84*
Yes	13(31.7)	22(51.2)	35(41.7)
No	28(68.3)	21(48.8)	49(58.3)
Total	41(100)	43(100)	84(100)

Notes: Chi square is 3.26852, significant at .05. Figures in parentheses are percentages.

Table 15.13 shows that of all the persons who admitted being sexually active, more than half, 58.3 per cent, did not use condoms as against 41.7 per cent who did. A total of 28 (68.3%) of the younger age group reported not using condom as against 21 (48.8%) of thc older age group. Majority of the older age group 22 (51.2%) respondents reported using condom as against only 18 (31.7%) respondents from the younger age group who used condoms.

In the light of our research findings, we reject the null hypothesis that condom use is not affected by age of the respondents and conclude that the age does affect condom use. The older persons are reportedly using condoms with higher frequency. From this reported findings, we conclude that the older group was found to be more responsible with regard to the non-transmission of HIV or protection of the partner from pregnancy or HIV.

In the research exercise, we are concerned with developing the infrastructure for prevention and control of the epidemic. Many initiatives were taken for this purpose. Identifying the core groups and bridge population and intensifying prevention activities were also the main agenda of this research. This included core groups like FSW (Female Sex Worker), MSM (Men having Sex with Men) and intravenous drug users alongwith bridge population like, long distance truck drivers along with migrants were outreached for HIV/AIDS prevention activities. Focus was on prevention of HIV to new persons by 'behaviour change communication'.

As has been understood that despite many awareness sessions for the HRG (High Risk Group) within the communities and the persons who are visiting ICTC (Integrated Counselling and Training Centre) of various hospitals, the data reflects that general awareness of HIV amongst the PLHA, i.e. 'persons living with HIV/AIDS' is far from satisfactory than expected. The respondents are suffering from the infection themselves. Hence, a better understanding is expected from them. Secondly, a rigorous effort from government is being made to increase their risk perception with an aim to change their risk behaviour. This is an alarming situation as NACO's (National AIDS Control Organization) call for behaviour change communication seems to have failed with HIV positive persons. Not using condoms especially by HIV + persons is like a volcano of HIV epidemic which is waiting to be erupted.

Emergence of Alarming and Worrisome Scenario

As is evident from the profile (refer to Table 15.3), the respondents were illiterate or semi-literate and with low income levels. Most of them have migrated to New Delhi. They originate from neighbouring states of Uttar Pradesh, Haryana, Punjab and Rajasthan. These migrants and long distance truck drivers are to be considered as bridge population which carries the HIV infection from core group of MSM/FSW to the general population. The most alarming trend found is that the age group of the majority PLHA-respondent falls in the category of youth migrants.

The behaviour of the young persons who were HIV positive was found to be risky, with more of young persons having opted for commercial sex activity and having chosen not to use condoms. As the age progresses, the choice seems to be more of persons of same sex than of the opposite sex. Age and income seem to be affecting the choices. Besides attraction, a majority of the respondents are able to form relation with person of their choice. However, it is noticeable that a majority of 84 per cent respondents are attracted to persons of opposite sex. Although attraction is affected by marital status, more unmarried respondents are getting sexually attracted to persons of same sex (MSM) or to both sexes (bisexual). But, if we look at it otherwise, probably the persons who get attracted to same sex choose to stay single. Attraction to same sex person was found in married persons too, and some of the married persons have reported getting attracted to persons of both sexes, which is a very risky behaviour.

Success in forming relationship is associated with marital status of the respondent with married persons being more successful than unmarried. Age too affect this behaviour, as younger persons are reported to be more successful than older ones. Of all the sexually active 84 respondents, the condom usage was reported by only 35 respondents (41.7%). The rest of the 49(58.3%) respondents reported that they do not use condoms. However, older persons were found to be using condoms than younger ones. Apart from older persons, married persons were found to be using condoms more than unmarried and 'ever married persons'. About 88.1 per cent of the unmarried respondents reported not using condoms in their recall of last sexual activity.

Yield and Insights from Qualitative Method

After hitherto having macro and quantitative statistical analysis and insights into PLHA respondents' risk behavioural patterns, it shall indeed be interesting to know about the qualitative responses on some of the perceptional and crucial determinants of risk behaviour of PLHA respondents. These challenging and sensitive field investigations on condom usage habits and sexual behaviour were conducted by using the methodology of Focused Group Discussions (FGD) separately with FSW and MSM. The following major insights were yielded from these FGDs:

1. *'Now when we are already HIV positive, what other threat can be there for us to insist on condom use. If we are getting good money, let the sex be without condom'* (Statement of one HIV+ FSW from Seema Puri in an FGD conducted in Jhilmil Colony).
2. *'I feel like giving it out (i.e. infecting) to everyone who comes to us. Even I got it from someone like them (i.e. infected) only. I am enraged; I want to infect it to all men out there who spread this virus'* (Another FSW in same FGD).

   In one of the FGDs conducted in Jehangirpuri with HIV positive, MSM and transgender respondents, there was an air of anger in the participants.
3. *'I do not want to use condom, I do not even tell my partner that I am (HIV) positive. Now since I have got it, I will give it to others out there who gave it to me,'* said one transgender.
4. At this juncture someone with a more balanced and sensitive outlook to life and more informed about HIV/AIDS said that: *'Pagal hai tu! Pehele maza, fir saza hai yeh to. Aur jyada bimar ho jayegi'* ('Are you mad! First indulge and enjoy, and then get this punishment. That way you will become more infected').
5. This was further retorted by the first transgender respondent as: *'Humain bhi to kissi ne diya hai ye virus, ab kuchh nahi kar shakte'* ('Someone has given this virus to us, now you cannot do anything').
6. Continuing the dialogue of despair, another respondent said that: *'Humain to pata hhi nahin tha is bimari ka. Pata hota to parhez karte. Ab jab sab khatam ho gaya, to kya fayada jankari ka?'* ('We did not know about this disease. Had we known, we would have refrained from it. Now what is the benefit of this information, when everything is finished?').

These statements of qualitative responses have truly captured the feelings of hopelessness, guilt, being cheated, anger, frustration and despair prevalent among the PLHA-FGD participants. There is a bitter but understandable base feeling of revenge prevailing in some of the sex workers and MSM, especially the transgender. These responses and situations need to be handled most carefully as the behaviour under consideration is very private and autobiographical. Unless a respondent-participant is ultra-sensitively motivated and adequately informed by a competent and well-trained social worker or socio-medical intervention specialist, such behaviour cannot be controlled as it is too deep-rooted, deceptive and private.

What is most worrisome is that these negative and 'anti-other' sentiments lead these HIV positive respondents to a feeling of victimization which, in turn, leads them to a state of hopelessness. It seems that there is a need to keep the HIV positive persons well informed about the ill effects of unprotected sex. Awareness about long asymptomatic stage of the infection must be created. Perceiving every client/partner as a potential carrier of HIV is important to encourage them to practice no risk or low risk behaviour.

Channeling youth energy towards positive and constructive activities is very important. The HIV infected youth must be involved in this awareness raising and behaviour-correctional campaigns. Such youth can become epitome of self-directed AIDS activists. If the youth of today's India is ill and undirected, a huge productive force of the country becomes a wasted resource. This resource can be utilized by guiding them well on the path of wellness.

Conclusion

Above findings of this research reflect that persons living with HIV/AIDS are following high risk behaviour. Besides, the diagnosis of having HIV infection has not changed their behaviour much. There is a need to look into the dynamics of risk behaviour as BCC needs to be strengthened. One also needs to look into the external factors affecting behaviour. Such factors like: (i) education level of the youth, (ii) the push factor which force a youth to migrate to greener pastures in search of jobs, (iii) poor living conditions at the place of destination with no outlet for excessive youthful energy, etc. can and must be guided in the right direction.

We as social scientists believe that inherently all the individuals can contribute to the society, but our behaviours govern our present as well as our future in the same way it has governed our past. Behaviours are largely learned, owing to the response to certain situations or environment. Even if we try to change the behaviour our surroundings push us back to same pattern. There is an insufficiently tested belief that 'an individual is a product of interaction between the nature and nurture'. This controversy is still not resolved. An individual with his vulnerabilities and environment with its pushes and pulls act upon a person to make him 'behave' in a certain way.

We must work on the environment to ensure that youth are well educated to take right decisions in times of peer pressure, or societal stigma and discrimination. They and their families are given social security during the times of lean periods owing to draught or floods. It must be ensured that their product gets comparable market price and they are not exploited in the hands of money-lenders, or wholesale buyers. Youth must be educated about the importance of small family, education of children and the government school be made better with a lower teacher-student ratio, so as to ensure that going to school is fun-filled. This shall deliver a well-informed and aware youth. All these small things can be achieved only if there is a political will and able execution of the existing schemes to make a change in environment.

There is a need to work on the education of the families towards youth sexuality so as to help him/her take an informed decision. Responsible, safe and accountable sexual behaviour must be either acquired or be inculcated from adolescent phase itself. This can be done by self-education and acquiring self-awareness. But this may not be possible for all strata of the young population. In the urban areas, it may be possible due to the presence of liberal and progressive climate. However, the real challenge posed in this matter is from among the illiterate, semi-literate, socially backward, economically weaker and religio-culturally conservative sections of rural (and in some cases peri-urban and urban) society. Gopinath (2007: 18–19) has made the following relevant observation for tackling the challenge of HIV/AIDS effectively in the rural areas:

> For rural youth, the favourable policy environment to engage Panchayati Raj Institutions in addressing HIV and AIDS is backed by flagship programmes for local development like NREGS, National Rural Health Mission and other rural development schemes. These flagship programmes aim at reducing health problems, by addressing the larger issues of livelihood, migration and overall welfare of the villages. Given the complexity of HIV and AIDS in terms of health, livelihood, stigma, right to live in dignity, etc. the grassroot leaders are best placed to address the problems, not only as communicators and facilitators but also in much more substantive ways.

HIV/AIDS is an infection with roots and persistence in poverty, inequality and ignorance ridden environment. If we work on these factors and make HIV positive persons responsible towards the self and society we can somewhat prevent the spread of this epidemic. Youth, as is rightly understood, are harbingers of any kind of change. They have led many social movements (Shah 2004), and time has come when the same youth has to lead a health movement in India. – be it either as an aware victim of HIV/AIDS or as a volunteer of anti-AIDS crusade.

References

Cox, David and Pawar, Manohar S. 2006. *International Social Work: Issues, Strategies and Programs*, New Delhi: Vistaar Publications.

Di Climente, Ralph J. 1997. 'Looking Forward: Future Direction for Prevention of HIV among Adolescents', in Lorraine Sherr (ed.), *AIDS and Adolescents*, Amsterdam: Harwood Academic Publishers.

Gopinath, Usha. 2007. *Role of Panchayats in Addressing Gender and HIV: A Trainers Handbook*, Bangalore: Institute of Social Sciences.

Gore, M.S. 2003. *Social Development: Challenges Faced in an Unequal and Plural Society*, Jaipur and New Delhi: Rawat Publications.

Government of India. 2012. *Annual Report 2010–11*, New Delhi: Department of AIDS Control, Ministry of Health and Family Welfare.

Midgley, James. 1995. *Social Development: The Developmental Perspective in Social Welfare*, London: Sage Publications.

Shah, Ghanshyam. 2004. *Social Movements in India: A Review of Literature*, New Delhi: Sage Publications.

The Economic Times, 2 November 2011. Retrieved from www.ehow.com/about_5438150_modern_social_work_theory (Accessed in April 2011).

CHAPTER 16

Gandhian Philosophy, Social Welfare and Social Development: Social Work Perspective

MAHAJAN P. MANI AND SREEPRIYA C.K.

Several biographers of Gandhian ideas, influences and contribution have stated that relevance of Gandhi continues uninterrupted. Louis Fischer (1997) was one of the renowned biographers of Gandhi. The nature of conflict, war and violence is changing continuously. The world is no longer the same as it was before Gandhi. He has ever been a gallant fighter against all social evils practiced in India in the most obnoxious manner. His thought was based on the values of ethical traditions of all religions that was why he could muster the dauntless courage against all social malpractices. He derived his strength from the Almighty that he could fight for a noble cause according to the dictates of his conscience. His uncompromising but peaceful fight against injustice and inequality made him an example worthy of emulation whose gospel influenced even the world.

Gandhi is an all time great social thinker and activist (Bharati 1995a). He had a very clear understanding of all sort of problems faced by the people and the nation. He presented before the public well thought suggestions and guidelines to overcome these limitations. The purity, freshness and simplicity made his thoughts unique. Gandhi emerged as a source of inspiration to all and he could influence people belonging to all walks of life because he not only preached what he thought but also practiced his ideas in life. Gandhi was, thus, a living example for the people to follow. The clarity, quality and depth of his thoughts have made Gandhi popular not only in his lifetime but even decades after his death.

One of the areas in which Gandhi has made an excellent contribution is the field of social welfare and development (Mazumdar 1964). Before getting into the Gandhian concept of welfare and development, let us first look into what these terms imply. Development is a concept that has relevance in various fields such as social, political, economy, spiritual, personal and emotional. In each field, the concept may have different purpose. However, the emphasis here is on social development. According to one view, 'Social development refers to an integral, value loaded cultural process encompassing the natural environment, social relations, education, production and consumption and well-being. The guide on development of the Food and Agricultural Organization states that the ultimate purpose of development is to provide everyone with ever increasing opportunities for a better life. It, therefore, requires an equitable distribution of income and other social resources in order to promote justice and efficient production, to raise the level of employment substantially, to expand and improve facilities for education, health, nutrition, housing, social and cultural well-being' (Mehta 1999: 43). Welfare, on the other hand, '... is an organized system of social services and institutions designed to aid individuals and groups to attain satisfying standards of life and health and personal and social relationship which permit them to develop their full capacities, to promote their well-being in harmony with the needs of the families and community' (Singh 1991: 86–87).

Gandhi had a clear vision regarding welfare and development. His concept of welfare and development is based on the philosophy of humanitarianism and spirituality (Mukherjee and Ramaswamy 1994). He believed that it is the moral responsibility of each and every human being to work for the welfare of the humanity and he visualized a society where there is no discrimination based on caste, class, colour and creed. He wanted all men to be free from all sorts of discrimination and exploitation. Hence, he questioned the evil practice of untouchability and advocated *harijan* (Scheduled Castes, *dalit*) welfare, pleaded for the equality of women, introduced his scheme of basic education, addressed the problems of health and sanitation and had special concern for lepers. Emergence of Gandhi in the Indian public life changed the basis of whole social and economic framework of India.

By development he meant that each and every individual and village should grow into self-sufficiency so that they do not have to depend on others. Gandhian *sarvodaya* and constructive programmes are the ways to attain his concept of welfare and development. Gandhi's versatility made every single object on earth a subject of his thought. Even the minute elements that were neglected by other thinkers captured his attention. He made wonderful observations and presented thought provoking and inspirational ideas to the public. The influences of his social thought are seen in the welfare policies pursued by the Government of India and many state governments since the achievement of political freedom.

His constructive programme aimed at changing the whole social and economic framework of India (Prasad 1958). He not only dedicated his entire life to serve the mankind as well as society but could also inspire several men to follow his path. There were several social and religious reformers and reform movements before the arrival of Gandhi, but none of them had been successful in gaining mass support. But Gandhi was capable of uniting them and gaining their support. Gandhi did not limit social work to a particular framework just like any other subject. His concept of social work was very deep and vast. The Gandhian concept of social work is linked to all other aspects that touches human and social life such as humanity, spirituality, morality, compassion, political freedom, role of state and government and co-operation. His ideas on all these areas are supported by a very strong philosophical background.

Gandhian Philosophy of Welfare and Development

Webster's *New International Dictionary* defines philosophy as: 'The science which investigates the most general facts and principles of reality, human nature and conduct: specially, and now usually, the science which comprises logic, ethics, aesthetics, metaphysics and the theory of knowledge'. Social work profession deals with human beings, their attitude, problems, well-being, etc. and hence the social work philosophy is based on humanitarianism, liberalism and democracy. Social work has not produced great philosophers and, hence, it has to use the thoughts of others and concern itself mainly with its methods (Misra 1994: 85). But Gandhi had his own vision of society and social work. He visualized that with genuine lead and guidance, the young men and women can fruitfully be employed for eliminating the social evils and re-installing the higher moral values in society. He presented before the Indian youth an excellent pattern of social work with a strong philosophical base and unique methods (Misra 1994 :85–91). Gandhian philosophy of social work which had influences of Hindu philosophy consists of the following components.

Value of Spirituality

A striking feature of Gandhian philosophy of social work is its emphasis on spirituality. His belief in god had served as the base for his philosophy. According to Gandhi, god is an unseen power that is present everywhere and controls everything and the faith in god will unite human beings. Belief in god will teach everyone to be truthful, to love and cooperate, and to be non-violent. To quote Gandhi: 'To me, god is truth and love; God is ethics and life and yet he is above and beyond all these. God is conscience. He is a personal god to those who need his presence. He is embodied to those who need his touch. He is the purest essence. He is all things to all men. He is in us and yet above and beyond us' (Gandhi 1925: 1). Gandhi said that god is beyond the reach of human senses but with a pure heart and strict moral and spiritual discipline one can feel the presence of god and there by attain self-realization.

Gandhi stressed the relationship between man and god. He said that every individual should try to realize the existence of god. Prayer, truth and self-discipline are the steps suggested by him to reach god. He believed that this relationship will regulate all aspects of human life. Gandhi declared that Truth is God. By this he meant that truth is the only finest and best attribute of god. Truth is eternal as god and is to be respected and worshipped as god. Gandhi also believed that whenever truth is present god is also present and that truth is just the other name of god. Prayer, according to Gandhi, is not mere demanding and asking but longing of the soul to reach god for his blessings. He said that one should have a pure heart to pray and, hence, prayer also implied admitting mistakes and weakness. Gandhi wanted men to shed their ego while praying and only then he can realize his inner self. He also believed in *karma* and re-birth. Gandhi, thus, points out that belief in god, search for truth and purification of minds are essential for people to help themselves as well as others which is the essence of social work.

Value of Individual

Gandhi considered individuals as the nucleus of all social concerns. He held the view that the focus of social transformation or development should be individuals. If individuals become perfect, then state will automatically become perfect. By perfection Gandhi did not mean the material comforts, luxuries and achievements of all individuals but the moral and spiritual well-being of each individual. This is a condition where each individual is able to love the whole mankind without any discrimination based on race, class, caste, etc. and are able to work for the unity of mankind.

The ten commandments of Gandhi that will help individuals to attain the state of perfection are truth, love, chastity, restraint of appetite, possess only of essentials, one's bread must be earned by the sweat of one's brow, man's duty is to serve his neighbour, equality of mankind, equality of all the great faith of the world and fearlessness. Apart from these commandments confession, *brahmacharya* (celibacy), fasting and prayer also contribute to the composite philosophy of Gandhi (Dadge 1997: 72).

Non-violence

This is another major component of Gandhian philosophy. In Mukherjee's words, 'Non-violence means non-appreciation and abhorrence of power for domination, control and profit. It concentrates on the development of majority. Through non-violence all the problems of the society can be solved' (1991: 19). Gandhi considered that truth and non-violence are the universal principles of morality and he considered them absolute. Gandhi believed that truth and non-violence are not matters for mere individual practice but for the practice by groups, communities and nations. Gandhi believed that non-violence will help individuals to realize truth. The evolution of non-violence in Gandhi was relatively a later development in his activities. During First World War Gandhi wanted Indians to take up arms to defend the British empire. He preferred violence to cowardice.

Gandhi considered non-violence as an attribute of the soul. It was a virtue to be practiced. He insisted that purification of mind is essential. Control over one's thought, speech and action too is essential. Gandhi was the first in human history to make use of non-violence from individual to social and political plane. He considered it as a civilized method that is capable of saving the mankind. He also believed that the practice of non-violence will make man fearless. According to Mukherjee, 'throughout his life Gandhi remained steadfast in his belief in non-violent mass action, though bulk of Congress men accepted it more as convenient strategy, rather than a creed, as Gandhi would like them to accept it' (1991: 21). Gandhi believed that non-violence will solve social problems and ensure social welfare.

Satyagraha

Satyagraha means insistence of truth or the use of truth as a force to achieve one's goal. *Satyagraha* aims at removing injustice and all forms of exploitation. But this is a long term process. The result is not seen in a day. Gandhi said that one should adopt this method only if the goal cannot be achieved through other means like verbal persuasion, legal action and constructive work. *Satyagraha* is the last phase of fight according to him. Gandhi said that *satyagraha* is a means to change the heart of the opponent by means of self-suffering. 'The underlying idea in *satyagraha* is to correct the wrong doer, to establish justice, to show him also that without the cooperation of the wrong that the wrong – doer cannot do the wrong intended by him. *Satyagraha* is nothing but search for truth. Gandhi believed that the non-cooperation and the heroic suffering in *satyagraha* will change even the stoniest of minds' (Dadge 1997: 7–8). This is a very strong weapon that Gandhi has given to us and he, in his lifetime itself, showed the strength of *satyagraha* through his struggle for the overall well-being of mankind.

In *satyagraha,* the attack is on the evil and not the evil doer. It annihilates the evil systems but not the person causing evil. When the evil is separated from the evil-doer, the doer will be transformed and a new and harmonious relationship is forged between the parties involved in the struggle. *Satyagraha* is based on the fundamental conviction that human nature is basically good and capable of being changed. The change, of course, had to be brought about by self-suffering and not by inflicting suffering on the opponent. To Gandhi, the law of love is the law of life. A true *satyagrah*i who has imbibed truth, non-violence and love will never fail to convert the opponent.

Gandhian concept of social work, his practices, his field of action and techniques differed significantly from those of the professional social workers. But Gandhi's contribution has been to prepare the background for the establishment of the profession of social work in India. Gandhi's philosophy as well as the plan of social work were grounded on a broad strategy of total social development resulting from a radical transformation from within the case of individual and of the community in which he lived. Social work was not to be directed merely to corrective or ameliorative activity, although this was important. It has to be geared to radical transformation, not merely to dealing with the consequences of an inequitable social order. Thus, it can be summarized that Gandhian philosophy of social work is not an individual problem oriented, ameliorative, but a community oriented process of rural development with much emphasis on the above mentioned values.

Gandhian Methods and Techniques

In his philosophy, Gandhi has put across to the Indian youth the values that they should adhere to in the practice of social work. To successfully carryout this task Gandhi suggested two methods, i.e. service to humanity and overall upliftment of mankind. This in his own terminology is known as constructive programme and *sarvodaya* movement. These methods, as viewed by Gandhi, are as follows:

Agenda of Constructive Programme

As Gandhi has said, the constructive programme is the truthful and non-violent way of winning *poorna swaraj*. Gandhi himself was aware of the practical difficulties that will arise in materializing his concept but he was confident and adamant that attempts in this direction will definitely bring some results. Constructive programme is designed to build the nation from the very bottom upwards. Gandhi's words, Bharati writes:

> My work of social work reform was no way less than or subordinate to political work. The fact is that when I saw that to a certain extent my social work would be impossible without the help of political work, I took to the later and only to the extent that it helped the former. I must therefore confess that the work of social reform or self purification of this nature is a hundred times dearer to me than what is called purely political work (1995a: 77).

Gandhi's constructive programme includes 18 items, which were 13 in 1940 and the rest were added later and these are aimed at complete development, upliftment and freedom in all areas of social life. Some followers of Gandhi later on added five more items such as cow protection, nature cure, *bhoodan, gramadan, shantiseva* to it. Gandhi, thus, gave a comprehensive eighteen point constructive programme for the upliftment of the nation (Gandhi 1983). To him, fulfilment of constructive programme is *swaraj* (Bharati 1995a). The principles of constructive programme are as follows:

1. It is performed on its own accord. It is purely a moral action which strengthens morality in man. It is not actuated by any temptation or fear.
2. Cooperation and mutual aid are important in constructive work. Voluntariness and sharing is the core of constructive activities.
3. Self-reliance and self-help.

4. Another principle is building up from below.
5. Constructive programme is the concrete expression of the spirit of non-violence.
6. Decentralization is stressed in constructive programme.

Constructive programme is not a strategy or technique of fighting to be adopted or discarded as expediency may suggest (Singh 1991). It connotes a way of life. It has to be adopted by heart as well as by intellect. The elements of constructive programme are as follows:

Achieve Communal Unity

This has always been a sensitive issue in the history of our nation. Communal unity is very significant in our country because of the fact that our nation is inhabited by people belonging to various faiths. According to Gandhi, communal unity is not something to be achieved through force or pressure. He felt that each individual should wholeheartedly accept the other faith. He wanted men to be tolerant to each other and to other's religions and beliefs. To inculcate this feeling, Gandhi believed that each person should possess a high level of thinking. They should come out of caste based and religion based thoughts and practices and instead should stand together and recognize himself and others as Indians. Gandhi firmly believed that only if the thought level of every Indian progresses to this level, communal unity is possible. Further, there should not be any privileges or discriminations based on religion or caste in schools, hospitals and social life. He viewed political unity as a by-product of communal unity.

In this context, Gandhi criticized the separate electorates for untouchables. He believed that this will only help in the continued existence of discrimination towards one section of population. Gandhi did not want communal unity to be enforced or imposed on people by means of political power or legal binding because he was well aware of the fact that such an imposed act or feeling is not static and there are always chances for breaking such rules. Instead, if it is achieved through an attitudinal change among the people, it can have long-lasting result. Being well aware of the dangers of communal disharmony, Gandhi undertook tours and addressed the people of different parts of the country and gave the message of tolerance to the people. In pre-Independent India, there were communal riots in different parts of the nation. Gandhi always called for the mass participation, irrespective of caste, colour and creed. He appealed them never to resort to violent measures and to rise above such narrow, foolish and low level of thoughts and deeds.

Removal of Untouchability

The practice of untouchability was a curse on Hindu religion and Indian society. This man made distinction based on certain myths was prevailing all throughout history which gave privileges to one section of population while this system made life miserable for the other section of population. This was a cruel form of discrimination against mankind. No one (except a few progressive social reformers during *Bhakti* movement) bothered to question this practice for a long time. Later social reformers took up this issue followed by Gandhi's involvement in the removal of this practice.

Gandhi, who believed in the idea of service to humanity, was never able to accept this practice and he invariably raised his voice against it. He always stood for the neglected and exploited group and one such group was the untouchables. Gandhi was convinced of the need to overcome this practice and called upon Congressmen to work in this direction as well. But, he was not happy about the idea of making it as an item in political agenda. Gandhi believed that the removal of untouchability is the moral responsibility of every Hindu and that they should adopt a friendly attitude towards the *harijans* (as Gandhi had named the untouchables). Gandhi felt that *swaraj* is impossible without the removal of untouchability because his vision of *swaraj* is the one in which all men are free from all sorts of exploitation. He considered this as one of the obstacles in way of attaining *swaraj*.

Advocated Prohibition

There had been a severe impact of alcoholism and drugs on lower income Indian families and our society at large. The addiction had not only affected the individuals physically, socially, financially and in behaviour but had also affected their families. These families were living in poverty and starvation and it had also led to moral degeneration in society. The children of such parents were also left alone to follow this path or end up fighting against poverty.

Gandhi was very much concerned about their future and that of the country and, hence, he wanted to help them to come out of this bad habit and turn them towards some creative and constructive work. He wanted the Congressmen to make some efforts in this regard but it did not happen. He made the women and students aware of their responsibility and role in advancing a reform against this evil practice that is craving the men and society. He thought the propaganda, friendly advices, and demonstration would go a long way in helping the people realize the ill effects of this habit and, hence, come out of it. He also suggested providing alternative recreation for them. Gandhi wanted this problem to be tackled at once and did not want it to be left for future.

Promotion of Khadi

Gandhi was well aware of the significance of economic self-sufficiency for individuals, families and the nation at large. He knew that economic freedom is essential for men to achieve political and social freedom. Hence, he always gave this message to the Indians and advocated the use of *khadi* for attaining this objective. By the use of *khadi*, Gandhi not only visualized economic self-sufficiency but also considered it as a fight against the large scale foreign clothes brought to India. He also considered it as a method to prevent the exploitation of our raw materials by the Britishers. This can also lead to the maintaining of the existing and the establishment of new trade centres in the country. He, thus, considered *khadi* as a strong measure capable of resisting all sorts of foreign attack on our economy and society.

Gandhi knew that the influences of western lifestyles on Indians were huge. A change in the attitude of Indians was required and believed that the use of *khadi* would help in this regard. He viewed that such a changed attitude will give each person an identity and would help in developing a sense of unity to Indians. Gandhi said: '*Khadi* to me is the symbol of unity of Indian people, of its economic freedom and equality' (1955).

Development of Village Industries

Gandhi visualized the life and soul of India in villages. He wanted each and every village to be self-sufficient in all aspects, which means that all the needs of the villagers were to be met from the village itself. For this purpose, apart from *khadi,* he also believed in the encouragement of village industries. Some of the essential village industries were hand grinding, hand pounding, soap-making, paper-making, match box-making and tanning. These were not huge industries but small units employing a limited number of workers where the production is also not large scale. All the raw material required for these needs were to be procured from the village itself. Gandhi did not mean purchasing or borrowing of the raw materials from other villages. In this way the villages will have a different face and the life in village will take a new phase. The result will be employment for all, meeting all the needs from the village itself and finally self-sufficiency. Gandhi believed that if all the villages in India follow this path and thus become self-sufficient, ours will become a wealthy nation in which poverty and starvation will be unknown.

Maintenance of Village Sanitation

Villages are always known for their simplicity and freshness. Compared to urban centres, we still receive fresh water and air in villages. This is because of less pollution due to the absence of huge industries, heavy traffic, etc. But on the other hand, the villages are not having a sense of cleanliness and beauty and they are not much bothered of maintaining cleanliness. They are not aware of the dangers of not maintaining hygiene and, hence, give less importance to it. As a result, they do not have proper drainage facilities and sanitation facilities and, hence, stagnant dirty water is seen in many places which give rise to mosquitoes and several diseases. They do not have separate places for washing and they use the rivers and public wells for bathing and washing. Unfortunately, these village practices pollute the fresh water. Villagers are more prone to water borne diseases. Though sanitation is not an issue of national importance, Gandhi gave greater importance to village sanitation along with any other issue and this makes his approach different. Gandhi was concerned about the minute details for bringing perfection to Indian social life. He realized that for a healthy personal and social life, the lack of village sanitation can act as a hurdle. Hence, he took up the task of spreading consciousness among the villagers and called for the Congressmen to do something in this regard.

Practice of Basic Education

Gandhi was very much concerned of the importance of education and convinced of the problems due to the lack of education in India. He realized that the superstitions and submissiveness of Indians were due to their ignorance and this will always keep them away from all sorts of development. The educational institutions promoted by the British at that time were only benefitting a small group of elites while the majority were neglected. Gandhi firmly believed that the future of India lies in the hands of the majority of village children and hence devised a new scheme of basic education for them. Gandhi realized the need for fostering a right attitude and right spirit in them. Gandhi's vision of education included occupational training along with the primary education. He believed that this will help them to learn a trade so that they can earn their livelihood in future. This system of education he thought would help them in learning self sufficiency and also dignity of labour at a very early age. This system will not leave hundreds and thousands of youngsters every year in search of jobs, instead they will be self-sufficient enough to choose a career straight and thereby they become confident and contribute their part to the nation's development.

Providing Adult Education

Gandhi had a very different outlook towards the concept of education. He firmly believed that it is essential for the people belonging to all walks of society to be educated. Hence, he not only visualized basic education for young children but also stressed the importance of adult education. By education he not only meant the ability to read and write. His concept had a much wider and deeper connotation. Gandhi wanted the education to help people to gain knowledge about his social, economic and political surroundings, to trigger their thoughts, make them think independently and prompt them to take right action at the right time. In short, Gandhi believed in such a system of education that will make people knowledgeable and think and act independently. He believed that the progress of our nation lies in the hands of such an educated human resource.

To quote him: 'My adult education means, therefore first, true political education of the adult by word of mouth. Side by side with the education by mouth will be the literary education. This itself is a speciality. Many methods are being tried in order to shorten the period of education. A temporary and permanent board of experts may be appointed by the working committee to give shape to the ideas here adumbrated and guide the workers' (Gandhi 1983: 7). He wanted the Congressmen to take up this highly specialized task.

Improvement in the Status of Women

Gandhi was very much worried about the low quality of life of the Indian women of his time. He realized that the Indian women were forced to live within the four walls of their own houses. They were not allowed to think or act freely. Their whole life was controlled by the significant others of their family. Gandhi wanted this situation to change. He believed that women have equal potentialities as men to contribute towards the social, economic and political development of the country. He wanted to make use of their unidentified talents and abilities which will give them better status in the family and society and is necessary for the nation's progress.

All efforts before Gandhi to help women were to give them some privileges or protection but within the control of men, guided by patriarchal, hierarchical social order. But Gandhi was the first person to view women as equal with men and, hence, wanted each woman to be an independent individual who recognizes her ability and plays her part. Two factors identified by Gandhi as responsible for the low status of women are the dominating nature of men and the submissive nature of women. He wanted the men and women of India to realize that women can be friends and co-workers of men. He wanted the Congressmen to imbibe this idea in themselves and spread this message to others and thereby lend women stairs to climb upwards. In order to give women opportunities of developing themselves, he gave membership to them in Congress, allowed to participate in *satyagraha* and other social and political movements. Gandhi said that – 'This revolution is easy, if the mind is made up. Let Congressmen begin with their homes. Wives should not be made dolls and objects of indulgence, but should be treated as honoured comrades in common service' (Gandhi 1983: 18).

Concern for Health and Hygiene

Sharpness of Gandhi's thoughts, the perfectionist in him and his excellent observational skills are revealed here in his concern for health and hygiene. While the authorities and people responsible had not given due importance to the poor state of the general health of public in those time, Gandhi realized the dangers of neglecting this area. Public suffered a lot of health problems in his time due to various reasons. One reason is that they were living in poverty and, hence, could not have a balanced diet or healthy food which adversely affected their health. Malnutrition was a very common problem and women and children were the worst hit. Since they did not have any formal education and lacked general awareness, they were ignorant of the need for maintaining hygiene and the dangers of unhygienic practices. The result was high death rate and diseases. This being the background, Gandhi decided to give necessary emphasis on educating the public on health and hygiene and included it in the constructive programme. Gandhi wanted the Congressmen to spread the message that: 'Your water, food and air must be clean and you will not be satisfied with mere personal cleanliness, but you will infect the surrounding with the same three fold cleanliness that you will desire for yourselves' (Gandhi 1983: 19).

Encouraging Provincial Languages

Effective communication is very essential in receiving the cooperation of various individuals in achieving a common objective and languages are very important in effective communication. Gandhi found out that the lifestyle and languages of the educated elite group of India were largely influenced by the British rule in India and the (western) education that they received from outside the country and there was a trend of neglect towards mother tongue. Gandhi also realized that the emergence of the English speaking Indians will create two separate classes in the society and the masses will be cut off from this elite group. This will make it difficult for them to work together towards the common objective of *swaraj*. Keeping this in mind, Gandhi stressed on the use of provincial languages so that they develop a sense of unity and work together.

Development of National Language

India is well known for its unity in diversity. One of the areas of diversity in Indian life is with regard to the languages. There are different regional languages spoken by the people of India in different areas. Gandhi realized the need for a common Indian language for the people of the country to give them unity in the midst of diversities. He also knew that this will not only create national and cultural unity but also facilitate effective communication. Gandhi held the view that Hindi or *Hindusthani* language which is spoken by the majority of Indians, especially in North India, would be the ideal language to be made as the national language or *rashtrabhasha*. The Congress Party in its famous resolution passed at the Kanpur Session in 1925, made Hindi the national language. At the same time, he also emphasized the need for developing the regional languages and instil and uphold the love for mother tongue.

Attainment of Economic Equality

Gandhi's idea of economic equality is expressed in his words as:

> 'Economic equality is the master key to non-violent independence. Working for economic equality should amount to mean abolishing the eternal conflict between capital and labour. It means the levelling down of the few rich in whose hands is concentrated the bulk of the nation's wealth on the one hand and a levelling up of the semi-starved naked millions on the other. A non-violent system of government is clearly an impossibility so long as so wide gulf between the rich and the hungry millions persists. The contrasts between the palaces of New Delhi and miserable hovels of the poor labouring classes cannot last even for a day in free India in which the poor enjoy the same power as the riches in the land. A violent and bloody revolution is a certainty one day, unless there is a voluntary abdication of riches and, the power that the riches should give them for the common good' (Gandhi 1983: 21).

Betterment of Kisans

During Gandhi's times, 80 per cent of our total population were peasants. They worked on land and produced food for others also. But the farmers of India were in a very deplorable position. They lived in poverty and debts, were exploited and suppressed by landlords, their life was no way better than that of slaves and they were trapped in bonded labour. Moreover, they were not protesting against this. Gandhi wanted this situation to change. He wanted them to be politically, aware of their own rights and wanted them to fight for their rights on non-violent terms and become free from all sorts of exploitation. He also wanted them to participate in the national and social movements. The efforts of Gandhi to organize them resulted in the *kisan* movements in various parts of the country. But in some areas they became violent and Gandhi was unhappy about it. Gandhi wanted the peasants not only to fight against the exploitation but also to join Congress in the fight for *swaraj.*

Welfare of the Labourers

Gandhi had his own vision, perception and understanding of labour problems and labour welfare. His view on this issue has become clearer from his following words:

> Ahmedabad Labour Union (ALU) is a model for all India to copy. It is based on non-violence. Its objectives are pure and simple. It has never had a setback in its career. It has gone on from strength to strength without fuss and show. It has its hospital, its school for children of the mill-hands, its classes for adults, its own printing

> press and khadi depot and its own residential quarters. The organization has never taken part in party politics. It influences the municipal policies of the city. It has to its credit very successful strikes which were wholly non-violent. Mill owners and labourers have maintained their relations largely through voluntary arbitration. If I had my way, I would regulate all the labour organizations of India after the Ahmedabad model. A time, I hope will come when it will be possible for the trade union congress to accept the Ahmedabad method and have the Ahmedabad Organization as part of the All India Union (Gandhi 1983: 24).

In the hindsight, it is disappointing to note that this dream of Gandhi remained half realized as the limits of moral force in resolving the labour disputes became manifest and distinctly visible. Labour militancy overtook this vision. Many leftist and centrist scholars on Gandhi's labour politics have questioned his assumptions. The complexities of capital-labour relations defy Gandhi's simplistic and somewhat romantic perceptions. Some have conceded that the ALU may be at best a case of exception rather than having any potential to become the rule.

Rights of Adivasis

They are the earliest inhabitants of India and numerically they are less in number (only 7 per cent of the total national population). However, this fact of demographic distortion should not deprive them of their equal rights with the rest of the population to live on this land. It is a sad story that even today after six decades of Indian Independence; their rights are not completely recognized and restored. In ancient days and even today, they are exploited by the rest and ignored by the government. But Gandhi did not ignore them. Their problems caught Gandhi's attention and their welfare was also his concern. *Adivasis* by their very nature live in isolation from the rest of the population and were ignorant of their rights and privileges and, hence, they never raised their voice. But Gandhi recognized their equal rights with rest of the population and hence included service of *adivasis* in his constructive programme.

Concern for Lepers

During Gandhi's times, the lepers were neglected in the country. They were much in need of receiving attention. The only institution run and working for them was the one near Wardha by Shri Manohar Dewan. Gandhi viewed an independent India without any beggars and lepers and included service for lepers in the constructive programme.

Guidance for Students

Gandhi believed that the future of the nation lies in the hands of the students, i.e. the educated youth. He encouraged them to participate in the non-cooperation movement. He wanted these young students not only to gain knowledge on subjects from education, but he wanted them to gain awareness on all that is happening around them, be able to think independently, to have a clear vision regarding every aspect of life, and to act in the right direction. Gandhi was unhappy about the corrupting foreign cultural influences. Their attraction to violence as a means of achieving political ends and indulgence in violent activities worried Gandhi a great deal. Gandhi suggested the following guidelines for students:

1. Keep away from party politics.
2. Avoid political and violent strikes.
3. Practice sacrificial spinning in a scientific manner.
4. Use *khadi* and other indigenous products.
5. Lead people to sing *Vande Mataram* and respect the national flag.
6. Be free from communal thoughts. Believe in inter-faith friendship and brotherhood.
7. To maintain compassion towards others and believe in the dignity of labour.
8. Learn national languages.
9. Translate into their own mother tongue everything new that they may learn and transmit it to the surrounding villages.
10. Lead an honest, pure and simple life.
11. To be scrupulously correct and chivalrous in their behaviour towards their fellow girl students.

He wanted the students not to waste their precious time in idleness but to use it for a noble purpose like national freedom by contributing their part. These are the components of Gandhian constructive programme described briefly. The constructive programme of Gandhi cannot be equated with present social work because Gandhi's constructive programme is very deep which has several dimensions and social work is only one of them.

Various Tenets as Architecture of Gandhian *Sarvodaya*

Gandhi was able to retain the loyalty of the common man as he instilled in each man an awareness of his social and economic responsibility. He inculcated a feeling of respect for self as well as for others. His emphasis was on duties rather than on rights. Gandhi's influence is strongly felt by the people throughout India. His philosophy permeates the social welfare policy of the government today. All that he stood for, worked for and died for was internalized in his immediate followers. Gandhi made his appearance in the Indian public life in 1920 and he received almost unanimous support for initiating multi-dimensional social reform activities. Gandhi's social welfare activities were part of his larger public life.

Ever since his public appearance, though the immediate concern of Gandhi was political freedom of the country from the British that was not his final goal. He addressed all the social issues of the time. His dream was *sarvodaya* – the rising of all, i.e, 'the welfare of each and every human being, total liberation from all that makes one not fully man'. *Sarvodaya* cannot be seen in isolation from other views of Gandhi, it was part of his larger vision. The dynamics of *sarvodaya* assumes a process that begins with the last and the least in the society and move on towards the dawn of a *moksha* (salvation) on earth or *Ramarajya*. This essentially offers a vision for future

Through *sarvodaya*, Gandhi attempted to recapture the spiritual heritage of India which has thrived in villages. *Swaraj* for him was not merely political independence but freedom from all sorts of oppressions. He advocated decentralization of power in all aspects of life. On political level, it meant distributing power from the centre to the villages, at the economic level, it meant discouraging foreign big industries and encouraging indigenous and small industries, and on the social level, it meant the equality for *harijans*, tribals and lower castes (Vettickal 2002).

Sarvodaya owes its origin to Gandhi. For him, '*Sarvodaya* was a concrete manifestation of several spiritual ideas found in many religious traditions' (Vattickal 2002). Gandhi borrowed the idea of *sarvodaya* from Ruskin Bond's book *Unto This Last.* This became his inspiration for the formation of *sarvodaya*. The ideal of *sarvodaya* is upliftment of all. Gandhi considered service to humanity as the key to this upliftment. For the total transformation of the Indian society on the lines of his vision, he also used other terms and methods like *swaraj, Ramarajya, ahimsa, satyagraha*, etc. and formulated various constructive programmes. The social aspects of Gandhi's *sarvodaya* are as follows:

Harijan Welfare

On one hand, India is a nation blessed with a rich tradition and culture. Even the West is influenced by Indian culture, tradition and philosophy. But, on the other hand, India's caste system has always been a curse on our society. It casts a shadow on the greatness of our culture. Untouchability is a man-made discrimination based on one's birth and was practiced in ancient India in an obnoxious manner. Unfortunately, this practice received some sort of encouragement by some sections of society and it continued to exist and even today (it is legally not allowed) is practiced by men in several forms.

The people belonging to the lower strata of this divisioning were called the untouchables, whom Gandhi had named as *harijans,* which means 'children of God'. Their life was miserable. For no fault of theirs, their freedom was limited, rights were denied and they were exploited in all sense. Their life was full of restrictions such as they were not allowed to touch the higher caste or even come within the vicinity of them. They were not allowed to enter public places and temples. Education was denied. They were not allowed to dress like upper caste and not allowed to construct houses like them.

As soon as Gandhi appeared on the Indian public scene, he took up this issue on a national level. He raised his voice against this evil practice and participated with them as one among them in the fight for equality. Gandhi could not stand any discrimination or exploitation of man. He was a man who always stood for justice and questioned whenever there was social, political, economic or religious injustice. While living the simplest form of human life and while working for and with the very ordinary men; his thoughts and deeds were of much higher level. The vastness of his thoughts permitted him to treat all men as equal. He wanted all men to tolerate each other. He wanted everyone to realize that each individual has his own unique part to play so that it is easy to develop the power of tolerance. Gandhi fought for them through Congress by mobilizing the masses in this struggle and also individually through his writings and speeches. He never allowed anything that encouraged the discrimination based on caste or religion and that is why he opposed the idea of separate electorates. He could foresee all possible dangers of allowing this system to continue and, hence, very strongly stood for its abolition.

He realized the need for changing the society's attitude and believed that the campaign against untouchability should be primarily carried on vigorously in villages and urged women to come forward in large numbers. He undertook the self-purification fast of 21 days from May 8–29, 1933 as a protest against the sluggishness of orthodox Hinduism to reform itself. He undertook an All India Harijan tour in November 1933 to break through deep rooted prejudices, orthodoxy and conservatism of the people. He also prepared his followers to accept the importance of enacting social legislations to remove the existing social barriers in the society. Mahatma Gandhi's influence gave rise to several voluntary organizations in the country for removing the social evils. In 1932, All India *Harijan Sevak Sangh* was started to promote this cause. Several other organizations also emerged. Mahatma Gandhi by his untiring efforts raised the problem of untouchability from the status of social reform issue to the greatest social and religious stirrings of modern Hinduism.

Women's Welfare

The status of women in India was always far from satisfactory. Though women in certain periods of the Indian history enjoyed some privileges, that was limited to a particular section of women and even that freedom was not absolute. The general picture of women's status was very poor. They were not allowed to think freely, move freely, were denied education, and to add up to their miseries, there were several evil practices like *sati,* child marriage, *purdah* system and ban on widow re-marriage. The socio-religious reform movements of the 19th century was the first ever attempt in improving the status of women. These movements though succeeded in certain aspects could not bring about an overall development and change.

The life of Indian women underwent complete transformation when Gandhi took up this problem. He could not tolerate this exploitation. He wanted his countrymen to treat women as their counterparts, with equal potentialities and give due respect. He was never willing to accept anything less than this from men towards women. He spread this message far and wide. The medium of his transformative message was his speeches, writings and the Congressmen (who acted as an oral carrier of his ideas). Gandhi expanded the world of Indian women and opened up new horizons for them. They were brought to the public life on equal rights and stand with men. Gandhi's concept of *sarvodaya* which means the upliftment of all would not be possible if the Indian women were left in such deplorable condition. Under the leadership of Gandhi, the Indian women who would otherwise not realize the existence of a world outside, came forward and participated in the freedom struggle. They participated in the civil disobedience movement, *satyagraha,* boycott movements, etc. This gave them a new identity, confidence, enlightenment and political emancipation. The thoughts, speeches and writings of Gandhi were so powerful and inspiring that life was not the same any more for the Indian women.

Today, there is not a single field (be it political, social, economic, spiritual or any other) untouched by women's contribution. For all opportunities they have, positions they hold, power they enjoy today, they owe a lot to this great man. Gandhi was the one who helped women to recognize and realize their own abilities and it was he himsef who cleared all the hardships that they might have faced from the society in this process of development. Gandhi made the path towards development smooth and easier for the Indian women.

Rural Welfare

Every passing day is a move towards modernization. Urbanization and industrialization are inevitable steps towards modernization. People get carried away by the colourfulness of urbanization and industrialization and call it development. They do not recognise the dangerous effects it can have on the social, economic and political spheres of our life and the nation. Gandhi could foresee the dangers of these trends and he realized the importance of village life in a country like India. The real development of the nation and people lies in the Gandhian concept of development. Since India is predominantly an agrarian country and a vast cluster of villages, he realized the need to stress the villages as the nucleus of development.

According to Gandhi, every village should develop, so will the nation. His concept of development is holistic. He held the view that social, economic, political, religious, educational and all other aspects of the village should develop and each village should be a self-sufficient unit. This means that all the needs of the villages should be met from within by utilizing its own resources. For him, rural welfare was not merely raising the material standards of living of the village folk, though that was also important but for laying the basis for peace, justice and freedom for all. The greatest advantage of Gandhian thought is that every idea he presented is well thought off and based on an in-depth understanding of the problem or need. He stressed rural welfare because he knew that the masses of Indian population will be worst hit if villages are neglected. The process of urbanization and industrialization may turn out to be helpful for a small percentage but the majority of rural population will be negatively hit. Moreover, the exploitation by the British rule had already damaged the village life. Unfortunately, this trend has continued till today.

Gandhi was convinced of the need to take up rural welfare and he lifted it to a plane of nationwide movement. Even before the arrival of Gandhi, though there were some attempts to improve the lot of rural folk, all these attempts remained to limited areas. According to Sarojini Naidu, Gandhi first empathized with one then reached out to the poor. In a vast nation like India, one cannot think of development of a nation in one single stretch. Here the Gandhian idea of rural welfare has much significance where the stress is on the development of each small unit and several such units contributing to the development of the whole nation. This idea appears to be more practical.

Gandhi had realized that the process of rural reconstruction is a tremendous task that requires patience, understanding, cooperation and necessitates the dealing with several other problems involved. He believed that if villages perish, so would India and, hence, the face of free India which he had depicted was the face of a rejuvenated rural India. Even in Independent India, Gandhi's vision of rural reconstruction is accepted and the process is accelerated through the community development programme.

Gandhi's Views on Village Panchayat

Gandhi could not visualize an India where the villages are ignored. He was very much convinced of the importance of villages in the development of our nation. He thought of rural development as the key to nation's development. Gandhi knew that the masses of Indian population lived in villages and, hence, any attempts of development ignoring villages would not bear fruit. Moreover, he was impressed by the several features of village life such as social, better inter-class or inter-community relations, co-operation among men, simplicity, small size and self-sufficient aspects. He wanted to preserve and develop all these features and could never think of all this being destroyed and hence Gandhi thought of village panchayat as a means to develop villages.

Gandhi equated village panchayat to *Ramarajya* where the ultimate power is in the hands of the people who for the convenience of governance will discharge the responsibilities temporarily through their chosen representatives. This is a process of democratic decentralization which gives the villagers the power to govern themselves. They can administer their own internal affairs. Not only that they can rule themselves, but they should be self-sufficient in all aspects such as education, economy, agriculture, industry, etc. According to him, every village should produce whatever is necessary to meet their needs from within and should not depend outside. Agriculture and small scale industries were encouraged for this purpose.

Gandhi was aware of the limitations of village life as well and hence suggested plans for its improvement. He took interest in aspects of health, hygiene and sanitation. This process of democratic decentralization consists of a three-tier system. They are the *gramsabha* for the administration of villages. *Gram sabha* would elect a panchayat annually to initiate plans of development, execute them. A second order of panchayat is established to deal with issues like education, transport and industries. A third order is also created. In such a decentralized *sarvodaya* democracy of Gandhi's understanding, people would take active interest in the management of its affairs.

Gandhi and Swaraj

The ideal of *swaraj* was for the first time enunciated by Gandhi. According to him *swaraj* had different perspectives – personal, economic and national. *Swaraj* is *sarvodaya* democracy, i.e. democracy of the masses for the masses. Since vast masses of India lived in villages, he perceived village as an oceanic circle and individual as its centre and both should be willing to perish for the other until the whole became one life organized as a state with decentralized functions. Such *sarvodaya* democracy had to be worked out from bottom by the people of every village. *Swaraj* according to him meant 'freedom for the meanest (i.e. the lowest) of our countrymen'. Gandhi's *swaraj* is known as poor man's *swaraj*. He did not recognize any racial or religious discriminations and advocated that the necessities of life should be enjoyed by the poor as the others also. He said that *poorna swaraj* will not be attained until that. Gandhi considered non-violence as the only way to attain *swaraj* which is the weapon of poor and exploited.

From a historical perspective, *sarvodaya* has a humble beginning in Gandhi. Gandhi initiated a momentum that is heading towards its fulfilment. It was humanly impossible for Gandhi to design the details of a future *sarvodaya* society, neither was able to see the full flowering of a *sarvodaya* society in his life time. However, Gandhi has sown the seeds of a revolution that is ongoing. The guidelines he suggested and the means he proposed towards establishing ideal *sarvodaya* society have stood the test of history and offer great potential for future. *Sarvodaya* vision of Gandhi leaves the door of future possibilities opens.

Theory and Practice of Social Work: A Gandhian Critique

If we analyse present social work practice on the basis of Gandhian concept of social work, it is observed that today's social work does not have a holistic approach to the idea of service to mankind or social welfare. According to Gandhian concept, social work not only implied solving the social or personal problems but included a total upliftment or development of the individual as well as society, covering all aspects like personal, social, political, economic, religious, educational and spiritual. This idea is very well depicted in Gandhian vision of *sarvodaya* and constructive programme. Today, social work is branched out into different specializations each consisting of a limited area of service, methods, particular target group, skills and techniques. A social worker who works in a particular field is only specialized in that particular field and, hence, is not competent in other fields and, therefore, deals with the client within their limited sphere. This may not always solve the problems properly and may not produce long-lasting results. Therefore, the social work profession today is almost becoming like that of medical profession where a client approaches with a specific problem and the worker tries to solve that specific problem and does not bother to look into the other areas or aspects of the client and do not attempt to bring about the total development of the individuals.

According to Gandhian concept, social work is the moral responsibility and duty of each and every individual and not a profession to be followed by a few. But today it is a profession. Professionalism does have its own positive aspects. But when too much professionalism creeps into social work practice, it brings about some problems as well. First of all, the social work practice gets limited to the hands of a few who are qualified for that and rest of the society believes that it is no longer their responsibility. Again those who practice social work consider it only as a means for bread-winning and fail to believe in and respect the nobility of the profession and, hence, their ethics and efficiency are affected. Thirdly, social workers rarely work independently. Mostly they work as part of some NGOs, welfare departments and other organizations. Therefore, the objectives of the organization are predominant in them than the interest of the client or community with which they are dealing. The social worker's freedom is limited by the interest of the agency. The policies of the organization are more valued than the emotions or needs of the clients and so the decisions regarding the cases are also taken by the higher authorities concerned rather than the client himself or the social worker. In this way professional aspect of social work sometimes act against the real purpose of the profession.

Besides, what we are practicing today is the western model of social work profession. The methods developed by them are used here as well. But the case work and group work methods are not always applicable and successful here. This is because we have not modified these methods according to the features and limitations of our society (Patel 2001). The Gandhian methods of constructive programme as well as *sarvodaya* are examples for us to follow. Those methods were developed after understanding the real problems and needs of our society and hence are competent enough to solve these problems and bring about development. These are some of the pertinent areas where present social work profession can be criticized on the basis of Gandhian concept of social work.

Summing Up

Gandhi's contribution in the Indian political field and national movement is largely acknowledged and highlighted. But that is only one aspect of his life. He has made excellent contributions to the social field as well. He had been successful in combining freedom movement, social reform and social welfare and in mobilising mass participation. Gandhi had original and unique idea of social work which is different from western social work and the social work profession in the country today.

Gandhian social work is different from the present social work practice in a number of ways. Gandhi considered social work practice as the duty and responsibility of the individuals where as in today's world, social work has been reduced to a profession. Since social work is viewed as a duty by Gandhi, no rewards are expected. Whereas today material benefits are expected for the services offered (as in all other professions like medical, legal, accounting, etc.). Gandhian social work has a different philosophy which emphasizes more on spirituality and suggests unique methods of constructive programme and *sarvodaya.* Whereas today, the philosophical emphasis is more on democracy, liberalism, secularism and possesses more sophisticated methods like case work, group work, community organization, etc. While the qualifications for the social worker according to Gandhi were his talents, commitment and devotion, today professional training and degree of social work are important. Gandhian concept stressed on the qualities of the worker like purified mind, self-respect, patience, loyalty, tolerance, faith. Whereas today, social worker should possess a different set of skills and techniques. Gandhian concept aims at helping all those who are in need irrespective of the fact that the needy approach the worker or not. But today, the services are mainly offered to those who approach the social worker or the agency. Gandhian social work has a broad outlook of providing well-being to the whole mankind and nation, whereas today's social work practice has a narrow outlook which aims at helping a particular person or a particular community at a time. In short, Gandhian social work is developmental in nature whereas today's social work is more remedial in nature.

When we analyse the present social work profession in the light of above mentioned factors, it becomes clear that the social work profession today is too narrow in its practice. Though theoretically there are several principles and ethics to guide this profession, in practice many of these values that the profession should adhere to are ignored and many of the objectives that the profession should strive for are not attained. This is because social work profession in India today is a blind imitation of the western model of social work and we are trying to solve the Indian problems with a western tool. Here surfaces the significance of Gandhian social work.

Gandhi had a right understanding of the problems and needs of our people, society and nation and he developed a social work perspective with unique philosophy, methods which is well suited to the Indian context. Gandhian social work has potential and promise to become one of the effective indigenous methods (Patel 2001), which can remain fresh and pure even today and, hence, remain superior to the present borrowed model of social work profession in the country. Gandhi had visualized a highly pragmatic approach which went a long way towards bringing in such a general climate of social welfare and development in Indian society through his broad concept of *sarvodaya* and constructive programmes.

References

Bharati, K.S. 1995a. *Thoughts of Mahatma*, Nagpur: Dattsons Publishers.

———. 1995b. *Thoughts of Gandhi and Vinoba: A Comparative Study*, New Delhi: Concept Publishers.

Dadge, M.S. 1997. *Dimensions of Gandhian Thought*, Aurangabad: Chhaya Publishing.

Fischer, Louis. 1997. *The Life of Mahatma Gandhi*, New York: Harper and Collins.

Gandhi, M.K. 1925. *Young India*, 5 March.

———. 1955. *Khadi: Why and How?*, Ahmedabad: Navjivan Publishing House.

———. 1983. *Constructive Programme: Its Meaning and Place*, Ahmedabad: Navjivan Publishing House.

Mazumdar, A.M. 1964. *Social Welfare in India: Mahatma Gandhi's Contributions*, New Delhi: Asia Publishing.

Mehta, S.R. 1999. *Dynamics of Development: A Sociological Perspective*, New Delhi: Gyan Publishing House.

Misra, P.D. 1994. *Social Work: Philosophy and Methods*, New Delhi: Inter India Publications.

Mukherjee, Subrata. 1991. *Gandhian Thought: Marxist Interpretations*, New Delhi: Deep & Deep Publications.

Mukherjee, S. and Ramaswamy, Sushila. 1994. *Facets of Mahatma Gandhi: Economic and Social Principles*, New Delhi: Deep & Deep.

Patel, Chhaya. 2001. 'Indigenization of Social Work Education: A Case Study from Baroda', *The Indian Journal of Social Work*, 62 (2), April, pp. 197–218.

Pradhan, B. 1980. *The Socialist Thoughts of Mahatma Gandhi*, New Delhi: G.D.K. Publications.

Prasad, R. 1958. *Constructive Programme: Some Suggestions*, Ahmedabad: Navjivan Publishing House.

Singh, R.S. 1991. *The Constructive Programmes of Mahatma Gandhi*, New Delhi: Commonwealth Publishers.

Vettickal, T. 2002. *Gandhian Sarvodaya: Realising a Realistic Utopia*, New Delhi: Gyan Publishing House.

CHAPTER 17

Impact of Gandhian Philosophy on Human Resource Management

JAYSHREE B. THAKORE AND RAM KUMAR BALYAN

A Synoptic Biographic Sketch of Gandhi: Life and Work

Mohandas Karamchand Gandhi (1869–1948), called Mahatma Gandhi, was the charismatic leader who fought for Indian Independence against the British colonial rule. His philosophy of non-violence, for which he coined the term *satyagraha*, has influenced both national and international movements for peaceful changes. By means of non-violent civil disobedience, Gandhi helped in inspiring other colonial people to work for their own independence, ultimately dismantling the British Empire to replace it with Commonwealth of Nations.

Gandhi was born at Porbandar on 2 October 1869. He belonged to *Bania* caste. His grandfather was *diwan* (minister) of the princely state of Porbandar. Gandhi was the youngest of the four children. His mother Putlibai was a very religious lady. She used to take her meals after prayers every day. His mother left deep impression on Gandhi. He started his education at Porbandar and later on shifted to Rajkot with his parents. During his school years, he never told lies and mythological plays like *Shravana Pitribhakti* and *Satyavan Harishchandra* and *Taramati* had great impact on his life. He wanted to become obedient to his parents like *Shravana* and truthful like *Harishchandra* in life. He was married when he was studying at high school. His wife Kasturbai was illiterate. He lost one year of education because of marriage and his teacher wanted to make good the loss by skipping a class. During his school time he started occasionally eating meat and smoking. But later on he realized that these were bad habits and decided to leave these habits. His father died when he was 16 years old. His autobiographical work *My Experiments with Truth* (Gandhi 1957) is the best account of his life as told by him (Sharma, R 2004).

After his matriculation examination in 1887, he wanted to go to England for higher studies. But his mother initially did not accept his proposal. After taking some vows of moral conduct, he went to England and became a barrister. Gandhi had promised his mother for not taking liquor and meat in England. He kept his promises. He started his practice in Bombay and later on in Rajkot. On the request of a firm from Porbandar, he accepted to go to South Africa to fight a case for the company. In 1893 he went to South Africa. There he faced a lot of difficulties. Gandhi was not allowed to travel in first class compartment in train. No doubt he found good friends also from Christian community. He studied the social, economic and political conditions of Indians in Transvaal and Orange Free state. He settled the case for which he went to South Africa. After three years of stay in South Africa, he returned to India. Again in 1897, he went to South Africa with his family. His this visit was opposed by the white people as Gandhi was against apartheid which discriminated Indians. He criticized their approach towards Indians. Back from South Africa, Gandhi met Pherozeshah Mehta, popularly known as the Lion of Bombay, Lokmanya Tilak and Gopal Krishan Gokhale. He described Pherozeshah Mehta to him like Himalaya, Lokmanya like Ocean and Gokhale as Ganges (Bourai 2004).

Gandhi opposed the Bills that were passed in Natal Legislative Assembly which adversely affected Indian traders and Indian immigration. He fought for racial equality for Indians. During Boer War, Gandhi and his corps provided voluntary service within the firing line and brought wounded soldiers on stretchers and nursed them. Thus, second time he returned to India and started working with Indian National Congress leaders like Gokhale and Pherozeshah. He settled in Bombay and started his practice in the court. Again the third time he went to South Africa. The principle called *satyagraha* came into being. It means passive resistance. Maganlal Gandhi coined the word *sadagraha* (*sat*-truth, *agraha*-firmness, insistence or hold).

It was modified by Gandhi as *satyagraha.* Calling on his fellow Indians to defy the new law and suffer the punishments for doing so rather than resist through violent means (Gandhi 1961). This plan was adopted, leading to a seven year struggle in which thousands of Indians were jailed. Gandhi himself was jailed on many occasions. There was total repression of protesting Indians. They were flogged or even shot at for striking, refusing to register, or engaging in other forms of non-violent resistance. While the government was successful in repressing the Indian protestors, the public outcry stemming from harsh methods employed by the South African government in the face of peaceful Indian protestors finally forced South African General Jan Christian Smuts to negotiate a compromise with Gandhi. This was the first major success of Gandhi's leadership.

Upon the outbreak of World War-I, Gandhi decided to return to India, bringing all that he had learnt from his valuable experiences in South Africa with him. When the Rowlett Act, empowering the colonial government to imprison those accused of sedition without trial, was passed, Gandhi called for a *satyagraha*. It soon led to violent outbreaks across the country. The most notable of them was the Jallianwala Bagh massacre of 379 Indian civilians by the British army, comprising Indian soldiers and led by General Dyer (who had imposed martial law in Amritsar). The violence led Gandhi to end the struggle, but he succeeded in placing himself at the centre of the Indian national movement. In April 1920, Gandhi was elected President of the All India Home Rule League. He was invested with executive authority on behalf of the Indian National Congress in December 1921. Under Gandhi's leadership, the Congress was reorganized and given a new constitution, with the goal of *swaraj* (self-rule). Membership in the party was open to anyone prepared to pay a token fee of twenty five paise.

Gandhi expanded his non-violence platform to include the *swadeshi* policy, the boycott of foreign-made goods, especially British goods. Gandhi urged the people to boycott British educational institutions and law courts, to resign from government employment, to refuse to pay taxes, and to forsake British titles and honours. This new programme enjoyed wide-spread appeal and success, empowering the Indian people as never before, yet just as the movement reached at its apex, it ended abruptly as a result of a violent clash in the town of Chauri Chaura, Uttar Pradesh, in February 1922. Fearing that the movement was about to take turn towards violence, and convinced that this would be the undoing of all his work, Gandhi called off the campaign of mass civil disobedience.

Now vulnerable, Gandhi was arrested on 10 March 1922, tried for sedition, and sentenced to six years. imprisonment.

Making good on his word in March 1930, he launched a new *satyagraha* against the tax on salt, highlighted by the Dandi March from 21 March to 6 April 1930, marching 400 kms (248 miles) from Ahmedabad to Dandi (located on Arabian Sea in South Gujarat) to make his own salt. Thousands of Indians joined him on this Salt March to the sea. This campaign was one of his most successful, resulting in the imprisonment of over 60,000 people. The government represented by Lord Irwin, decided to negotiate with Gandhi.

The Gandhi-Irwin Pact was signed in March 1931. In it, the British Government agreed to set all political prisoners free in return for the suspension of the civil disobedience movement. Furthermore, Gandhi was invited to attend the Round Table Conference in London as the sole representative of the Indian National Congress. The conference was a disappointment to Gandhi and the nationalists as it focused on Indian minorities rather than the transfer of power. Further, Lord Irwin's successor, Lord Willington, embarked on a new campaign of repression against the nationalists. World War-II broke out in 1939 when Nazi Germany invaded Poland. Gandhi was fully sympathetic with the victims of fascist aggression. After lengthy deliberations with colleagues in the Congress, he declared that India could not be party to a war ostensibly being fought for democratic freedom while that freedom was denied in India to India herself.

As the war progressed, Gandhi increased his demands for independence, drafted a resolution calling for the British to leave vide Quit India Movement in 1942. Gandhi and his supporters made it clear they would not support the war effort unless India was granted immediate independence. The last British authority was forced to hand over power to Indians. But it was planned to divide India into two separate countries. Gandhi did not like it. He did not celebrate the India's Independence. He was assassinated in Birla House, New Delhi on 30 January 1948 by Nathuram Godse, a radical Hindu who was later tried, convicted and executed. This way the eventful life of Gandhi came to an end.

Principles of Mahatma Gandhi

Mahatma Gandhi was a great Indian leader but essentially he was a universal man of the entire humanity. Mahatma means great soul. This title was accorded to Gandhi in 1915 by his admirer Rabindranath

Tagore, the first Asian to win the Nobel Prize for literature. Gandhi called him *Gurudev* and Tagore called him Mahatma. Gandhi was nominated for Nobel Prize five times but to the misfortune of the award authority, he could never be awarded the coveted peace prize. There are statues of Mahatma Gandhi in his memory in different cities of world like San Francisco, Houston, New York, Atlanta, Moscow, Paris, Amsterdam, Barcelona, Lisbon, Manitoba, Ontario and London (Chavan 2001). Philosophy and ideas of Mahatma Gandhi were influenced by the *Bhagavad Gita,* Hindu and Jain religions and teachings of Leo Tolstoy (Betai 2002). Mahatma advocated the following ideas:

1. *Untouchability:* He advocated that all people are equal. God made all people equal. He did not accept untouchability. A person does not become untouchable by birth, but should become untouchable due to lust, anger and evils.
2. *Mobilizing Resources:* Gandhi put up the idea of mobilizing resources to meet the existing requirements. He collected money and manpower from the society to help the untouchables.
3. *Communication Skills:* Communication means sharing of message or making common between two or more parties. Communication skill is the ability to make messages common. Gandhi appealed to the people to help the weak and untouchables with proper words, phrases and language. This is a very good example of communication skill.
4. *Scientific Interview and Participative Discussion:* Scientific interview means, during interview, certain guidelines are to be followed and in discussion active part should be taken. Interviewing is a process for scientific selection. During interview, negotiation is also necessary to finalize the terms and conditions of the employment. He advocated for deciding the terms and conditions of employment for workers.
5. *Satyagraha*: The concept of *satyagraha* was developed when Gandhi was in South Africa. '*Satya*' means truth and '*agraha*' means firmness. It means truth-force or force of truth. It comprises two main elements, i.e. of truth and non-violence. *Satyagraha* is described as non-violent resistance. *Satyagraha* is applicable to all situations of person, group, national and international. *Satyagraha* is gentle and it never causes wounds. *Satyagrahis* do not exploit a position of weakness of opponent. *Satyagrahi* never humiliates opponent. *Satyagraha* has been designed as an effective substitute for violence. *Satyagraha*

teaches us the art of living as well as dying. *Satyagraha* does not depend on the outside help but it derives its strength from within. *Satyagrahi* should never lose hope up to the last. There is no enemy in the dictionary of *satyagraha*. Since *satyagraha* is a method of conversion and conviction. It does not accept the use of coercion.

6. *Truth:* Truth means '*sat*'. Truth means the voice within you which tells you how to resolve moral dilemma in favour of right conduct. Truth is the right designation of God. The more truthful we are, the nearer we are to the God. The truth is like a tree. The more we nurture it, the more fruits we get. Truth alone will endure and all the rest will be swept away before the tide of time. Truth makes one fearless.
7. *Non-violence:* Non-violence means action without physical force. Violence begets violence and non-violence means *ahimsa*. Non-violence is the means and truth is the end. Non-violent resistance brings out the issues into open and reaches to the peaceful solution (Sharma 2001).
8. *Self-suffering:* Self-suffering means the person who exercises it only suffers. It does not mean submission to the will of opponent. It puts one's soul against the will of the opponent. It is the chosen substitute of violence to others. Self-suffering appeals to others and, thereby, shapes the opinion of public. It does not make others suffer.
9. *Faith in Human Goodness:* Gandhi had faith in human goodness. We all are a mix of good and evil. Whatever respect or credit we want for ourselves the same should be given to opponents also. Even if the opponent is repeatedly false, the *satyagrahi* should be ready to trust him.
10. *Fearlessness: Satyagrahi* should not have fear. The courage of *satyagrahi* comes from within and not due to physical strength. Gandhi did not accept cowards. A violent person could become non-violent but never a coward. Act of bravery is always better than cowardly submission.
11. *Sarvodaya:* This concept was coined by Mahatma Gandhi and guided the activities of Sevagram. It is the combination of two words from Sanskrit. *Sarva* means all and *udaya* means rise, welfare or prosperity. It means welfare of all. Gandhi felt that *sarvodaya* should guide us in our efforts to build ourselves, families, organizations and communities.

12. *Trusteeship:* Based on the concepts of *nishkam karma* and *loksangraha*, Gandhi was inspired and introduced the theory of trusteeship. Trusteeship is the natural answer to *nishkam karma*. It gives the owner a chance of reforming himself. It does not recognize any right to private property except to the extent it may be permitted by society for its own welfare. It proposes to fix the decent minimum wages for workers and maximum income limit to any person in the society. Trusteeship is not inheritable. Gandhi believed that the children would inherit only if they proved their fitness for it. It establishes good and long lasting relationships between employees, employer and management. Trustee must take care of his/her employees. Their needs and requirements must be considered sympathetically. The theory of trusteeship includes the human and the human values such as welfare of workers, employee needs, service, human development and share-holder requirements (Veerraju 1999; Das 2002).
13. *Profit-sharing:* In an industrial or non-industrial organization, the owners invest their capital and workers invest their labour. Due to these factors the organization earns profit. Therefore, this profit should be shared between workers and owners. This would prove helpful to maintain a sense of partnership and loyalty among the workers. Ultimately, it leads to motivation of employees and good industrial relations. Owners must consider workers as partners.
14. *Open to Change:* Gandhi described himself as an average man with less than an average ability. He admitted that intellectually he was not sharp. He did not care much for bookish learning. But he was interested to learn more from actual living of the life in its variety of shades. He kept his mind open to accept the changes and adjust accordingly (Dash 2004).
15. *Solution to Industrial Conflicts:* Conflicts are likely to take place due to differences in opinion, attitude, lifestyle or approach in our life. Similarly, it takes place in industry also. The main reasons are wages, management policies, behaviour, grievances, etc. For avoiding industrial disputes, the labour should have equal status to capital. Employees should have same access to the transactions of the mills as the shareholders. If disputes take place, they must be settled through peaceful methods like

negotiation and arbitration. Gandhi used these methods in South Africa for settlement of a case (Goel 2002).

16. *Vegetarianism:* Gandhi advocated for vegetarian diet. He was influenced by the traditions of Hindu and Jain religions. No doubt he tasted meat in his early age but decided not to take later on. He met Henry Salt at the meeting of Vegetarian Society in London. Later on he wrote on this subject. He experimented with different diets, analysed and concluded that the vegetarian diet is good and sufficient to meet minimum requirements of the body.
17. *Brahmacharya*: When Gandhi was in South Africa and fighting for civil rights of Indians, he decided to follow the principle of *brahmacharya*, a spiritual and practical purity derived by practicing celibacy. Gandhi started spending one day in a week in silence. He believed that abstaining from speaking would give him inner peace. It is a practice which is used for minimizing stress and strain from work.
18. *Labour Organization:* Gandhi thought that labour is very important in the industry. Labour problems could be avoided if given equal status and treatment. For this purpose workers must be united. Labourers are intelligent enough to organize and to act as one. They will have equal status to capital. But organizing labour should come through Satyagraha. This way the owner would not dominate them. Gandhiji organized the workers of textile mills in Ahmedabad to put their demand to the management.
19. *Women Empowerment:* Gandhi supported the belief that women are equally competent. In non-violence women are more powerful than men. There is no reason to consider women inferior or subordinate to men. Women are companion of men and possess equal mental competence. In case of non-violence, the future of the ideal would be with the women world. But today this is not realized.
20. *Non-cooperation:* Non-cooperation means refusing to behave with the desire of a tyrannical sinner. It is neither to help nor to get help. Non-cooperation is a measure of discipline and sacrifice. Non-cooperation means refuse to accept the evil and help that is good. Non-cooperation paves the way for real and honourable cooperation based on mutual respect and understanding. Real non-cooperation is against the evil and not the person. Non-cooperation is with methods and system but never

with men. Non-violence is the foundation on which structure of non-cooperation as a tool of civil disobedience is built.

21. *Democracy:* Democracy means the government of the people, for the people and by the people. The main essence of democracy is that where every person has the right to represent his interest. It is possible only when everybody has the right to represent his interest. It is possible only when everybody has the right to represent. Democracy is disciplined and enlightened. It is the finest thing in this world. Under democracy all should have equal opportunity. The spirit of democracy is from within and not imposed. In real sense, democracy works when it works at the lower level first.

Impact on Human Resource Management

Gandhi advocated the principles of truth and non-violence. In the course of his life and work, Gandhi got involved and associated with several issues and activities of public and personal nature. *Satyagraha,* mobilizing resources, communication skills, scientific selection, self-suffering, fearlessness, faith in human goodness, *sarvodaya*, trusteeship, profit-sharing, open to changes, solution of industrial conflicts, vegetarianism, *brahmacharya*, labour organization, women empowerment, non-cooperation and village democracy are some of the examples of this aspect of his life. The modern practices of Human Resource Management (HRM) in organizations are directly or indirectly impacted by one or the other of these issues, values and principles. Gandhian philosophy is increasingly being viewed as an indirect approach to human resources management. The impact noticed on HRM is as follows:

1. Gandhi founded *Sevagram Ashram* on 25 May 1915. The entire procedure of deciding policies, preparing people to accept untouchables and preparing untouchables to join the main stream was a big experiment. He discussed the questions of untouchability with his friends in Ahmedabad. The first step in this direction was admitting untouchable inmates into the *ashram*. The entire process is based on principle of belief and faith in the inherent worth of human. At present, HRM considers the merit of the candidates and not caste and creed in their selection. This looks like endorsement of Gandhi's principle. But Thorat and Newman's (2007) researches have produced altogether a different picture and argue otherwise.

2. As the next step that Gandhi tried was mobilizing resources, he collected money and mobilized manpower from the society for the cause of untouchables. In the present time also, HRM recruits the employees from different areas and countries to meet the personnel requirements of an organization.
3. Gandhi's appealing speeches, convictions for the right causes, proper words, phrases, idioms and language used for the appeal to the masses is the best example of communication skill. These are fundamental tools for HRM and being used by all branches of management to steer and coordinate the various activities in the organization.
4. Gandhi's approach to the cause of abolition of indentured emigration of labourers was also a process of social change. Under the Smuts-Gandhi Settlement of 1914, the three taxes in respect of the indentured emigrants to Natal had been abolished for the general emigration from India.

In February 1917, Pandit Madan Mohan Malaviya asked for leave to introduce a bill for the immediate abolition of indentured emigration of labourers but Lord Chelmsford refused permission that led Mahatma Gandhi to travel through the country for an all India agitation. Gandhi planned for his rigorous struggle. He also decided his actions step by step. Gandhi also applied for interview with M.V. Muffey who, without giving promise, assured him of probable help. The principle of scientific interview and participative discussion was used by Mahatma Gandhi during 1915 to 1917 and today interview and participative discussion are used by HRM to carry out its functions more effectively. These are considered to be the best methods and skills of professional human resources manager and industrial relations manager.

5. While dealing with conditions of Champaran farmers, Gandhi carried out realistic SWOT (Strength, Weakness, Opportunity and Threat) analysis of the problem. Workers were illiterate, harassed and exploited. It was the right cause for a leader like Gandhi to fight for protecting the interests of the weak people. Gandhi launched a righteous non-violence agitation against the government but he did not violate the laws. He accepted summons. He was abiding by the law and at the same time was fighting for the rights of the workers. Gandhi also helped the officials like the district collector, magistrate, and police officials. He only legally resisted the notices served on him. Gandhi's love

for people and his tremendous faith in *ahimsa* could bring him the solution of the problem peacefully. Nowadays, this approach is accepted by HRM also for solution of industrial conflicts.

6. Gandhi advocated that the solutions to disputes and grievances require trust and faith in non-violence, acceptance of legal measures and true love for people. The problems may arise but the solution of the industrial conflicts must be peaceful. He solved the problems of textile workers with management through collective bargaining. This principle has been accepted by HRM today also to solve the industrial problems and solved many other problems.
7. In order to become a pure vegetarian, Gandhi read number of books on vegetarianism. He was impressed by Howard William's classic work *The Ethics of Diet* (1883, 1896, 2003) which was a biographical history of the literature of human dietetics from earliest period to the present day. In short, Gandhi was such a social scientist who studied every problem and analysed it with cause and effect relationship and arrived at a right solution. Today, this is the approach of HRM to study people's grievances, diagnose their maladies and arrive at a solution of the problem. Gandhi after reaching England for a study of Bar of Law compared Indian culture with western culture and after scientific analysis adopted the simple way of living. Gandhi was elected as an executive member of the vegetarian society.
8. Gandhi's acquaintance with religion and first exposure to *Bhagavad Gita* was interesting. Verses of second chapter of *Gita,* dealing with human desires and how human needs go on multiplying, particularly impressed Gandhi (Betai 2002). It is related to theories of motivation applicable in dealing with human desires. Theory of hierarchy of human needs advocated by Maslow is similar to this. Of course, *Gita* tells about minimizing needs in order to get peace of mind, motivation theory tells us about meeting and satisfying human needs that might increase productivity, efficiency and improved quality of work life. This has been used by HRM to keep the employees motivated and prevent many labour problems.
9. Gandhiji had strong devotion for labour class. When he received a letter from Ansuyaben Sarabhai about the conditions of labour in Ahmedabad he was moved and intervened with sympathy. Workers were paid low wages. The labourers had been agitating

long for an increment. Gandhi guided them in their struggle. Similarly, Gandhi worked in Champaran for cow protection, rural satisfaction and education. As Gandhi practiced the principles of HRM, he also considered workers as very valuable assets and treated them as partners.

10. Mahatma Gandhi's all programmes were people oriented. He believed in the inherent worth of human beings that is the basic principle of human resource management. Potentialities and capacities of individuals cannot be developed unless you trust their basic ability to achieve the desired goal. While designing organization structure, HRM trusts inherent capability of the employees and tasks are assigned to them accordingly.
11. Gandhi's belief in the dignity of labour was his basic message. No work could be considered inferior. In Gandhi's all preaching, the value of self-help is emphasized. His life itself is a great message of dignity of labour. They were amply reflected in the working of the institutions he had established in Ahmedabad, like the Sabarmati Ashram, Kochrab Ashram or Gujarat Vidyapeeth. At all the above places, most of the work was done by the inmates themselves. They never considered any work inferior. *Work is worship* is the real message of Mahatma Gandhi's philosophy. Principle of individual development that is important for any HR manager has its roots in Gandhian philosophy. Everyone who joined Gandhi's *satyagraha* movement or Dandi March was coloured by his spirit. Gandhi sharpened inner abilities of individuals and helped them to develop their abilities.
12. People's participation in their common public/societal affairs was emphasized in every activity. In human resource management and industrial relations too we find that the worker's participation in management is given priority. Joint management councils were created for the workers to participate in the dispute-resolving processes. According to Gandhi, the life of the labourer, tiller of the land and handicraft man is worth living. To Gandhi, serving the cause without serving the person was a bad thing. His identification with labourers, farmers and socially deprived people was totally on humanitarian ground.

    When Gandhi rushed from Champaran in response to a call by Ansuyaben Sarabhai for the cause of mill workers of the cotton textile industry in Ahmedabad in February 1918, it resulted in starting of a unique labour movement in India. There was unrest amongst weavers of textile industry. Weavers demanded higher wages since bonus was withdrawn by mill owners. Gandhi studied the entire issue. He used to have his own diagnosis of the situation. After detailed study and analysis, he realized that workers' demand and grievances were genuine. He negotiated with mill owners but it was not fruitful. Then he suggested for arbitration but mill owners were not prepared for third party intervention. Ultimately strike was the last resort. Gandhi prepared and trained workers to fight till the last. Their demands were either to be accepted or the process of arbitration was to be initiated. Entire process is similar to HRM process of study, diagnosis and solution. Rather one can say that HRM has to learn many principles from Gandhian philosophy. Gandhi accepted everybody in his fold – be it capitalist rulers or the toiling workers. But he did not accept any injustice done by either of them.

13. Gandhi believed in change-management which is the requirement of modern organizational development. Gandhi wanted major changes in the approach and attitude of workers and management towards each other. Instead of having master and servant relationship, Gandhi emphasized on paternalistic approach or real brotherhood approach amongst both the capitalist and the labour as industry cannot survive without the support of either party.
14. According to Gandhi, wealth and intellect of employer should be used for the health and welfare of workers. Employers should be the trustees of well-being of employees who are pouring their sweat and blood for keeping the industry in motion. Modern HRM has partially accepted the principle of trusteeship for developing industrial relations. Concept of trusteeship aims at bringing about changes in the outlook of management and workers. It really bridges the gap of trust between employers and employees. Gandhi's concept of trusteeship aimed at minimizing the distance between the minimum and maximum ownership of wealth that could be adjustable with the space of time, morals and ethics of society from time to time. Gandhi also believed that production should be based on social requirement rather than on personal ambition of an individual. In order to bring a change in the heart and mind of people, Gandhi launched non-cooperation movement. Gandhi emphasized on training and

education of workers so that they can understand their rights and duties along with acquiring necessary skills for earning livelihood. According to Gandhi, the basic emphasis was on education, knowledge of human affairs and human relations. Same approach is also followed by HRM to deal with the employees in the industry at present. The terms used today are different, but substance has remained the same (Gangal and Gangal 1995).

Conclusion

Mahatma Gandhi was a great personality from India (Sharma S.R. 2004). He lived a simple life but his principles were very rich. He fought for the interest of the Indian immigrant labourers-cum-settlers in South Africa and later on participated in Indian freedom struggle. He sacrificed a lot for the nation. He fought against the British rule in South Africa and later in India. India got freedom in 1947 due to efforts of Gandhi. He advocated the principles of truth, non-violence, *satyagrah*, *sarvodaya,* trusteeship, vegetarianism and *brahmacharya.*

These principles are eternally relevant and very valuable. These Gandhian principles have become visible in the functioning of contemporary HRM practices. This has a very good influence in the areas of communication, interview and participative discussion, worker's development, motivation of workers, profit-sharing, workers' participation in management activities, settlement of disputes, labour strike, dealing with workers, etc. In nutshell, it is to be concluded that Gandhian philosophy has a great impact on HRM functioning.

Acknowledgement

We are thankful to Professor Hardik Shah, Nirma Institute of Management, Professor Sandhya Thakkar, Director, HRM Programme, Gujarat Vidyapeeth, Professor Sheetal, Gujarat Vidyapeeth, Students of HRM Programme and (Late) Sadhana Vora, Gandhi Peace Foundation, Gujarat Vidyapeeth, for their help in providing relevant material for composing this chapter.

References

Betai, Ramesh S. 2002. *Gita and Gandhiji*, New Delhi: National Gandhi Museum.

Bourai, Himanshu. 2004. *Gandhi and Modern Indian Liberals*, Delhi: Abhijeet Publishers.

Chavan, Sheshrao. (ed.). 2001. *Mahatma Gandhi: Man of Millennium*, New Delhi: Authors Press.

Das, Ratan. 2002. *Gandhi in Twenty-First Century*, New Delhi: Swarup Publishers.

Dash, Nibedita. 2004. *Life and Thoughts of Gandhi and Nehru*, New Delhi: Dominant.

Gandhi, M.K. 1957. *An Autobiography: The Story of My Experiments with Truth*, Boston: Beacon Press.

____. 1961. *Non-violent Resistance (Satyagraha)*, New York: Schocken.

Gangal, S.C. and Gangal, Anurag. 1995. *Contemporary Global Problems: A Gandhian Perspective*, Jammu: Vinod.

Goel, S.K. 2002. *Gandhian Perspective on Industrial Relations: A Study of Textile Labour Association, Ahmedabad, 1918–48*, New Delhi: Shipra Publishers.

Sharma, Rashmi. 2004. *Autobiographical Writings of Mahatma Gandhi*, New Delhi: Deep & Deep.

Sharma, S.R. (ed.). 2001. *Gandhi: Ahimsa and Non Violence in Practice*, Delhi: Cosmo.

Sharma, S.R. 2004. *Gandhi: The Man among Men*, New Delhi: Radha Publications.

Thorat, Sukhadeo and Newman, Katherine S. 2007. 'Caste and Economic Discrimination: Causes, Consequences and Remedies', *Economic and Political Weekly*, XLII (41), 13 October, pp. 4121–4124.

Veerraju, Gummadi. 1999. *Gandhian Philosophy: Its Relevance Today*, New Delhi: Decent Books.

William, Howard. 1883, 1896. *The Ethics of Diet: A Catena of Authorities Deprecatory of the Practice of Flesh-Eating*, London: F. Pitman. (In November 2003, The University of Illinois Press re-published it as a popular anthology of vegetarian thought with an additional introduction by eco-feminist author Carol J. Adams).

CHAPTER 18

Gandhian Approach to Rural Development

MAHAJAN P. MANI

One of the most formidable and fundamental aspects of India's developmental effort has been to evolve a strategy to ameliorate the social and economic conditions of those who continue to live below the poverty line expecting something to turn up. Many half-baked theories have been advanced, ad-hoc projects and schemes conceived and implemented, but the problem continues to evade solution (Bhagwati 2007: 46). Hirway and Terhal have correctly raised a set of pertinent and critical questions such as '... how has this development treated the poor and what are the future prospects of economy as far as the poor are concerned? On the face of it, it seems that the incidence of poverty is still quite high .... And that the prospects for the poor at the bottom of the economy are not very bright. How can this happen in a state (Gujarat) which is at the forefront of economic development in the country and which is growing at a rapid rate at present?' (2002: 38). It demands that there is something else to be done. Gandhi was conscious of this growing deprivation of rural classes. In such a vast rural economy, as India is, nothing can be achieved unless adequate stress is given to the development of rural economy. In India, nothing can be achieved unless adequate stress is given to the development of rural sector. He, therefore, wished to raise a strong India on rural pedestal. His earnest desire was to see rural millions as the formidable partners of Indian polity and economy.

The relevance of development by attempting to examine its broad concepts can be known in terms of theory and practice. In conclusion to her definitive study of the political economy of India since Independence, Frankel emphasizes the point that radical agrarian reform in the rural sector is necessary if India is to achieve the economic, social and political goals that were announced at Independence. She concludes that 'Whether the aim is to achieve sustained economic growth, or to reduce social disparities, or to consolidate strong political institutions that can bypass local elites to penetrate the villages, it is essential to alter the pattern of economic concentration in the rural sector. This involves some significant redistribution of productive assets, particularly land, to ensure minimum levels of viability to larger numbers of small holdings. It also requires some degree of change in agrarian organizations from individual to co-operative patterns of economic activity .... The entrepreneurial approach adopted in the mid–1960s ended with the worst possible result from the point of view of the multiple economic and social goals of planning. The new economic policies appeared unlikely to achieve the goals of economic growth, and they were certain to increase economic disparities' (Frankel 1978: 334). The condition of the landless poor in village India was, of course, a key concern of Gandhi.

Development has been attracting a lot of attention for the last couple of decades and many different perspectives and theories have been put forward to explain and implement it. Gandhian philosophy is one of the studies that has introduced into development while having a large impact in people's lives, especially in India. The studies by Dasgupta (1996) and Ghosh (2007) have found that Gandhism has good potential to offer an alternative model of economic development which will do justice to the questions of equitable distribution, creating jobs and protecting environment. More importantly, Gandhian philosophy incorporates ethics and morality into the practical aspects of life. Human Development theory and Gandhian philosophy will be examined to show a contrast to the prevailing ideas of development. It should be noted that this is not only an exploratory exercise, but also an exercise into evolving a critique of ideas and theories. Haq has succinctly observed that '... after many decades of development, we are rediscovering the obvious – that people are both the means and the end of economic development ... Economists often talk about investment capital. Physical capital has taken centre – stage, to the exclusion of many other factors of production. Human capital is measured neither quantitatively nor qualitatively. Nor does it receive the attention it deserves' (1995: 3).

Recent Trends in Development

Development, generally, means bettering people's standard of living on a mass scale. It involves many areas and will have different meanings to different people. Development cannot be limited to economics, sociology, philosophy, politics, environment, health, but encompasses all of these and more. A better standard of living does not have to be defined by higher consumption or income, but will depend on more satisfaction of life and that is also very personally defined.

Development, as it is popularly understood, is also equated with words such as progress and growth, in other words, a change for the better, the better being open to interpretation. It always implies a change, for instance, from the traditional to the modern, as has been popular especially during the fifties and sixties. This change is always calculated and implemented by those in powers and seldom by those going through the change, colonialism being a good example. Today's position of North and South is not very different. The economics and resource power have not shifted hands regardless of what the political situation points to. The term development is also at a very large geographic and demographic scale to be considered. Scale in this case means levels of analysis such as global, national and/or communal issues, down to the personal level of a single person and the geography of the body. The demography of one nation was to be developed and national programmes of progress and growth were to be implemented by the national government. Concepts of national interdependence and global community were introduced only after World War-II. The call for communal and grassroots development has been popularized more recently.

Needless to say, popular concepts of development have left little room for personal and individual development. Models and methods of calculation and analysis have been formed to approach large-scale demographic units. It is an approach for and of the masses and not the individual. Subsequently the role of the individual is virtually non-existent in development.

Development, Economics and the Disillusion of the Two

For many, economic development has been synonymous with economic growth. Economic development has a broader approach, one facing structural and systemic change or in some cases completes overhauling of the system. While economic growth implies only to the expansion of the national economy as it is making only slight changes necessary. Both involve economics as well as politics and other various aspects of society.

Economics are entangled with the political and cultural systems. There is no such thing as free markets in the real world; it is only at the theoretical level. Having said this, it should be recognized that economic theory has been very influential in all aspects of the world today. Although difficult to perceive, the conflict of ideas and the hegemony of one form of understanding do impact our day-to-day life.

Economic theory is based on certain assumptions. At the individual scale, or microeconomics, classical economists work with the assumption that the individual is rational, consistent, and attempts to maximize profits to meet self-interest. Production, labour, prices, allocation of resources, and wealth are all explained by the concept of supply and demand of the individual, whose actions and motivations are predictable. More sophisticated and elaborate models are built on these assumptions. These concepts may not necessarily be wrong, but they are not complete.

It needs to be recognized in all sciences that ethics and spiritually do impact and motivate people. The degree of impact rests on the culture and traditions that the people identify with. Whereas in some cases it may be valuable to separate aspects of life, such as politics, economics and religion, it may not be valuable to do so in other cases. One system is not necessarily better than the other and the enforcement of one over the other will not be successful.

Human Development Indicator

Human Development (HD) theory is a new addition to the theories of development and a reaction to the traditional understanding of development. Recent theorists of HD have attempted to put the people back into the equation. The human dimension of development is not just another addition to the development dialogue. The value of HD theory can be realized by looking at its essential components, which are very different than purely economic based development. The equity needs to be brought about by enlarging people's choices and allowing them equitable access to opportunities and resources. Sustainability points out that the next generation deserves the same standard as the current generation and today's progress should not be pushed forward at the cost of the future. Productivity is the economic aspect of HD theory with emphasis on investing in people and creating an environment where they achieve their maximum potential. Empowerment demands development by the people and participation of the people in creating the policies that impact and define their lives.

Another vital part of this perspective is their concept of sustainable development. The concept breaks down the importance on growth at any cost by emphasizing the importance of people's needs and those of coming generations. It makes development a responsibility of the developed and developing nations. A new global ethic makes consumers responsible for their consumption today and takes into account hidden costs such as environmental and energy costs that are not reflected in the prices. This looks like we are heading towards slow collective suicide.

Although the environment is a major component of sustainability, it also looks at other related concepts. This includes financial, social and demographic sustainability. The current population does not have the moral or legal right to accrue debts that they cannot themselves pay and, thereby, hinder the development of the future generations. They should try to meet their present needs with consideration of the future.

Gandhian Perspective

In his work to organize the people into a potent political force during the Independence movement, Gandhi simultaneously advocated their personal and spiritual growth. This was absolutely a new dimension of mass mobilization in the 20th century. His ideas of development and progress included the search for truth, love, and non-violence. All of these three values are to be viewed as very personal decisions and searches in the lives of every individual, although the society and environment will influence their decisions. No global or federal structure can implement or oversee these developments.

Gandhi persisted that India must not copy the West in development and must find its own route to development. His approach to development was to concentrate on the village and communal development. Gandhi stressed on the development of the individual and evolving philosophy that deals with personal growth and in this way changing the larger society (Gandhi 1947). Herein lies Gandhi's true worth as a visionary and an actionist.

One of the most relevant concepts proposed by him was the necessity of equality to achieve non-violence and peace. The type of equality advocated by Gandhi is very different from the ones we may be most familiar with say liberalism, socialism, communism or Marxism. Gandhi's perspective of equality was dependent on access to resources and not necessarily the equal allocation of resources. Gandhi deeply believed that: Nature produces enough for our wants from day to day; and if only everybody took enough for himself and nothing more, there would be no pauperism in this world, there would be no man dying of starvation.

Gandhi's concepts of development are much more practical rather than theoretical. India's development lies in the villages by educating the villagers with better diet, hygiene, and monetary and productive practices. According to Gandhi, the goal is to convert the villages of India, so that it may be easy for anyone to live in them as it is supposed to be in the cities. This puts the villages and the cities on somewhat equal footing. Part of the development also needs to be in areas of spirituality and culture. With literacy and poverty relief, the villagers will be able to use and reflect on their freedom and responsibilities as a citizen (Gandhi 1967).

Unemployment is a challenge that every economy has faced in the past and continues to face in the present too. It is and has been a strong factor in theories from industrial revolution to Marxism to today's reformation of stagnant European economies. This is true even for Gandhian philosophy. While describing an ideal economy, he stated that the choice to work is the right of every human being and great disturbances and socio-political upheavals have developed when this right has been taken away. For India, the issue of unemployment and underemployment that the villages face leads to lessening of productivity and limiting of individual's choices. One thing that the city dwellers could learn from the villagers is the work ethic. He recognizes that villagers are the producers of what the cities consume. The city depends on the village for its existence and yet the villagers are looked down upon by the city dwellers. Gandhi makes it a point to show that the two are interdependent and can learn from each other for mutual and collective benefit.

Gandhi has some indigenous theoretical and socially relevant practical ideas as to how problems such as unemployment and underemployment could be alleviated (Gangrade 1999: 217–218). According to him, one way to increase employment is to downplay large-scale and widespread industrialization and eliminate the use of machinery if there is human labour to perform the same job. Although this concept of large-scale industrialization is applauded by classical economists and industrialists on the ground of creating employment, efficiency in production and reduction of cost, Gandhi points out the evil of it by showing the suffering that the people go through. For this reason, some have termed Gandhi as anti-industrial and anti-machinist. But his concern is first the people and then the machine, so that people's well-being is not sacrificed for the sake of increasing efficiency produced by the giant machines.

Another method of increasing labour opportunities, in addition to the elimination of machines, is to keep production of basic goods and services in the villages. An example of this is the case of textile and tannery sector in India. Due to its colonial past, British policies of exporting raw material and importing finished products led to an emergence of a large unskilled, unemployed population. This form of exploitation was well thought out and planned, clearly a misuse of power by the alien colonial rulers and not a shortcoming of Indian society. The challenge was to reverse this and re-teach Indians their traditional skills, social development concepts and human rights which had got left behind.

Gandhi was also an advocate of all forms of labour. This was his way of getting rid of untouchability. The untouchables are not only one of the poorest sections of the Indian society but also the oppressed and discriminated group with the least rights. And this is due to their form of labour. According to Gandhi, the implementation of labour division in every aspect of social and economic life has held India back from realizing its full potential. All his life he lamented the fact that the glory and dignity of labour was overlooked and neglected by his countrymen.

The other step towards higher employment is for the village to produce what is needed for the city dweller with concerted communication and organization. The producers should have the full use of their products. The farmer as a food-producer should not go hungry and a coal miner should not lack fuel. Therefore, as Gandhi believed, we have to concentrate on the village being self-contained and manufacturing mainly for self-use. This could be done with the help of the government. In terms of fiscal policy, Gandhi was a strong advocate of government involvement and social funding. In accordance with his views of non-violence, he was very much against any spending on military and weaponry. This corresponds with theories of HD theory, where higher expenditure per GDP on defense is cause of a negative rank.

One of the most important aspect of Gandhian theory is its emphasis on the person as the catalyst for change. Unlike other schools which have pushed for institutional change, reform and involvement, Gandhi begins with the person as the central point and asks them to change the conditions. The person is not only asked to change her/his perception of the world but also to take on the labour of the villagers and to alter her/his consumption patterns. For Gandhi, exploitation is a form of violence. The rich taking from the poor what is needed for their survival actually amounts to a form of violence. Obviously, the rich cannot be rich without the help of the poor, there needs to be a form of co-existence, where the two can benefit and greater equality can be reached.

This can be achieved by Gandhi's concepts of trusteeship. As mentioned above, he is not for equal distribution, but equitable distribution, allowing people to earn through their labour. Equitable distribution lies with the wealthy, since they are entrusted with the wealth and are to come and redistribute it. The ideal situation would be when they do not own or possess more than their neighbour, but distribute their earnings willingly. By working for the good of the society and state through giving and non-violence, then person will change internally and reach a higher state of peace and *ahisma* (non-violence).

Conclusion

In conclusion, it should be stressed that Gandhian theory can improve today's concepts of development and personal satisfaction. But his ideas cannot exist in a vacuum without the incorporation of other great philosophies and systems of thoughts. His concepts of personal development and social justice are idealistic, if not completely utopian. They encourage and assume that the individual is better and can be better than what they exhibit at the moment, providing us with a scope for prescriptive analysis of the world rather than a descriptive analysis. His theories fit especially well and with HD theory, which also recognizes people, if not the person, as central to development and change. In this way, Gandhian theories are supplementary but vital to the creation of a silent but substantive transformation. They have potential to offer revolutionary understanding of development in contemporary times.

References

Bhagwati, Jagdish. 2007. 'What Went Wrong?', in Rahul Mukherji (ed.), *India's Economic Transition: The Politics of Reforms*, New Delhi: Oxford University Press.

Dasgupta, Ajit K. 1996. *Gandhi's Economic Thought*, London: Routledge.

Frankel, Francine. 1978. *India's Political Economy–1977: The Gradual Revolution*, Princeton, N.J.: Princeton University Press.

Gandhi, M.K. 1947. *India of My Dreams* (Compiled by R.K. Prabhu), Ahmedabad: Navjivan Publishing House.

____. 1967. *The Mind of Mahatma Gandhi* (Compiled by R.K. Prabhu and U.R. Rao), Ahmedabad: Navjivan Publishing House.

Gangrade, K.D. 1999. 'Gandhi through Five Generations: A Personal Account of Rural Social Work', in Chhaya Patel (ed.), *Social Work Practice: Religio-Philosophical Foundations*, Jaipur and New Delhi: Rawat Publications.

Ghosh, B.N. 2007. *Gandhian Political Economy: Principles, Practices and Policy*, Hampshire: Ashgate.

Haq, Mahbub Ul. 1995. *Reflections on Human Development*, New Delhi: Oxford University Press.

Hirway, Indira and Terhal, Piet. 2002. 'Contradictions of Growth', in Ghanshyam Shah et al. (eds), *Development and Deprivation in Gujarat: In Honor of Jan Breman*, New Delhi: Sage Publications.

A Life of Relentless Praxis for Social Development: Professor Anil S. Navale

CHHAYA PATEL

Battle for Primacy: Theory vs Praxis

Much of what should find a place here at the beginning of this narrative on academic profiling has already been done in the first few opening pages of this volume under the caption: '*Festschrift:* An Ennobling Academic Tradition' in chapter one on Introduction. This introductory note on Professor Navale is only a somewhat detailed and contextualized narrative on his life and work which is mostly centred on the other end of an idea or theory, namely, practice or praxis. A bird's eye-view on his life and work brings out this fact rather well. Ideally the preference and/or orientation to theory and praxis or idea and action should hang in balance. But this is rarely found to be happening. In most cases, as in this too, the imbalance is found to have tilted in favour of either theory or praxis.

However, the ultimate enrichment of social science domains continues happening from both the ends of theory and practice or idea and action. The field of social work essentially is that of pre-dominant primacy of practice and action. Helping the needy in as much an institutionalized format as possible is one of the several *avtaars* (forms, versions, aspects) of social work understanding and theoretical assumptions. There is one more understanding of this binary process. That, no action is possible without some latent or manifest informing or guidance by theory. Some *a priori* imagination – howsoever raw, unfinished and unarticulated – gets formed before the action.

Socialization could be one of its sources. Priority and urgency for action may be getting determined by the socio-economic conditions in which one is born, reared and grown. Pressure for instant action, as a situation may demand, hardly leaves one with the luxury of sufficient time for robust imagination, detailed conceptualization and organizing a deliberative thought process.

Group or mass based actions require altogether a different set of leadership skills. The process of mobilization of any social group for a constructive and corrective social action is at once a challenging task. It often tests the patience of the mobilizing leader and his ability to persist in the face of non-responsive behaviour and uncooperative attitude of the targeted group. Getting the people together for an action and retaining their interest is important. These thoughts come to mind when we view and reflect on the life and work of Professor Navale. He gave primacy to action, practice or praxis and relegated the written, printed word of idea, theory, philosophy or ideology to secondary level. Right from the early student days, he was more keen on translating Gandhian philosophical and normative ideas into practice, rather than extracting and binding them into some theoretical and/or interpretative thought systems of no less academic values. One of the key sources of this early orientation to Gandhian values and their inculcation in young Navale was his teacher and mentor Professor Indira Patel.

Contextualizing Navale's Normative Baptism and Institutional Affiliation at Baroda School

This calls for a little dig into the early years of Baroda School of Social Work at The M. S. University (henceforth referred to as MSU) of Baroda, Baroda; Gujarat. It is fairly well known that since 1950, the Baroda School is engaged in the task of imparting professional social work education and training at post-graduate level in Western India by setting a new trend of initiating the generic approach, instead of the then (and subsequently too) prevailing trend of specialization. This breaking away from the tradition (practiced by Tata Institute of Social Sciences, Mumbai and Delhi School of Social Work) amounted to a radical academic departure. The rationale for introducing generic approach to professional social work education at Baroda School was primarily based on the conception of man in Indian philosophical tradition and realistically locating him in contemporary socio-economic conditions of Indian society. It was ingeniously perceived and correctly realized that immediately after India's

Independence in 1947, the Indian youth was in need for such a professional course which trained and engaged them in the complex task of nation-building through social service and social development.

It was a matter of great academic courage, conviction and leadership qualities of such illustrious founders and pioneers of the School as Professors Parin Vakharia (Founding Dean), Indira Tayal, Ammu M. Muzumdar, G.G. Dadlani, Indira Patel, Olive Swoboda, Meher Nanavatty, Pervez Bhatt and P.D. Kulkarni, that Baroda School was finally able to establish itself as a reputed academic centre for teaching and training in generic social work. Subsequent academic leadership at the School made conscious efforts to continue these institutional ethos and practices. In 1960, Professor Ammu M. Muzumdar began to research and write a doctoral thesis on: *Mahatma Gandhi's Contribution to Social Welfare in India*. Gandhian ideals of social service were included into the curriculum and the practical demonstration was given by organizing rural reconstruction camps. The students were exposed to rural life and study tours were made to various Gandhian institutes and centres in and around Gujarat.

Professor Indira Patel was one of the few earliest products of the School who imbibed all these new values, ethos and inherited glorious institutional traditions as its faculty later. Her doctoral thesis on: *Oriental Approach to Social Work* (later on published as a book, *Vivekanand's Approach to Social Work*. Madras: Ramkrishna Math, 1987) bears testimony to the centrality and continuity of a philosophical and normative tradition at Baroda School.

One of the many dimensions of this institutional engagement and commitment of Professor Patel's work at the School was to spot, cull, cultivate and nurture the second generation of academics to carry on this glorious tradition of Baroda School. The youth of the University was her special area of academic and community extension work interest. She was a pioneer in housing the National Service Scheme (NSS) at the Faculty of Social Work and took deep and persistent interest in its working from its premises. One of the very few individuals (among others) who could pass the test of her stringent and exacting demands of Spartan discipline, unsullied moral character and integrity was a local youth from the underdeveloped lower middle class area of Baroda city, namely Fatehpura (which was disreputed for such illegal activities like gambling, liquor sale, sex working, communal rioting etc). This youth won the trust and confidence of Professor Patel and others by sheer hard work, complete dedication and devotion and set on a long professional journey as a second generation torch-bearer of Baroda School, who not only ensured continuity but effected multipronged academic expansion of the school. This in later years won the School fourth and fifth rank as the best School of Social Work in the country.

A Brief Biographic Sketch

This youth mentioned in the ending lines of the previous section was no other than Professor Anil Shankarrao Navale. His humble origins and bringing up made his efforts to rise in life more strugglesome and testing but also rewarding. The humble origin in the midst of socio-economically lower-wrung people instilled in him a strong sense of affinity and loyalty to his immediate neighbourhood community. His bringing up as an eldest son in the joint family of seven members in relatively harsher income conditions emboldened his resolves for strong family values which extended to all those who later on joined him in his numerous mobilization campaigns and myriad social development activities centring on youth, NSS, NGOs, the industry and the needy sections of the society.

Behind Professor Navale's hard work for upholding the inherited institutional values and ethos with the stringent personal discipline, deep involvement and sustained single-minded dedication was his wife Smt. Maltiben (M.Sc. B.Ed.), herself a dedicated school teacher and home maker, who took charge of the affairs of a large joint family and also of their children – Kunal and Sanskriti – in a manner that left Professor Navale free for his 365 days and almost round the clock work for NSS, University, society, community, academics, civic and governmental organizations and the profession. Professor Navale's humility, simplicity, duty-consciousness and complete commitment to work during the long career of thirty five years are just amazing. He is one of the few professionals who have served the institutions on a priority basis, often by sacrificing the family time at home. The evidence of Professor Navale being a friendly but uncompromising task master, trusted associate, caring teacher and dependable colleague is to be found in the vast band of his admirers (the ex-students or colleagues of many campaigns) who are spread across the globe in varying capacities and spheres of work.

His entire higher education was obtained from the world renowned The M. S. University of Baroda, Baroda. He obtained his BA (1965), MSW (1967), Post-graduate Diploma in Labour Practice (1970) and LL.B. (1974) degrees from this University. During his student life at the MSU from 1963 to 1974, Professor Navale tried to receive life shaping mentoring influences, inputs, feedbacks and career-moulding counsels with both the hands wide open. During these years, a major metamorphosis occurred in his world view. A new direction for life of work was emerging. His emergence as Gandhian youth and student leader became discernible. He contested MSU Students Union elections and became Faculty representative in Faculty of Law in 1967–68. He got elected as Vice-President, MSU Students Union in 1968–69 and represented it at National Council of University Students of India at New Delhi (of which he was elected National Secretary for 1968–69). He also represented MSU at All India Meet on National Integration Scheme (NIS), convened by University Grants Commission, New Delhi in 1968–69.

He had a rare honour on being appointed by the Government of India in the Committee of the Vice Chancellors and student leaders of Indian Universities, New Delhi during 1969–70. In 1969, he participated as MSU Student Union's Vice-President in National Meeting convened for introduction of NSS in Indian Universities; and in World Assembly of Youth Conference at International Youth Centre, New Delhi. This wide-ranged exposure gradually shaped him as a credible student leader of youth movement in Gujarat and in Western and Northern India. So far as the beginnings are concerned it can be said for Professor Navale that it was a case of: 'as in life, so in work'. He began his academic and professional work career from very humble assignments and gradually rose to higher steps on a long career ladder. Youth mobilization, welfare and leadership activities; youth movements; social work teaching; practice and extension; social development initiatives and engagements have remained his main fields of praxis and contribution.

However, in two major student protest movements of his time in his city and the state, his role had come under criticism and unfavourable characterization. Firstly, in 1969 the students of the MSU had risen in protest against the Baroda Municipal Corporation and city Mayor's deceitful slicing away of university's prime track of land for widening the road between railway station and Kaala Ghoda Circle in Sayajiganj area. Navale's pacifist and non-violent Gandhian approach had not found many takers. It got him branded by the rival student leaders as a secret agent and collaborator of one man power centre which was common to MSU and the city. Secondly, during the Gujarat state's well-known students-led *Navnirman* Movement, his role continued to be like the moderates of the Indian National Congress party in early twentieth century. Whatever be the level and intensity of his involvement, he continued to face the criticism as a pacifist Gandhian leader with a faith in dialogue, debate, negotiation and compromise rather than one to pick up stone at a drop of a hat and throw it on a bus, building or police.

These two brief sketches inform us that early Navale of student phase was an 'in-system' activist, a pacifist, often a collaborator with the power-be, rather than being an extremist in approach, a ruthless challenger, fierce fighter and violent protester against the system from outside it. These experiences had taught two important lessons to him which, in turn, guided his rest of the career. He believed that political neutrality is indispensable for resourcing, building, administering and thereby strengthening academic institutions. Professor Navale came to believe that being an overt part of the periodically erupting protest mobilizations along the political party lines on one or the other issue weakens your genuinely deserving demands from being made and met. What one can do from inside the system cannot do it from outside it. This personal ideology could be the result of his baptism in early social work education and later its practice as the inductee in the Baroda School as its faculty member. It seems the Gandhian values offered scope for remaining above and higher over partisan politics on polarized lines of narrow personalized loyalties. It offered an aura and an image of saintliness and legitimacy for practicing traditional, patriarchal and hierarchical values which often bordered on autocracy and authoritarianism of sorts. Once in a while, this tendency manifested in some activities as the case below brings out.

Bangladesh Refugee Relief Camp in Bihar, 1971–72: A Case in Point

The most outstanding hallmark of Professor Navale is his organizing the NSS Camps. The preparations for such myriad camps were no different than preparing a lecture series to be delivered at any reputed centre of academics. Forging a common agenda in form of camp objectives for students of all backgrounds – ranging from law, medicine, arts, commerce, engineering, science, fine arts and home science – and then carrying them out without any normative or operational compromise was no small feat. Throughout his life, Professor Navale must have organized hundreds of such rural camps, awareness campaigns, study tours, disaster relief missions and so on. A synoptic profiling of one such camp, based on the then student NSS volunteer participant-observer's account shall illuminate his contribution on this front.

A word or two regarding the wider context and nature of human tragedy shall be helpful in getting correct picture about the case. As is known, in 1971–72 the political refugees from then East Pakistan had crossed over the border *en masse* and come to India for safe shelter in big number. It was one of the familiar faces of recurring human tragedies in one or the other part of the world. They were Bengali Hindus hounded away by Pakistani army and local Muslim civilians. It was somewhat like a partition type of tragedy. Women were raped and made pregnant. The pregnant victims were ashamed of this uncivilized treatment and did not move about in the relief camp site during the daylight. They used to move about only after sunset and dusk. The absence of female student volunteers in the team had become regrettable. In such sensitive situations, they could have worked among them and provided emotional support to the raped pregnant victims. The young and the elderly too needed support. Food supply, medical care, cleanliness, hygiene, sanitation and informal education to the children were to be provided in a rationed and make-shift manner.

Professor Navale had led one team of MSU's NSS student volunteers to Panchanpur Refugee Relief Camp in Gaya district. It was set up on a huge sprawling area of an abandoned World War–II military airport site. Participation in this camp was a life-shaping experience for the volunteers. The tasks of the relief activities were meticulously divided and rotated among volunteers mostly according to their study background. Every evening the stock-taking was done. The experience was shared. The problems, if any, were discussed. Monitoring of self and group functioning was done by discussions. Professor Navale taught us to see and treat them as our neighbourhood guests in distress rather than see them as thrown out helpless political refugees.

At the end of the camp we found that we had become assimilated as one community - blurring the distinction of our being host country's volunteers and them being distressed guests. Some graduates of Dhaka University invited a few of us to their new 'home' – which was a small shanty like furniture-less space allotted to them by the relief camp administration. In one such visit, we were welcomed as guests by offering a *chapatti* rolled with a few sugar grains on it as a handy sweet. This hospitality in such uprooted and harsh conditions touched us and became a lifetime memorabilia. This cultural practice and form of *Atithi Devo Bhava* was so heart-warming that it got etched in our young hearts forever.

Despite physically and mentally tiring routines at the relief camp, Professor Navale would keep pouring the periodical dozes of encouragement and inspiration. After the camp, we went to Rajgir, Nalanda University site and *ghats* at Gaya on a study tour visit. One of the signs of backwardness is lack of proper transport. Bihar was atrocious then. In one instance, we could not walk to the site of our visit and there was no transport. One cycle-rickshaw was spotted and all of us got on to it beyond its carrying capacity. The weak and the famished cycle-rickshaw owner found the load too heavy. Seeing this Professor Navale immediately got down and started walking along and pushing it during slopes. After some distance, we rotated the ride among us and Professor Navale relieved the profusely perspiring driver by taking over cycling himself. This small random act of kindness was not like today's TV camera photo-op sessions, in which we saw everyone well-dressed and sweeping 'clean' roads or areas by wielding the *jhadoos* in hand and looking at the cameras during recently launched *Swachha Bharat Abhiyan*!

Hierarchies are particularly our bane and difficult to escape them. They intermittently surface in one or the other forms. Young Navale was no exception. It was observed during this camp that the student volunteers from medicine, engineering, science and law somehow had got placed higher than those from arts and commerce in several significant and not so significant matters. In one group meeting during the camp, this practice of differential treatment among volunteers was pointed out loud and clear by stating that Gandhian values of equality and *sambhav* were getting violated. This shocked Navale and a few elite volunteers. But the happy outcome was that on collective realization of this lapse, it was instantly corrected and suitable changes were made amicably in a true spirit of team volunteerism. This is just one personal synoptic narrative of a camp. Each of the hundreds of such camps, campaigns and missions which were conceived, organized and executed by Professor Navale throughout his active (and even retired) life is a lesson in learning cardinal values of good teamwork and thereby enhancing and shaping one's life in general irrespective of the domain being legal, medical, management, business, homemaking, academic, engineering, commerce or administration.

Academic, Governance and Administrative Positions Held

Professor Navale has travelled a diverse work track. He began his academic journey from a small station. In 1967, he worked as

Research Assistant to Professor Kurdo's (University of Osaka, Japan) research project on: *Study of Cousin Marriage Patterns among Muslims of India and Pakistan*. Then he worked as Junior Research Fellow in *P.L. 480 Scheme*, Faculty of Home Science, MSU, Baroda in the same year. In 1969, he joined Faculty of Social Work as Research Assistant for a brief stint. He acquired valuable experience as Community Worker in Baroda Community Development Services during 1970. The next step proved immensely consequential. He became Programme Coordinator of National Service Scheme at the MSU, Baroda during 1970–1974 and then onwards worked in honorary capacity till 2005. He became a Lecturer in Faculty of Social Work from 1973–1983; Reader from 1983–1994 and Professor from 1994–2005.During this long productive period at the MSU, he became Head and Dean of the Faculty of Social Work (1997–2003); Co-ordinator, UGC-DSA in Social Work (1997–2005); Founder Director of self-financed programme of Master of Human Resource Management (1999–2005) and Founder Director, Post-Graduate Diploma in Human Resource Management (2001–2005). He was Founder Director of other three Post-Graduate Diplomas in: (i) Social Development and Organizational Management (SDOM), (ii) Health Management and Intervention (DHMI), and, (iii) Criminology and Correctional Management (DCCM) during 2001–2003.

Apart from this, he shouldered responsibility of heading several other programmes and institutions in the M. S. University of related interest to social development and social work. During 1979–2000, he worked as Honorary Director, National Adult Education Program Unit, Centre for Continuing Adult Education and Community Services at the MSU; and, worked also as Honorary Director, V.T. Krishnamachari Institute of Rural Development, Samiala Campus, MSU from 1987–2002. He headed the Nodal Agency for Childline at the Faculty as its Director during 1997–2003. He was the President of Students Union at the MSU in 1983. As a Director, Department of Students Welfare at the MSU during 1983–2005, he got an opportunity to continue his lifelong concern of having interface with the youth (of such a large year after year growing student body from 18,000 to 30,000 in one university).

His long association first as a teacher (1980–2005) and later as Director of Post-graduate Diploma in Industrial Relations and Personnel Management (1997–2005) provided a window into the domain of industry as a useful resource to design new programmes and build institutions and truly enrich social work practice and profession. This experience led to the founding of new self-financed courses in human resource management during his tenure as Head and the Dean of the Faculty during this period as well as Member, Senate (1982–87 and 1997–2003) and Member, Syndicate (1982–1985 and 2000–2003) of the MSU.

As a Chief Warden of girls and boys hostels in the MSU campus, his contact with the youth deepened and expanded as student inmates' issues of lodging, boarding, safety, comfort, indiscipline, fights, recreation etc brought him closer to them and made him more intimate and sensitive. Male and female inmates of the hostels took professor Navale far beyond the religio-cultural and ethnic bounds of Baroda city into other areas of the state, country and the world as students came to MSU from as far as North-Eastern states, Jammu & Kashmir, Orissa, Tamil Nadu, Bihar, West Bengal, Kerala and from African, Middle-eastern and South East Asian countries. The diversities and pluralities of cultures, faiths, languages, food habits, ethnicities, colour, ideologies and orientations that these students brought with them may have amazed and enriched the *weltanschauung* of Professor Navale as a keen and committed interlocutor between them and the MSU administration on one hand and between them and Baroda city students and society on the other. No wonder he was appointed as Co-ordinator, Campus Diversity Initiative at the MSU during 1998–2005. Professor Navale contributed hugely by becoming a member of many administrative and governance committees of the MSU such as Investment Committee, Annual Report Committee, Staff Welfare Committee, Information Cell (1984), Construction Committee, Central Students Union Election Committee (1983–84), Examination Vigilance Committees (1985), Member-Secretary, University Advisory Committee for NSS (1970–2005), Committee for Improving Conditions in the University Halls (i.e., Hostels) of Residence (1984), and Press Supervisory Committee during his twin tenures as Senate and Syndicate member.

In the city of Baroda, he was associated with several civic, voluntary and cultural associations and organizations in various capacities of being resource person, adviser, trainer and collaborator in their activities. These bodies were: *Vikas Jyot* Trust, Worker's Education Centre, NSS Training and Orientation Centre, *Shramik Vikas Sansthan*, Community Service Centre, *Jagrut Grahak*, Shri Kamlashankar Pandya Foundation and *Jan Shiksha Sansthan*. He held positions in various other such bodies like: Director, Navrachana Co-operative Society; Trustee, *Seva Sahayog* Trust; Trustee, *Malhaar Mahalsakant Maratha Mangal Karyalaya Sangathan (MMMMKS)*; Executive Secretary, *Antar Bharati*; President, Youth Council; Trustee, Beautiful Baroda Council; President, Centre for Industrial Relations and Social Development, Baroda. According to him, community education is an important means for bringing about necessary awareness regarding social change and social development. In order to further this objective Professor Navale took to popular writing. A series of articles on social education for the youth were published in *Vadodara Samachar*, a Gujarati language daily newspaper and *M.S.U. News*. In order to reach out to the multi-lingual youth community in the city and region, Marathi, Gujarati, Hindi and English languages were intermittently used. These articles were published under columns/titles: *Juvanini Jyot (*A series of 91 articles in Gujarati), 1979–80; *M.S.U. News,* 1983–1990 and *Emester,* 1967–68.

In accordance with the evolution of such a career and the chequered track record, Professor Navale held various positions in other institutions and carried out various assignments. He was an Expert Member, Academic Council, Tata Institute of Social Sciences, Bombay; Panel Member, National Eligibility Test (NET) Examinations, University Grants Commission, New Delhi; Panel Member, SET Examinations, Maharashtra State Eligibility Test, Pune; Project Director, Documentation & Evaluation Project, sponsored by Gujarat Ecology Commission; Members, Review Committees, Special Assistance Programme, UGC-DRS and UGC-DSA (of Department of Social Work, Andhra University; Department of Social Work, Lucknow University, Lucknow; School of Social Work, Udaipur; Department of Social Work, Jamia Millia Islamia, New Delhi; Tata Institute of Social Sciences, Mumbai and Department of Social Work, University of Delhi, Delhi). He worked as Members, Review Committees, UGC-SAP, Centre for Advanced Study in Social Work for Department of Social Work, Lucknow University and Department of Social Work, Jamia Millia Islamia, New Delhi.

Professor Navale was similarly associated in different capacities in GOs-NGOs and institutions located outside Baroda city such as: Gujarat State Crime Prevention Trust, Ahmedabad; Indian Council for Social Welfare, Gandhinagar, Gujarat State; NSS Training Centre, Anand; *Gram Vikas* Kendra, Panelav, Panchmahal district; Rajiv Gandhi National Institute of Youth Development, Government of

India, New Delhi; Member, Central Executive Committee, Indian Council of Social Welfare, Mumbai; and, Member, Advisory Committee, Gujarat State Gazetteer, Government of Gujarat.

Teaching, Research & Extension Activities

As a formal social work educator Professor Navale taught innumerable batches of post-graduate students of MSW, MHRM, IRPM and DHRM the courses in urban community development, labour welfare and industrial relations, social legislations, social group work and methods of working with people. The students of regular course work researches and doctoral researches were guided in the subject areas of: women workers, indebtedness among working class, Legal Aid Scheme and its implementation, Employee's State Insurance Scheme and its Implementation, Women Learners under National Adult Education Programme, NEAP and its Implementation, Physically Handicapped Employees, Welfare Officer's Role and Responsibilities, Mass Program for Functional Literacy, Trade Unions and *Mahila Antyodaya Kendra*, Workers' Education Scheme, CSR and Human Resource Management, and, Impact of Narmada Dam Displaced Tribal Peoples' Rehabilitation Programme.

One more mutually helpful component of the academic programme at the Faculty came handy to Professor Navale in initiating, monitoring and expanding his horizons through field work students who were regularly placed round the year in such industries and agencies as: Labour Welfare Centre, Fatehpura and Akota, *Balbhavan* Society, Alembic Chemicals Ltd, Sarabhai Chemicals Ltd., New India Industries, Dinesh Mills, Ambica Mills, Precision Bearings India Ltd., Novino Batteries, and, Gujarat Alkalies and Chemicals Ltd. Professor Navale quite often along with his students gave a series of Radio Talks and frequently conducted Panel Discussions on various topical themes of social work interest and relevance on *Yuva Vani* (Youth Voice) Programmes of All India Radio, Vadodara Station during 1970s and 1980s. He produced video cassettes on AIDS Awareness and tried to spread awareness through frequently organized rallies, Quiz Programmes, *Bhavai* (a form of popular regional folk play/theatre), posters, slides and magic shows for spreading social messages.

Professor Navale worked on several research assignments and held positions as subject expert in other governmental, civic, voluntary, academic and regulatory bodies across the city, state and the country. Professor Navale conducted several research studies and directed some other research projects such as: Project on *Human Development Study in Villages of Bharuch and Surat Districts*, sponsored by Birla Cellulosic (2000); *Impact Assessment of Partnerships for Sexual Health on HIV/AIDS*, Baroda Citizen Council, sponsored by Gujarat State AIDS Control Society (2000); Project on *District Mapping Exercise of Population Groups Vulnerable to HIV/AIDS*, sponsored by Gujarat State AIDS Control Society and Gujarat Institute of Development Research, Ahmedabad (2001); Project on *Social Need and Impact Assessment of Earthquake Affected People of Gujarat*, sponsored by the World Bank (2001–2003); and, *Integrated Community Development Project*, sponsored by GAIL (2003).

This wide range of exposure and experience, gathered over the years of intense involvement and participation in numerous activities, agencies, institutions and organizations, sharpened Professor Navale's insights into the concerns of social work practice – some of which became evident in his authored and co-authored publications in various forms (which are listed in Appendix-I) as articles, books, reports, monographs, mimeographs, edited issues of Faculty's Journal, *Social Work Review* and popular writings.

The post-retirement period has not deterred Professor Navale from being actively associated with ideas, agencies, institutions and organizations involved in broad engagements with issues of social development. Apart from continuing with his earlier associations with such bodies in and around Baroda, it has now extended far beyond it. He participated in *Make Difference a Day* Programme, conducted by Ms. Sugi Shiva, Human Services Department, City of Fremont, California, USA, October 2009 and also in its *Pen-Pal Project*, conducted by Ms. Sugi Shiva, in January 2010. He became member to an *Online Group: Human Service Professionals*, and also to *Online Group: Global Organization of Social Work Educators and Practitioners* initiated by Ms. Deona Hooper, Durham, North Carolina, USA, April 2012.

Awards and Felicitations

Such a career as that of Professor Navale cannot remain unnoticed. Institutional and organizational persistence does get noticed as the nature, scope and importance of work expands and draws attention of society and the state. In the course of his career he received several honours, awards and felicitations as follows:

- Community Service Award for Blood Donation Camp, Lions Club Baroda, 1980.

- Outstanding Young Person of Baroda City: Baroda Jaycees, Baroda, 1982.
- Felicitation for Contribution to Co-op. Banking: Shri Krishna Co-op. Bank, Baroda, 1983.
- Honorary Member, Organization for Indian Affairs, New Delhi, 1983.
- Felicitation for Contribution to organizing National Integration Camp with *Antar Bharti* Trust, India, 1992.
- Comets of Social Work: Alumni Association of Faculty of Social Work, The M.S. University of Baroda, Baroda, 1994.
- Best Programme Coordinator Award, NSS, NSS State Cell, Government of Gujarat, 1994.
- Sardar Patel Youth Development National Award, Commonwealth Association for the Education and Training of Adults, International Association of Educators for World Peace and The Global Open University, Milan, Italy, 1999–2000.
- Honoured with Dedicated Teacher's Felicitation Award by Lion's Club International, District 232 F1 on Teacher's Day, 5 September 2014.

Continuing the Worship of Work

Professor Navale's worship of work has not stopped. In the post-retirement period from November 2005 till date, he has remained active with several organizations and institutions in and around Baroda in various leadership capacities. They are as follows:

- Director, SMKS Hospital and Educational Complex, Karjan, Baroda District.
- Chairman, Community Care Initiatives, SMKS Homeopathy Medical College, Karjan, Baroda District.
- President, Centre for Industrial Relations and Social Development, Baroda.
- Chairman & Managing Director, Search Foundation for Social Development, Baroda.
- President, Indian Council of Social Welfare, Baroda.
- Treasurer, V-ONE Society, Baroda.
- Trustee and Treasurer, *Antar Bharati* Trust, Baroda.
- Founder Director, Navrachna Cooperative Society of Baroda, Baroda.

In the course of about five decades of limitless varied engagements and work, Professor Navale has built a vast network of relationships spread all over the city, state, country and abroad in form of his numerous students, colleagues, professionals and peers. He has devoted his life and work to the cause of social work education, profession, practice, training, discipline and pedagogy. Professor Navale is well known as the man of extension, organization and an academic administrator. He has been a modest teacher-researcher; a team-builder and zealous, resource mobilizer and executor of ideas, programmes, and schemes.

Appendix-I — Publications

Books

2006. (Co-authored with Mona Sharma). *An Action-oriented Research and Field Experiment: University, Industry and Community Interface*, Baroda: The M.S. University of Baroda, Baroda Publication.

2006. (Co-authored with Aruna Khasgiwala and Saroj Vardiwale). *An Innovative Field Experiment on Alcohol and its Management: An Intervention in Rural Community*, Baroda: The M.S. University of Baroda, Baroda Publication.

Mimeographs, Monographs and Reports

1970–71. *NSS News,* NSS Unit, Faculty of Social Work, The M.S. University of Baroda, Baroda, December.

1971, 1972. *National Service Scheme,* NSS Unit, Faculty of Social Work, The M.S. University of Baroda, Baroda.

1972. 'Bangladesh Refugee Relief Camps at Panchanpur, Gaya District, Bihar,' *NSS News,* Special Issue, NSS Unit, Faculty of Social Work, The M.S. University of Baroda, Baroda.

1973. *NSS Youth Against Famine*, NSS Unit, Faculty of Social Work, The M.S. University of Baroda, Baroda.

1978. *Integrated Rural Development and Social Work Education: Compilation of Case Studies in Rural Development,* Faculty of Social Work, The M.S. University of Baroda, Baroda.

1979. *Block Development Plan for Jabugam*, Baroda District, May.

1982. *Handbook of NSS*, NSS Unit, Faculty of Social Work, The M.S. University of Baroda, Baroda.

1982. *Youth Accepts Challenge: NSS in Gujarat Helps Flood Victims of Morbi,* Gandhinagar: Government of Gujarat.

1985. *News Bulletin*, Special Issue, NSS News, Ahmedabad: Gujarat State Resource Centre, International Youth Year.

1988. *Youth Power in National Development: A Study of Antar Bharti Campers,* Faculty of Social Work, The M.S. University of Baroda, Baroda.

1991. *Reforming Industrial Relations*: *Seminar Proceedings,* Faculty of Social Work, The M.S. University of Baroda, Baroda.

1991. *Training, Monitoring and Evaluation of Urban Community Development Project*, Municipal Corporation, Baroda, Faculty of Social Work, The M.S. University of Baroda, Baroda.

1991. Training Course for Counselors (Produced reading material on counseling techniques for social workers and report 1990–91).

1992. University Talks about AIDS: A Compilation of Reading Material, 1991–92.

1992. Readings in NSS: A Compilation of Reading Material 1991–92.

1992. Anti-addiction Awareness Campaign 1990–91, NSS Unit, Faculty of Social Work, The M.S. University of Baroda, Baroda.

1995. LEC News (Lifestyle Education Centre Newsletter), Special Issue on HIV/AIDS Education, NSS Unit, Faculty of Social Work, The M.S. University of Baroda, Baroda,

1998. *Role and Competencies of Human Resource Professionals in New Millennium*, Management Convention.

1998. *Age-Related Health Problems and Economic Activities of the Elderly in Rural Villages: A Study Conducted Among Elderly Members of the Households in Seven Villages in Panchmahal District.* Faculty of Social Work, The M.S. University of Baroda, Baroda.

1998. *Status of Women and Atrocities on them in Rural Villages: A Study Conducted on Women in Seven Villages in Panchmahal District*, Faculty of Social Work, The M.S. University of Baroda, Baroda.

1998. *Maternal Health Care in Rural Villages: A Study Conducted on Women in Seven Villages in Panchmahal District*, Faculty of Social Work, The M.S. University of Baroda, Baroda.

1998. (ed.). *Social Work Review*, Annual Number on 'Women and Social Development'.

1998. (Co-authored with Danny Koshi). *Report on Trainers' Training: Skill Development for Elected Women Representatives*, Sponsored by British Council, Mumbai.

1999. (ed.). *Social Work Review*, Annual Number on 'Poverty Alleviation and Social Development'.

1999. *Report on Monitoring and Evaluation of Projects of NGOs*, supported by Gujarat Ecology Commission under World Bank aided 'NGO Environment Action Fund', Gujarat, August.

2000. *Managing Organizational Change and Leadership in New Millennium*, HRM Convention, January.

2000. *Achieving Competitive Edge through People*, HRM Conclave Proceedings, December.

2000. (ed.). *Social Work Review*, Annual Number on 'Social Work Profession at the Dawn of the New Millennium'.

2000. *Report on Campus Diversity Initiative Program*, The M.S. University of Baroda, Baroda.

2003. (Co-ed.). *Social Work Review,* Annual Number on 'Development of SC and ST in Indian Society: Issues and Challenges'.

2004. *Report on Women and Environment: State Level Seminar,* Faculty of Social Work, The M.S. University of Baroda, Baroda.

2004. (Co-ed.). *Social Work Review,* Annual Number on 'Social Work in Industry'.

2005. (Co-ed.). *Social Work Review,* Annual Number on 'Social Work and Human Resource Education'.

2005. (ed.). *Social Work Review,* Annual Number on 'NGOs and Corporate Sector for Social Development: Issues and Challenges'.

2006. (ed.). *Social Work Review,* Annual Number on 'Corporate Social Responsibility and Rural Development: Issues and Challenges'.

2006. (ed.). *Social Work Review,* Annual Number on 'Corporate Social Responsibility and Rural Development'. An UGC-DSA supported Publication.

2006. (ed.). *Social Work Review,* Annual Number on 'Integrating Human Rights Perspective with Social Work Education'. An UGC-DSA supported Publication.

Articles

1972. 'Program of the National Service Scheme: A Review and Prospect', *National Service Scheme,* Publication No. 7, Delhi School of Social Work, New Delhi.

1986. 'Youth and Development: IYY and NSS Program, *Rashtriya Seva Publication,* Department of Social Work, University of Delhi, New Delhi. Also published in *Social Work Review,* Annual Number, Faculty of Social Work, The M.S. University of Baroda, Baroda, 1986.

1987. 'Camping Activity as an NSS Program', *Social Work Review,* Annual Number, Faculty of Social Work, The M.S. University of Baroda, Baroda.

1988. 'Youth and Development: Curricular Significance of NSS', *NSS Unit,* Tata Institute of Social Sciences, Bombay.

1988. 'NSS Involvement of Youth in Drought Relief Program', *The M.S. University Epigraph on Drought,* Faculty of Social Work, The M.S. University of Baroda, Baroda.

1990. 'Youth and Development: Participation of Youth in Program of Mass Functional Literacy Campaign', *Social Work Review,* Annual Number, Faculty of Social Work, The M.S. University of Baroda, Baroda.

1992. 'National Integration and Environment Protection Camp at Kevadia,' *IFM Socialist Educational International Bulletin,* October.

2003. (Co-authored with Mona Sharma) 'Adolescent Needs, Interest and Concerns: Contextual Imperatives for Family and Life Skill Education' in Bhagban Prakash (ed.), *Adolescents and Life Skills,* New Delhi: Tata-McGraw Hill India Ltd.

Index